INTERNATIONAL RELATIONS

INTERNATIONAL RELATIONS

Ravi Ranjan

ANMOL PUBLICATIONS PVT. LTD.
NEW DELHI-110 002 (INDIA)

ANMOL PUBLICATIONS PVT. LTD.

Regd. Office: 4360/4, Ansari Road, Daryaganj,
New Delhi-110002 (India)
Tel.: 23278000, 23261597, 23286875, 23255577
Fax: 91-11-23280289
Email: anmolpub@gmail.com
Visit us at: www.anmolpublications.com

Branch Office: No. 1015, Ist Main Road, BSK IIIrd Stage
IIIrd Phase, IIIrd Block, Bangalore-560 085 (India)
Tel.: 080-41723429 • Fax: 080-26723604
Email: anmolpublicationsbangalore@gmail.com

International Relations

First Edition, 2010

ISBN 978-81-261-4556-0

PRINTED IN INDIA

Printed at Mehra Offset Press, Delhi.

Contents

Preface

International relations (IR) or International studies (IS) represents the study of foreign affairs and global issues among states within the international system, including the roles of states, inter-governmental organizations (IGOs), non-governmental organizations (NGOs), international nongovernmental organizations (INGOs), and multinational corporations (MNCs). It is both an academic and public policy field, and can be either positive or normative as it both seeks to analyse as well as formulate the foreign policy of particular states. It is often considered a branch of political science (specially after 1988 UNESCO nomenclature), but an important sector of academia prefer to treat it as an interdisciplinary field of study. Apart from political science, IR draws upon such diverse fields as economics, history, international law, philosophy, geography, sociology, anthropology, psychology, and cultural studies. It involves a diverse range of issues including but not limited to: globalization, state sovereignty, ecological sustainability, nuclear proliferation, nationalism, economic development, global finance, terrorism, organized crime, human security, foreign interventionism and human rights.

The hyperglobalist perspective contends that history and economics have come together to create a new order of international relations in which states are either converging economically and politically, or are being made irrelevant by the activities of transnational business. Economic policies are determined more by markets than by governments and in the economically developed portions of the world, the telecommunications media have facilitated the spread of global mass culture. According to the hyperglobalist perspective, key production factors such as capital technology and even labor are globally mobile and the notions of national products, national industries and national corporations have become redundant, as have the nation-state and its strategies.

—*Author*

1

Post-First World War Peace Settlement

International Relations

International relations (IR) or International studies (IS) represents the study of foreign affairs and global issues among states within the international system, including the roles of states, inter-governmental organizations (IGOs), non-governmental organizations (NGOs), international nongovernmental organizations (INGOs), and multinational corporations (MNCs). It is both an academic and public policy field, and can be either positive or normative as it both seeks to analyse as well as formulate the foreign policy of particular states. It is often considered a branch of political science (specially after 1988 UNESCO nomenclature), but an important sector of academia prefer to treat it as an interdisciplinary field of study. Apart from political science, IR draws upon such diverse fields as economics, history, international law, philosophy, geography, sociology, anthropology, psychology, and cultural studies. It involves a diverse range of issues including but not limited to: globalization, state sovereignty, ecological sustainability, nuclear proliferation, nationalism, economic development, global finance, terrorism, organized crime, human security, foreign interventionism and human rights.

History

The history of international relations is often traced back to the Peace of Westphalia of 1648, where the modern state system was developed. Prior to this, the European medieval organization of political authority was based on a vaguely hierarchical religious order. Westphalia instituted the legal concept of sovereignty, which essentially meant that rulers, or the legitimate sovereigns, had no internal equals within a defined territory and no external superiors as the ultimate authority within the territory's sovereign borders. A simple way to view this is that sovereignty says, "I'm not allowed to tell you what to do and you are not allowed to tell me what to do." Classical Greek and Roman authority at times resembled the Westphalian system, but both lacked the notion of sovereignty.

Westphalia encouraged the rise of the independent nation-state, the institutionalization of diplomacy and armies. This particular European system was exported to the Americas, Africa, and Asia via colonialism and the "standards of civilization". The contemporary international system was finally established through decolonization during the Cold War. However, this is somewhat over-simplified. While the nation-state system is considered "modern", many states have not incorporated the system and are termed "pre-modern".

Further, a handful of states have moved beyond the nation-state system and can be considered "post-modern". The ability of contemporary IR discourse to explain the relations of these different types of states is disputed. "Levels of analysis" is a way of looking at the international system, which includes the individual level, the domestic nation-state as a unit, the international level of transnational and intergovernmental affairs, and the global level.

What is explicitly recognized as International Relations theory was not developed until after World War I, and is dealt with in more detail below. IR theory, however, has a long tradition of drawing on the work of other social sciences. The use of capitalizations of the "I" and "R" in International Relations aims to distinguish the academic discipline of International Relations from the phenomena of international relations. Many cite Thucydides' *History of the Peloponnesian War* as the inspiration for realist theory, with Hobbes' *Leviathan* and Machiavelli's *The Prince* providing further elaboration. Similarly, liberalism draws upon the work of Kant and Rousseau, with the work of the former often being cited as the first elaboration of democratic peace theory. Though contemporary human rights is considerably different than the type of rights envisioned under natural law, Francisco de

Vitoria, Hugo Grotius and John Locke offered the first accounts of universal entitlement to certain rights on the basis of common humanity. In the twentieth century, in addition to contemporary theories of liberal internationalism, Marxism has been a foundation of international relations.

Study of IR

Initially, international relations as a distinct field of study was almost entirely British-centred. In 1919, the Chair in International Politics established at the University of Wales, Aberystwyth (renamed Aberystwyth University in 2008), from an endowment given by David Davies, became the first academic position dedicated to IR. In the early 1920s, the London School of Economics' department of International Relations was founded at the behest of Nobel Peace Prize winner Philip Noel-Baker.

The first university entirely dedicated to the study of IR was the Graduate Institute of International Studies (now the Graduate Institute of International and Development Studies), which was founded in 1927 to form diplomats associated to the League of Nations, established in Geneva some years before. The Graduate Institute of International Studies offered one of the first Ph.D. degrees in international relations. Georgetown University's Edmund A. Walsh School of Foreign Service is the oldest international relations faculty in the United States, founded in 1919. The Committee on International Relations at the University of Chicago was the first to offer a graduate degree, in 1928.

Theory

Epistemology and IR Theory

IR theories can be roughly divided into one of two epistemological camps: "positivist" and "post-positivist". Positivist theories aim to replicate the methods of the natural sciences by analysing the impact of material forces. They typically focus on features of international relations such as state interactions, size of military forces, balance of powers etc. Post-positivist epistemology rejects the idea that the social world can be studied in an objective and value-free way. It rejects the central ideas of neo-realism/liberalism, such as rational choice theory, on the grounds that the scientific method cannot be applied to the social world and that a 'science' of IR is impossible. A key difference between the two positions is that while positivist theories, such as neo-realism, offer causal explanations (such as why and how power is exercised), post-positivist theories focus instead on constitutive questions, for instance what is meant by 'power'; what makes it up, how it is experienced and how it is reproduced. Often, post-positivist theories explicitly promote a normative approach to IR, by considering ethics. This is something which has often been ignored under 'traditional' IR as positivist theories make a distinction between 'facts' and normative judgments, or 'values'. During the late 1980s/1990 debate between positivists and post-positivists became the dominant debate and has been described as constituting the Third "Great Debate" (Lapid 1989).

Paris Peace Conference, 1919

The Paris Peace Conference was the meeting of the Allied victors in World War I to set the peace terms for Germany and other defeated nations, and to deal with the empires of the defeated powers following the Armistice of 1918. It took place in Paris in 1919 and involved diplomats from more than 30 countries. They met, discussed and came up with a series of treaties (Peace of Paris Treaties) in an attempt to maintain a lasting peace throughout the world. At its centre were the leaders of the three "Great Powers": President Woodrow Wilson of the United States, Prime Minister David Lloyd George of Britain, and Georges Clemenceau of France. Germany was not allowed to attend, and Russia, in the middle of a civil war, could not attend, but numerous other nations did send delegations, each with a different agenda. Kings, prime ministers and foreign ministers with their crowds of advisers rubbed shoulders with journalists and lobbyists for a hundred causes, ranging from independence for the countries of the South Caucasus to women's rights. For six months the city was effectively the centre of a world government, as the peacemakers wound up bankrupt empires and created new countries. The most important results included a punitive peace treaty that declared Germany guilty, weakened it militarily, and required it to pay all the costs of the war to the winners. This was known as the War Guilt Clause that was included in the Treaty of Versailles. The Austro-Hungarian Empire was also dissolved and its disparate peoples created new states. The Conference also created the League of Nations.

Historians debate whether or not the terms imposed on Germany helped the rise of the Nazis and cause World War II, or whether the terms were the best that could be expected, given the mood of the victors.

Overview

The conference opened on 18 January 1919. It came to a close on 21 January 1920 with the inaugural General Assembly of the League of Nations.

The following treaties were prepared at the Paris Peace Conference (with, in brackets, the affected countries):

- the Treaty of Versailles, 1919, 28 June 1919), (the German Empire in Weimar Republic form)
- the Treaty of Saint-Germain, 10 September 1919), (Austria)
- the Treaty of Neuilly, 27 November 1919), (Bulgaria)
- the Treaty of Trianon, 4 June 1920), (Hungary)
- the Treaty of Sèvres, 10 August 1920; subsequently revised by the Treaty of Lausanne, 24 July 1923, (Ottoman Empire).

The disposition of the lands of the former Ottoman Empire were also considered. These discussions included competing European and American aims generally, and competing nationalist Zionist and Arab claims in Palestine. The latter were conditionally agreed to previously by the Faisal-Weizmann Agreement on 3 January 1919. On 30 January the Conference decided that the Arab provinces should be wholly separated from the Ottoman Empire and the newly conceived mandate-system applied to them. This decision clashed with the expectation of Faisal's Arab delegation that his state would include Palestine, and the conditional understandings reached in the Faisal-Weizmann Agreement.

On 3 February Chaim Weizmann, the leader of the Zionist delegation, presented its case in a Statement, together with a map of the proposed country. The statement supported the creation of a mandate entrusted to Britain, it detailed this affinity and stated the Jewish historical connection with the area. It also declared the Zionist's proposed borders and resources "essential for the necessary economic foundation of the country" including "the control of its rivers and their headwaters". It included statements by others. On 6 February, Faysal addressing the Conference noted previous Allied promises, demanded independence of the whole of Arab Asia, and suggested the establishment of a confederation. He stated that the Arabs needed help but not at the price of their independence. Subsequently a dispute between Great Britain and France concerning the geographical area of Syria and the previously secret Sykes-Picot Agreement delayed decision on various claims.

The Paris peace treaties, together with the accords of the Washington Naval Conference of 1921-1922, laid the foundations for the so-called Versailles-Washington system of international relations. The remaking of the world map at these conferences gave birth to a number of critical conflict-prone international contradictions, which would become one of the causes of World War II.

The decision to create the League of Nations and the approval of its Charter both took place during the conference.

The "Big Four" — Georges Clemenceau, Prime Minister of France; David Lloyd George, Prime Minister of Great Britain; Woodrow Wilson, President of the United States; and Vittorio Orlando, Prime Minister of Italy — were the dominant diplomatic figures at the conference. The conclusions of their talks were imposed on the defeated countries.

Australia's Approach

The Australian delegates were Billy Hughes (Prime Minister), and Joseph Cook (Minister of the Navy), accompanied by Robert Garran (Solicitor-General). John Greig Latham later Sir, was also part of the delegation. Frederic Eggleston had been invited, but left in disgust at Hughes' behaviour. Indeed, Latham was to run successfully for the Federal seat of Kooyong on a policy of 'Get Rid of Hughes', so appalled was he at Hughes' behaviour. Their principal aims were war reparations, annexation of German New Guinea and rejection of the Japanese racial equality proposal. Hughes had a profound interest in what he saw as an extension of the White Australia Policy. Despite causing a big scene, Hughes had to acquiesce to a class C mandate for New Guinea. President Wilson asked Hughes if Australia really wanted to flout world opinion by profiting from Germany's defeat and extending its sovereignty as far north as the equator; Hughes famously replied: "That's about the size of it, Mr. President".

China's Approach

The Chinese delegation was led by Lou Tseng-Tsiang, accompanied by Wellington Koo.

Before the Western powers, Koo demanded that Japan return Shandong to China. He further called for an end to imperialist institutions such as extraterritoriality, legation guards, and foreign lease holds. Despite American support and the ostensible spirit of self-determination, the Western powers refused his claims. Thus the Chinese delegation at the Paris Peace Conference was the only one not to sign the Treaty of Versailles at the signing ceremony.

France's Approach

The French Prime Minister Georges Clemenceau's chief goal was to weaken Germany militarily, strategically and economically. Having personally witnessed two German attacks on French soil in the last forty years, he was adamant that Germany should not be permitted to attack France again. In particular, Clemenceau sought an American and British guarantee of French security in the event of another German attack. Clemenceau also expressed skepticism and frustration with Wilson's Fourteen Points: "Mr. Wilson bores me with his fourteen points," complained Clemenceau. "Why, God Almighty has only ten!"

Another alternative French policy was to seek a rapprochement with Germany. In May 1919 the diplomat René Massigli was sent on several secret missions to Berlin. During his visits Massigli offered on behalf of his government to revise the territorial and economic clauses of the upcoming peace treaty. Massigli spoke of the desirability of "practical, verbal discussions" between French and German officials that would lead to a "collaboration franco-allemand". Furthermore, Massagli told the Germans that the French thought of the "Anglo-Saxon powers", namely the United States and British Empire, to be the major threat to France in the postwar world. He argued that both France and Germany had a joint interest in opposing "Anglo-Saxon domination" of the world and warned that the "deepening of opposition" between the French and the Germans "would lead to the ruin of both countries, to the advantage of the Anglo-Saxon powers". The Germans rejected the French offers because they considered the French overtures to be a trap to trick them into accepting the Versailles treaty "as is" and because the German foreign minister, Count Ulrich von Brockdorff-Rantzau thought that the United States was more likely to reduce the severity of the peace terms than France. In the final event it proved to be Lloyd George who pushed for more favourable terms for Germany.

There were also some strange intrigues with President Wilson playing the delegates off against one another in order to increase their trust and dependence on him.

Italy's Approach

Italy had been persuaded first to join the Triple Alliance and then to join the Allies in order to gain land. In the Treaty of London, they had been offered the Trentino and the Tyrol as far as Brenner, Trieste and Istria, all the Dalmatian coast except Fiume, full ownership of Albanian Valona and a protectorate over Albania, Antalya in Turkey and a share of Turkish and German Empires in Africa.

Vittorio Orlando was sent as the Italian representative with the aim of gaining these and as much other territory as possible. The loss of 700,000 Italians and a budget deficit of 12,000,000,000 Lire during the war made the Italian government and people feel entitled to these territories. There was an especially strong opinion for control of Fiume, which they believed was rightly Italian due to the Italian population.

Nevertheless, by the end of the war the allies had made contradictory agreements with other nations, especially in Central Europe and the Middle-East. In the meetings of the "Big Four," in which Orlando's powers of diplomacy were inhibited by his lack of English, the Great powers were only willing to offer Trentino to the Brenner, the Dalmatian port of Zara, the Island of Lagosta and a couple of small German colonies. All other territories were promised to other nations and the great powers were worried about Italy's imperial ambitions. As a result of this, Orlando left the conference in a rage (Jackson, 1938).

Japan's Approach

The Japanese delegation was headed by Prince Saionji Kinmochi (former Prime Minister), with Baron Makino Nobuaki (fomer Foreign Minister), Viscount Chinda Sutemi (ambassador in London), Matsui Keishiro (ambassador in Paris) and Ijuin Hikokichi (ambassador in Rome) and others making a total of 64. Neither Hara Takashi (Prime Minister) nor Yasuya Uchida (Foreign Minister) prioritised travelling so far away from Japan so shortly after their election.

The delegation focused on two demands: (a) the inclusion of their racial equality proposal and (b) territorial claims for the former German colonies; Shandong (including Jiaozhou Bay) and the Pacific islands north of the Equator i.e., the Marshall Islands, Micronesia, the Mariana Islands, and the Carolines. Makino was *de facto* chief as Saionji's role was symbolic, limited by ill health. The Japanese delegation became unhappy after receiving only one-half of the rights of Germany, and walked out of the conference.

The Racial Equality Proposal

After the end of seclusion, Japan suffered unequal treaties and demanded equal status with the Powers. In this context, the Japanese delegation to the Paris peace conference proposed the "racial equality clause" in the Covenant of the League of Nations. The first draft was presented to the League of Nations Commission on 13 February as an amendment to Article 21:

The equality of nations being a basic principle of the League of Nations, the High Contracting Parties agree to accord as soon as possible to all alien nationals of states, members of the League, equal and just treatment in every respect making no distinction, either in law or in fact, on account of their race or nationality.

It should be noted that the Japanese delegation did not realize the full ramifications of their proposal, and the challenge its adoption would have put to the established norms of the (Western dominated) international system of the day, involving as it did the colonial subjugation of non-white peoples. In the impression of the Japanese delegation, they were only asking for League of Nations to accept the equality of Japanese nationals; however, a universalist meaning and implication of the proposal became attached to it within the delegation, which drove its contentiousness at the conference.

Makino Announced at a Press Conference

We are not too proud to fight but we are too proud to accept a place of admitted inferiority in dealing with one or more of the associated nations. We want nothing but simple justice.

The proposal received a majority vote on 28 April 1919. 11 out of the 17 delegates present voted in favour to its amendment to the charter, and no negative vote was taken. The votes for the amendment tallied thus:

- Japan (2) Yes
- France (2) Yes
- Italy (2) Yes
- Brazil (1) Yes
- China (1) Yes
- Greece (1) Yes
- Serbia (1) Yes
- Czechoslovakia (1) Yes

Total: 11 Yes

- British Empire (2)-Not Registered
- United States (2)-Not Registered
- Portugal (1)-Not Registered
- Romania (1)-Not Registered
- Belgium (2)-absent

The chairman, U.S. President Woodrow Wilson, overturned it saying that although the proposal had been approved by a clear majority, that in this particular matter, strong opposition had manifested itself, and that on this issue a unanimous vote would be required. This strong opposition came from the British delegation. Though the proposal itself was compatible with British stance of equality for all subjects as a principle for maintaining imperial unity, there were significant deviations in the stated interests of its Dominions, notably Australia. As it risked undermining the White Australia Policy, behind the scenes Billy Hughes and Joseph Cook vigorously opposed the proposal, and so advocated against it through the British delegation. Without the support of its Dominions, the British delegation could not take such a stand on principle. According to Cecil, the delegate representing the British Empire at the Conference, in his diary

...it is curious how all the foreigners[sic] *perpetually harp on principle and right and other abstractions, whereas the Americans and still more the British are only considering what will give the best chance to the League of working properly.*

Though in a diary entry by House it says that President Wilson was at least tacitly in favour of accepting the proposal, but in the end he felt that British support for the League of Nations was a more crucial goal. There is not much evidence to show that Wilson agreed strongly enough with the proposal to risk alienating the British delegation over it. The Japanese media fully covered the progress of the conference, leading to an alienation of Japanese public opinion towards the United States of America, leading to broader conflicts later on.

As such, this point could be listed among the many causes of conflict which lead to World War II, which were left unaddressed at the close of World War I. The rejection of the racial equality clause provoked important factor in turning Japan away from cooperation with West and toward nationalistic policies. It is both ironic, and indicative of the scale of the later changes in the mood of the international system, that this contentious point of racial equality would later be incorporated into the United Nations Charter in 1945 as the fundamental principle of international justice.

Territorial Claims

The Japanese claim to Shandong was disputed by the Chinese. In 1914 at the outset of First World War Japan had seized the territory granted to Germany in 1897. They also seized the German islands in the Pacific north of the equator. In 1917, Japan had made secret agreements with Britain, France and Italy as regards their annexation of these territories. With Britain, there was a mutual agreement, Japan also agreeing to support British annexation of the Pacific islands south of the equator. Despite a generally pro-Chinese view on behalf of the American delegation, Article 156 of the Treaty of Versailles transferred German concessions in Shandong, China to Japan rather than returning sovereign authority to China. The leader of the Chinese delegation, Lu Zhengxiang, demanded that a reservation be inserted before he would sign the treaty.

The reservation was denied, and the treaty was signed by all the delegations except that of China. Chinese outrage over this provision led to demonstrations known as the May Fourth Movement. The Pacific islands north of the equator became a class C mandate administered by Japan.

Britain's Approach

Maintenance of the British Empire's unity, holdings and interests were an overarching concern for the British delegates to the conference, but it entered the conference with the more specific goals of:

- Ensuring the security of France
- Removing the threat of the German High Seas Fleet
- Settling territorial contentions
- Supporting the Wilsonian League of Nations with that order of priority.

The Racial Equality Proposal put forth by the Japanese did not directly conflict with any of these core British interests. However, as the conference progressed the full implications of the Racial Equality Proposal, regarding immigration to the British Dominions (specifically Australia), would become a major point of contention within the delegation.

Ultimately, Britain did not see the Racial Equality proposal as being one of the fundamental aims of the conference. The delegation was therefore willing to sacrifice this proposal in order to placate the Australian delegation and thus help satisfy its overarching aim of preserving the unity of the British Empire.

Britain also managed to rebuff attempts by the envoys of the newly-proclaimed Irish Republic to put its case to the Conference for self-determination, diplomatic recognition and membership of the proposed League of Nations. The Irish envoys' final "Demand for Recognition" in a letter to Clemenceau, the Chairman, was not replied to. Britain had planned to legislate for two Irish Home Rule states, and did so in 1920.

United States' Approach

Prior to Wilson's arrival in Europe, no American President had ever visited Europe while in office. Wilson's Fourteen Points, of a year earlier, had helped win the hearts and minds of many as the war ended; these included Americans and Europeans generally, as well as Germany, its allies and the former subjects of the Ottoman Empire specifically. Wilson's diplomacy and his Fourteen Points had essentially established the conditions for the armistices that had brought an end to World War I. Wilson felt it was his duty and obligation to the people of the world to be a prominent figure at the peace negotiations. High hopes and expectations were placed on him to deliver what he had promised for the postwar era. In doing so, Wilson ultimately began to lead the foreign policy of the United States toward interventionism, a move strongly resisted in some domestic circles.

Once Wilson arrived, however, he found "rivalries, and conflicting claims previously submerged." He worked mostly trying to sway the direction that the French (Georges Clemenceau) and British (Lloyd George) delegations were taking towards Germany and its allies in Europe, as well as the former Ottoman lands in the Middle East. Wilson's attempts to gain acceptance of his Fourteen Points ultimately failed, after France and Britain refused to adopt some specific points and its core principles.

In Europe, several of his Fourteen Points conflicted with the other powers. The United States did not encourage nor believe that the Article 231 placed on Germany was fair or warranted. It would not be until 1921, when the United States finally signed separate peace treaties with Germany, Austria and Hungary.

In the Middle East, negotiations were complicated by competing aims, claims, and the new mandate system. The United States hoped to establish a more liberal and diplomatic world, as stated in the Fourteen Points, where democracy, sovereignty, liberty and self-determination would be respected. France and Britain, on the other hand, already controlled empires, wielded power over their subjects around the world, and still aspired to be dominant colonial powers.

In light of the previously secret Sykes-Picot Agreement, and following the adoption of the mandate system on the Arab province of the former Ottoman lands, the conference heard statements from competing Zionist and Arab claimants. President Woodrow Wilson then recommended an international commission of inquiry to ascertain the wishes of the local inhabitants. The Commission idea, first accepted by Great Britain and France, was later rejected. Eventually it became the purely American King-Crane Commission, which toured all Syria and Palestine during the summer of 1919, taking statements and sampling opinion. Its report, presented to President Wilson, was kept secret from the public until the New York Times broke the story in December 1922. A pro-Zionist joint resolution on Palestine was passed by Congress in September 1922.

France and Britain tried to appease the American President by consenting to the establishment of his League of Nations. However, because isolationist sentiment was strong and some of the articles in the League's charter conflicted with the United States Constitution, the United States never did ratify the Treaty of Versailles nor join the League of Nations, which President Wilson had helped create, to further peace through diplomacy rather than war and conditions which can breed it.

The United States had proved itself to be a major world player and a dominant military and economic power, but it had still failed to win the peace at Paris. The separate treaties with Germany, Austria, and Hungary in 1921 reserved for the United States all reservations it might have had if it had joined the League of Nations, but accepted none of the obligations, because of the constitution. By this time, Warren G, Harding was President of the United States, and these separate treaties broke the deadlock on the League of Nations. These separate treaties kept the United States out of the League.

Statement of the Zionist Organization regarding Palestine

The Zionist Organization submitted their draft resolutions for consideration by the Peace Conference on February 3, 1919. This shortly followed the Conference's decision that the former Arab provinces of the Ottoman Empire should be separated from it and the newly conceived mandate-system applied to them.

The statement included five main points:

- Recognition of the Jewish people's historic title to Palestine and their right to reconstitute their National Home in Palestine.
- The boundaries of Palestine were to be declared as set out in an attached Schedule.
- The sovereign possession of Palestine would be vested in the League of Nations and the Government entrusted to Great Britain as Mandatory of the League.
- Other provisions to be inserted by the High Contracting Parties relating to the application of any general conditions attached to mandates, which are suitable to the case in Palestine.
- The mandate shall be subject also to several noted special conditions.

Statement

The statement reiterates the historic title Zionist Jews claim regarding Palestine. It sets out five main considerations.

- The land is the historic home of the Jews. It is the place where they achieved their greatest development and spiritual and moral influences of value to mankind. They were driven from Palestine by violence and have long hoped for a return.
- Millions of Jews in some parts of the world have experienced deplorable conditions. The need for new opportunities is urgent. Palestine is chosen "above all others in which they would most wish to cast their lot." With economic development, "Palestine can be made now as it was in ancient times, the home of a prosperous population many times as numerous as that which now inhabits it."
- Palestine is not large enough to contain more than a portion of the Jews of the world. The majority of the approximately fourteen million Jews scattered throughout the world must remain in their present locations, and it will be one of the concerns of the Peace Conference to ensure for them equal rights and humane conditions. A Jewish National Home in Palestine will be of high value to the Jews; its influence will permeate the Jews of the world, it will inspire millions,

often despairing, with a new hope and a higher standard; it will help to make them even more useful citizens in the lands in which they currently reside.

- Such a Palestine would be of value also to the world at large, whose real wealth consists in the healthy diversities of its peoples
- The land of Palestine needs redemption and development; much of it is desolate and its present condition is poor. Two things are necessary for that redemption-a stable and enlightened government, and additional people to the present population, which shall be energetic, intelligent, devoted to the country, and backed by the large financial resources that are indispensable for development. The Jews alone can supply such a population.

The statement notes that the historic title of the Jews to Palestine was recognized by the British Balfour Declaration, 1917 and quotes it in full. The Boundary Schedule set out the general lines of the boundaries of Palestine from a point on the Mediterranean Sea near Sidon in the north and following the watersheds of the foothills of the Lebanon, east and then south to Hermon, then east following the northern watersheds of the Nahr Mughaniye to just west of the Hedjaz Railway; south along the railway to the Gulf of Akaba; west along a frontier to be agreed with the Egyptian Government, to the Mediterranean Sea.

The statement notes that Palestine must have its natural outlets to the seas, the control of its rivers and their headwaters and secure water resources. The boundaries were those considered essential for the necessary economic foundation of the country.

The sparsely populated lands east of the Jordan were proposed as an area for economic development. Free access to the Hedjaz Railway was seen as important for both Palestine and Arabia. Intensive development of agriculture in Trans-Jordania would require access to the Red Sea by Palestine. The ports to developed in the Gulf of Akaba were to be free ports to support commerce.

Versailles Peace Settlement

Versailles Peace Settlement (1919–23) Sometimes referred to as the Paris Peace Settlement, a collection of peace treaties between the Central Powers and the Allied powers ending World War I. The main treaty was that of *Versailles* (June 1919) between the Allied powers (except for the USA, which refused to ratify the treaty) and Germany, whose representatives were required to sign it without negotiation.

Another treaty, that of *St Germain-en-Laye* (September 1919), was between the Allied powers and the new republic of AUSTRIA. A third treaty, that of *Trianon* (June 1920), was with the new republic of HUNGARY, in which some three-quarters of its old territories (i.e., all non-Magyar lands) were lost to Czechoslovakia, Romania, and Yugoslavia, and the principle of reparations again accepted. The treaty of *Neuilly* (November 1919) was with BULGARIA, in which some territory was lost to Yugoslavia and Greece, but some also gained from Turkey; a figure of £100 million reparations was agreed, but never paid. These four treaties were ratified in Paris during 1920. A fifth treaty, that of *Sèvres* (August 1920), between the Allies and the old OTTOMAN EMPIRE, was never implemented as it was followed by the final disintegration of the empire and the creation by Mustafa Kemal ATATÜRK of the new republic of Turkey. The treaty was replaced by the Treaty of *Lausanne* (July 1923), in which Palestine, Transjordan, and Iraq were to be mandated to Britain, and Syria to France. Italy was accepted as possessing the Dodecanese Islands, while Turkey regained Smyrna from Greece.

Russian Revolution (1917)

The Russian Revolution is the collective term for the series of revolutions in *Russia* in 1917, which destroyed the Tsarist autocracy and led to the creation of the Soviet Union. In the first revolution of February 1917 (March in the Gregorian calendar) the Czar was deposed and replaced by a Provisional government. In the second revolution of October that year the Provisional Government was removed and replaced with a Bolshevik (Communist) government.

The February Revolution (March 1917) was a revolution focused around St Petersburg. In the chaos, members of the Imperial parliament or Duma assumed control of the country, forming the Russian Provisional Government. The army leadership felt they did not have the means to suppress the revolution and Czar Nicholas II of Russia, the last Czar of Russia, abdicated, effectively leaving the Provisional Government in power. The Soviets (workers' councils) which were led by more radical socialist factions initially permitted the Provisional government to rule, but insisted on a perogative to influence the government and control various militias. The February Revolution took place in the context of heavy military setbacks during the First World War, which left much of the army in a state of mutiny.

A period of dual power ensued, during which the Provisional Government held state power while the national network of Soviets, led by socialists, had the allegiance of the lower-class citizens and the political left. During this chaotic period there were frequent mutinies and many strikes. When the Provisional Government chose to continue fighting the war with Germany, the Bolsheviks and other socialist factions campaigned for the abandonment of the war effort. The Bolsheviks formed workers militias under their control into the Red Guards (later the Red Army) over which they exerted substantial control.

In the October Revolution (November on the Gregorian calendar), the Bolshevik party, led by Vladimir Lenin, and the workers' Soviets, overthrew the Provisional Government in Petrograd. The Bolsheviks appointed themselves as leaders of various government ministries and seized control of the countryside, establishing the Cheka to ruthlessly quash dissent. To end the war, the Bolshevik leadership signed the Treaty of Brest-Litovsk with Germany in March 1918. However a brutal civil war erupted between the "Red" (Bolshevik), and "White" (anti-Bolshevik), factions, which was to continue for several years, with the Bolsheviks ultimately victorious. In this way the Revolution paved the way for the USSR. While many notable historical events occurred in Moscow and Petrograd, there was also a broadly-based movement in cities throughout the state, among national minorities throughout the empire, and in the rural areas, where peasants took over and redistributed land.

Background

At the start of 1917 the country was ripe for revolution — growing rapidly, creating expanded social opportunities but also great uncertainty. Poor villagers more and more often migrated between agrarian and industrial work environments, and many relocated entirely, creating a growing urban labor force. A mid class of white-collar employees, businessmen, and professionals (the latter group comprising doctors, lawyers, teachers, journalists, engineers, etc.) was on the rise. Even nobles had to find new ways to subsist in this changing economy, and contemporaries spoke of new classes forming (proletarians and capitalists, for example), although these classes were also divided along crisscrossing lines of status.

It was becoming harder to speak of clearly-defined social groups or boundaries. Not only were groups fractured in various ways, their defining boundaries were also increasingly blurred by migrating peasants, worker intellectuals, gentry professionals, and the like. There was a general sense that the texture of people's lives was being transformed by a spreading commercial culture which remade the surfaces of material life (buildings, store fronts, advertisements, fashion, clocks and machines) and nurtured new objects of desire.

By 1917, the growth of political consciousness, the impact of revolutionary ideas, and the weak and inefficient system of government (which had been debilitated further by its participation in World War I), should have convinced the emperor, Nicholas II, to take the necessary steps towards reform. In January 1917, in fact, Sir George Buchanan, the British Ambassador in Russia, advised the emperor to "break down the barrier that separates you from your people to regain their confidence." In response to his advice, Nicholas effectively disowned Buchanan.

Many of the people of Russia resented the autocracy of Czar Nicholas II and the corrupt and anachronistic elements in his government. He was seen as being out of touch with the needs and aspirations of the Russian people, the vast majority of whom were victims of the wretched socio-economic conditions which prevailed. Socially, Tsarist Russia stood well behind the rest of Europe in its industry and farming, resulting in few opportunities for fair advancement on the part of peasants and industrial workers. Economically, widespread inflation and food shortages in Russia contributed to the revolution. Militarily, inadequate supplies, logistics, and weaponry led to heavy losses that the Russians suffered during World War I; this further strengthened Russia's view of Nicholas II as weak and unfit to rule. Ultimately, these factors, coupled with the development of revolutionary ideas and movements (particularly during the years following the 1905 Bloody Sunday Massacre), led to the Russian Revolution.

Economic and Social Changes

An elementary theory of property, believed by many peasants, was that land should belong to those who work it. At the same time, peasant life and culture was changing constantly. Change was facilitated by the physical movement of growing numbers of peasant villagers who migrated to and from industrial and urban environments, but also by the migration of city culture into the village through material goods, the press, and word of mouth.

Workers also had good reasons for discontent: overcrowded housing with often deplorable sanitary conditions, long hours at work (on the eve of the war a 10-hour workday six days a week was the average and many were working 11–12 hours a day by 1916), constant risk of injury and death from very poor safety and sanitary conditions, harsh discipline (not only rules and fines, but foremen's fists), and inadequate wages (made worse after 1914 by steep war-time increases in the cost of living). At the same time, urban industrial life was full of benefits, though these could be just as dangerous, from the point of view of social and political stability, as the hardships. There were many encouragements to expect more from life. Acquiring new skills gave many workers a sense of self-respect and confidence, heightening expectations and desires. Living in cities, workers encountered material goods such as they had never seen while in the village. Most important, living in cities, they were exposed to new ideas about the social and political order.

The social causes of the Russian Revolution mainly came from centuries of oppression of the lower classes by the Tsarist regime, and Nicholas's failures in World War I. While rural agrarian peasants had been emancipated from serfdom in 1861, they still resented paying redemption payments to the state, and demanded communal tender of the land they worked. The problem was further compounded by the failure of Sergei Witte's land reforms of the early 1900s. Increasing peasant disturbances and sometimes full revolts occurred, with the goal of securing ownership of the land they worked. Russia consisted mainly of poor farming peasants, with 1.5% of the population owning 25% of the land. The rapid industrialization of Russia also resulted in urban overcrowding and poor conditions for urban industrial workers (as mentioned above). Between 1890 and 1910, the population of the capital, Saint Petersburg, swelled from 1,033,600 to 1,905,600, with Moscow experiencing similar growth. This created a new 'proletariat' which, due to being crowded together in the cities, was much more likely to protest and go on strike than the peasantry had been in previous times. In one 1904 survey, it was found that an average of sixteen people shared each apartment in Saint Petersburg, with six people per room. There was also no running water, and piles of human waste were a threat to the health of the workers. The poor conditions only aggravated the situation, with the number of strikes and incidents of public disorder rapidly increasing in the years shortly before World War I.

World War I only added to the chaos. Conscription swept up the unwilling in all parts of Russia. The vast demand for factory production of war supplies and workers caused many more labor riots and strikes. Conscription stripped skilled workers from the cities, who had to be replaced with unskilled peasants, and then, when famine began to hit due to the poor railway system, workers abandoned the cities in droves to look for food. Finally, the soldiers themselves, who suffered from a lack of equipment and protection from the elements, began to turn against the Tsar. This was mainly because, as the war progressed, many of the officers who were loyal to the Tsar were killed, and were replaced by discontented conscripts from the major cities, who had little loyalty to the Tsar.

Political Issues

Many sections of the crown had reason to be dissatisfied with the existing autocracy. Nicholas II was a deeply conservative ruler and maintained a strict authoritarian system. Individuals and society in general were expected to show self-restraint, devotion to community, deference to the social hierarchy, and a sense of duty to country. Religious faith helped bind all of these tenets together as a source of comfort and reassurance in the face of difficult conditions and as a means of political authority exercised through the clergy. Perhaps more than any other modern monarch, Nicholas II attached his fate and the future of his dynasty to the notion of the ruler as a saintly and infallible father to his people.

This idealized vision of the Romanov monarchy blinded him to the actual state of his country. With a firm belief that his power to rule was granted by Divine Right, Nicholas assumed that the Russian people were devoted to him with unquestioning loyalty. This ironclad belief rendered Nicholas unwilling to allow the progressive reforms that might have alleviated the suffering of the Russian people. Even after the 1905 revolution spurred the Tsar to decree limited civil rights and democratic representation, he worked to limit even these liberties in order to preserve the ultimate authority of the crown.

Despite constant oppression, the desire of the people for democratic participation in government was strong. Since the Age of Enlightenment, Russian intellectuals had promoted Enlightenment ideals such as the dignity of the individual and of the rectitude of democratic representation. These ideals were championed most vociferously by Russia's liberals, although populists, Marxists, and anarchists also claimed to support democratic reforms. A growing opposition movement had begun to challenge the Romanov monarchy openly well before the turmoil of World War I. Dissatisfaction with Russian autocracy culminated in the huge national upheaval that followed the Bloody Sunday massacre of January 1905, in which hundreds of unarmed protesters were shot by the Tsar's troops. Workers responded to the massacre with a crippling general strike, forcing Nicholas to put forth the October Manifesto which established a democratically elected parliament (the State Duma). The Tsar undermined this promise of reform but a year later with Article 87 of the 1906 Fundamental State Laws, and subsequently dismissed the first two Dumas when they proved uncooperative. Unfulfilled hopes of democracy fueled revolutionary ideas and violent outbursts targeted at the monarchy.

One of the Tsar's principal rationales for risking war in 1914 was his desire to restore the prestige that Russia had lost amid the debacles of the Russo-Japanese war. Nicholas also sought to foster a greater sense of national unity with a war against a common and ancient enemy. The Russian Empire was an agglomeration of diverse ethnicities that had shown significant signs of disunity in the years before the First World War. Nicholas believed in part that the shared peril and tribulation of a foreign war would mitigate the social unrest over the persistent issues of poverty, inequality, and inhuman working conditions. Instead of restoring Russia's political and military standing, World War I led to the horrifying slaughter of Russian troops and military defeats that undermined both the monarchy and society in general to the point of collapse.

World War I

The outbreak of war in August 1914 initially served to quiet the prevalent social and political protests, focusing hostilities against a common external enemy, but this patriotic unity did not last long. As the war dragged on inconclusively, war-weariness gradually took its toll. More important, though, was this deeper fragility: although many ordinary Russians joined anti-German demonstrations in the first few weeks of the war, the most widespread reaction appears to have been skepticism and fatalism. Hostility toward the Kaiser and the desire to defend their land and their lives did not necessarily translate into enthusiasm for the Tsar or the government.

Russia's first major battle of the war was a disaster: in the 1914 Battle of Tannenberg, over 30,000 Russian troops were killed or wounded and 90,000 captured, while Germany suffered just 20,000 casualties. However, Austro-Hungarian forces allied to Germany were driven back deep into the Galicia region by the end of the year. In the autumn of 1915, Nicholas had taken direct command of the army, personally overseeing Russia's main theatre of war and leaving his ambitious but incapable wife Alexandra in charge of the government. Reports of corruption and incompetence in the Imperial government began to emerge, and the growing influence of Grigori Rasputin in the Imperial family was widely resented. In the eyes of Lynch, a revisionist historian who focuses on the role of the people, Rasputin was a "fatal disease" to the Tsarist regime.

In 1915, things took a critical turn for the worse when Germany shifted its focus of attack to the Eastern front. The superior German army — better led, better trained and better supplied — was terrifyingly effective against the ill-equipped Russian forces, driving the Russians out of Galicia, as well as Russian Poland, during the Gorlice-Tarnow Offensive campaign. By the end of

October 1916, Russia had lost between 1,600,000 and 1,800,000 soldiers, with an additional 2,000,000 prisoners of war and 1,000,000 missing, all making up a total of nearly 5,000,000 men.

These staggering losses played a definite role in the Mutinies which began to occur, and, in 1916, reports of fraternizing with the enemy started to circulate. Soldiers went hungry, and they lacked shoes, munitions, and even weapons. Rampant discontent lowered morale, only to be further undermined by a series of military defeats.

Casualty rates were the most vivid sign of this disaster. Already, by the end of 1914, only five months into the war, around 390,000 Russian men had lost their lives and nearly 1,000,000 were injured. Far sooner than expected, scarcely-trained recruits had to be called up for active duty, a process repeated throughout the war as staggering losses continued to mount. The officer class also saw remarkable turnover, especially within the lower echelons, which were quickly filled with soldiers rising up through the ranks. These men, usually of peasant or worker backgrounds, were to play a large role in the politicization of the troops in 1917.

The huge losses on the battlefields were not limited to men. The army quickly ran short of rifles and ammunition (as well as uniforms and food), and, by mid-1915, men were being sent to the front bearing no arms; it was hoped that they could equip themselves with the arms that they recovered from fallen soldiers, of both sides, on the battlefields. With patently good reason, the soldiers did not feel that they were being treated as human beings, or even as valuable soldiers, but rather as raw materials to be squandered for the purposes of the rich and powerful.

By the spring of 1915, the army was in steady retreat, which was not always orderly; desertion, plunder and chaotic flight were not uncommon. By 1916, however, the situation had improved in many respects. Russian troops stopped retreating, and there were even some modest successes in the offensives that were staged that year, albeit at great loss of life. Also, the problem of shortages was largely solved by a major effort to increase domestic production. Nevertheless, by the end of 1916, morale among soldiers was even worse than it had been during the great retreat of 1915. The fortunes of war may have improved, but the fact of the war, still draining away strength and lives from the country and its many individuals and families, remained an oppressive inevitability. The crisis in morale (as was argued by Allan Wildman, a leading historian of the Russian army in war and revolution) "was rooted fundamentally in the feeling of utter despair that the slaughter would ever end and that anything resembling victory could be achieved."

The war devastated not only soldiers. By the end of 1915, there were manifold signs that the economy was breaking down under the heightened strain of wartime demand. The main problems were food shortages and rising prices. Inflation shoved real incomes down at an alarmingly rapid rate, and shortages made it difficult to buy even what one could afford. These shortages were especially a problem in the capital, Petrograd (formerly the City of Saint Petersburg), where distance from supplies and poor transportation networks made matters particularly bad. Shops closed early or entirely for lack of bread, sugar, meat and other provisions, and lines lengthened massively for what remained. It became increasingly difficult both to afford and actually buy food.

Not surprisingly, strikes increased steadily from the middle of 1915, and so did crime; but, for the most part, people suffered and endured — scouring the city for food — working-class women in Petrograd reportedly spent about forty hours a week in food lines — begging, turning to prostitution or crime, tearing down wooden fences to keep stoves heated for warmth, grumbling about the rich, and wondering when and how this would all come to an end.

Government officials responsible for public order worried about how long the people's patience would last. A report by the Petrograd branch of the security police, the Okhrana, in October 1916, warned bluntly of "the possibility in the near future of riots by the lower classes of the empire enraged by the burdens of daily existence."

Nicholas was blamed for all of these crises, and what little support he had left began to crumble. As discontent grew, the State Duma issued a warning to Nicholas in November 1916. It stated that, inevitably, a terrible disaster would grip the country unless a constitutional form of government was put in place. In typical fashion, however, Nicholas ignored them, and Russia's Tsarist regime collapsed a few months later during the February

Revolution of 1917. One year later, the Tsar and his entire family were executed. Ultimately, Nicholas's inept handling of his country and the War destroyed the Tsars and ended up costing him both his rule and his life.

February Revolution

This revolution broke out without definite leadership and formal plans, which may be seen as indicative of the fact that the Russian people had had quite enough of the existing system. Petrograd, the capital, became the focus of attention, and, on 23 February (8 March) 1917, people at the food queues started a demonstration. They were soon joined by many thousands of women textile workers, who walked out of their factories—partly in commemoration of International Women's Day but mainly to protest against the severe shortages of bread. Already, large numbers of men and women were on strike, and the women stopped at any still-operating factories to call on their workers to join them. The mobs marched through the streets, with cries of "Bread!" and "Give us bread!" During the next two days, the strike, encouraged by the efforts of hundreds of rank-and-file socialist activists, spread to factories and shops throughout the capital. By 25 February, virtually every industrial enterprise in Petrograd had been shut down, together with many commercial and service enterprises. Students, white-collar workers and teachers joined the workers in the streets and at public meetings, whilst, in the still-active Duma, liberal and socialist deputies came to realise a potentially-massive problem. They presently denounced the current government even more vehemently and demanded a responsible cabinet of ministers. The Duma, consisting primarily of the bourgeoise, pressed the Tsar to abdicate in order to avert a revolution.

On the evening of Saturday the 25th, with police having lost control of the situation, Nicholas II, who refused to believe the warnings about the seriousness of these events, sent a fateful telegram to the chief of the Petrograd military district, General Sergei Khabalov: "I command you tomorrow to stop the disorders in the capital, which are unacceptable in the difficult time of war with Germany and Austria." Most of the soldiers obeyed these orders on the 26th, but mutinies, often led by lower-ranked officers, spread overnight. On the morning of the 27th, workers in the streets, many of them now armed, were joined by soldiers, sent in by the government to quell the riots. Many of these soldiers were insurgents, however, and they joined the crowd and fired on the police, in many cases little red ribbons tied to their bayonets. The outnumbered police then proceeded to join the army and civilians in their rampage. Thus, with this near-total disintegration of military power in the capital, effective civil authority collapsed.

By nighttime on the 27th, the cabinet submitted its resignation to the Czar and proposed a temporary military dictatorship, but Russia's military leaders rejected this course. Nicholas, meanwhile, had been on the front with the soldiers, where he had seen first-hand Russia's defeat at Tannenberg. He had become very frustuated and was conscious of the fact that the demonstrations were on a massive scale; indeed, he feared for his life. The ill health of his son (suffering from the blood disorder hemophilia) was causing him difficulties, too. Nicholas accepted defeat at last and abdicated on 13 March, hoping, by this last act of service to his nation (as he stated in his manifesto), to end the disorders and bring unity to Russia. In the wake of this collapse of the 300-year-old Romanov dynasty—Nicholas's brother, to whom he subsequently offered the crown, refused to become Czar unless that was the decision of an elected government; he wanted *the people* to want him as their leader—a minority of the Duma's deputies declared themselves a Provisional Government, chaired by Prince Lvov, a moderate reformist, although leadership moved gradually to Alexander Kerensky of the Social Revolutionary Party.

October Revolution

The October Revolution was led by Vladimir Lenin and was based upon Lenin's writing on the ideas of Karl Marx, a political ideology often known as Marxism-Leninism. It marked the beginning of the spread of communism in the twentieth century. It was far less sporadic than the revolution of February and came about as the result of deliberate planning and coordinated activity to that end. Though Lenin was the leader of the Bolshevik Party, it has been argued that since Lenin wasn't present during the actual takeover of the Winter Palace, it was really Trotsky's organization and direction that led the revolution, spurred by the motivation Lenin instigated within his party. Critics on the Right have long argued that the financial and logistical assistance of German intelligence via their key agent, Alexander Parvus was a key component as well, though historians are divided, for the evidence is sparse.

On 7 November 1917, Bolshevik leader Vladimir Lenin led his leftist revolutionaries in a revolt against the ineffective Provisional Government (Russia was still using the Julian Calendar at the time, so period references show a 25 October date). The October revolution ended the phase of the revolution instigated in February, replacing Russia's short-lived provisional parliamentary government with government by soviets, local councils elected by bodies of workers and peasants. Liberal and monarchist forces, loosely organized into the White Army, immediately went to war against the Bolsheviks' Red Army.

Soviet membership was initially freely elected, but many members of the Socialist-Revolutionary Party, anarchists, and other leftists opposed the Bolsheviks through the soviets. When it became clear that the Bolsheviks had little support outside of the industrialized areas of Saint Petersburg and Moscow, they barred non-Bolsheviks from membership in the soviets. Other socialists revolted and called for "a third Russian revolution." The most notable instances were the Tambov rebellion, 1919–1921, and the Kronstadt rebellion in March 1921. These movements, which made a wide range of demands and lacked effective coordination, were eventually defeated along with the White Army during the Civil War.

Civil War

The Russian Civil War, which broke out in 1918 shortly after the revolution, brought death and suffering to millions of people regardless of their political orientation. The war was fought mainly between the Red Army ("Reds"), consisting of radical communist revolutionaries, and the "Whites"—the monarchists, conservatives, liberals and moderate socialists who opposed the drastic restructuring championed by the Bolsheviks. The Whites had backing from nations such as Great Britain, France, USA and Japan. Also during the Civil War, Nestor Makhno led a Ukrainian anarchist movement, the Black Army allied to the Bolsheviks thrice, one of the powers ending the alliance each time. However, a Bolshevik force under Mikhail Frunze destroyed the Makhnovist movement, when the Makhnovists refused to merge into the Red Army. In addition, the so-called "Green Army" (peasants defending their property against the opposing forces) played a secondary role in the war, mainly in the Ukraine.

Death of the imperial family

In early March, the Provisional Government placed Nicholas and his family under house arrest in the Alexander Palace at Tsarskoe Selo, 15 miles (24 km) south of Petrograd. In August 1917 the Kerensky government evacuated the Romanovs to Tobolsk in the Urals, allegedly to protect them from the rising tide of revolution during the Red Terror. After the Bolsheviks came to power in October 1917, the conditions of their imprisonment grew stricter and talk of putting Nicholas on trial increased. As the counter revolutionary White movement gathered force, leading to full-scale civil war by the summer, the Romanovs were moved during April and May 1918 to Yekaterinburg, a militant Bolshevik stronghold. During the early morning of 16 July, at approximately 01:30, Nicholas, Alexandra, their children, their physician, and several servants were taken into the basement and killed. According to Edvard Radzinsky and Dmitrii Volkogonov, the order came directly from Vladimir Lenin and Yakov Sverdlov in Moscow. That the order came from the top has long been believed, although there is a lack of hard evidence. It has been argued that the execution was carried out on the initiative of local Bolshevik officials, or that it was an option approved in Moscow should White troops approach Yekaterinburg. Radzinsky noted that Lenin's bodyguard personally delivered the telegram ordering the execution and that he was ordered to destroy the evidence.

The Russian Revolution and the World

Trotsky said that the goal of socialism in Russia would not be realized without the success of the world revolution. Indeed, a revolutionary wave caused by the Russian Revolution lasted until 1923. Despite initial hopes for success in the German Revolution, in the short-lived Hungarian Soviet Republic and others like it, no other Marxist movement succeeded in keeping power in its hands.

This issue is subject to conflicting views on the communist history by various Marxist groups and parties. Stalin later rejected this idea, stating that socialism was possible in one country.

The confusion regarding Stalin's position on the issue stems from the fact that he, after Lenin's death in 1924, successfully used Lenin's argument—the argument that socialism's success needs the workers of other countries in order to happen—to defeat his competitors within the party by accusing them of betraying Lenin and, therefore, the ideals of the October Revolution.

Impact of the Russian Revolution: Ideology Matters Comments to the Meeting of the Western Front Association

Backdrop: German Idealism and Russian Revolutionaries

German philosophers in the 19th century were often "Idealists," that is, they held that ideas have a force, power, and reality that is more "real" than that concrete, reality that so consume us in our daily lives.

German idealism dominated the 19th-century Russian revolutionary movement from the Decembrist Revolt of 1825 until long after Lenin's successful revolutionary coup that we call the October (or Bolshevik or Communist) Revolution of 1917.

I never want to downplay the central role of raw hypocrisy in human affairs. We in the United States have seen the dissonance between the sublime humanism of Marx's ideas and the coarse violence of the Stalinist dictatorship as rank hypocrisy. Yet, we can also see the conflict as the desperate attempt to coerce reality through the power of belief—through the power of the Idea.

And one way to interpret the final collapse of the Soviet Union in 1991 was that the Soviets had lost their ability to convince themselves that the Leninist/Stalinist Idea had the power to transform reality into a better future. With the collapse of this self-justifying, central Myth that legitimized the Soviet experience, the Soviet Union died not with a bang but rather whimpered into Lev Trotsky's "dust bin of history." With this introduction, I would now like to offer three examples in the Russian Revolutionary experience where Ideas deeply affected the course of events. Only toward the end of the twentieth century have these effects begun to run out of steam.

Three Examples

"Moderate" Socialism and the February Revolution of 1917

The first example involves the reaction of moderate socialists to the February Revolution in Petrograd in 1917. Moderate Socialists, including the Marxist Mensheviks in contrast to Lenin's Bolsheviks, had adopted a position that Russia was not yet ready for a Socialist Revolution. Reading Marx's Stages of History literally, they understood the Bourgeois Revolution had to come first and had to take place under the leadership of the bourgeoisie. The working-class movement thus had to satisfy itself with playing the role of a party of the extreme opposition. The bourgeois revolution had to come first and be developed. The responsibility of the proletariat was to encourage this historical necessity.

Real consequences flowed from this belief. When the women, workers, and soldiers of Petrograd spontaneously took to the streets in February 1917, it took only several days for them to overthrow the 300-year-old Romanov dynasty. They then handed power they had won in the streets to their moderate socialist leadership—none of whom were philosophically or psychologically ready to assume the mantle of power. Consistent with their beliefs, the socialists in turn handed power to the bourgeoisie who set up the Provisional Government. Not having the complete courage of their convictions, however, the moderate socialists also created the Petrograd Soviet. This organization held veto-power over the actions of the bourgeois Provisional Government.

This "compromise" established the period of "Dual Power" which was inherently unstable. In retrospect, it is amazing that the Provisional Government, amidst the catastrophe of World War I, managed to hold on to power until October of 1917 when Lenin's and Trotsky's Bolsheviks managed a *coup d'etat* to take power. Lenin, like his Menshevik cousins, was a Marxist, but his Marxism focused less on the determinist element of Marx's Stages of History than on the ability of the individual to assert his will on history. For him, there was no need to wait patiently for the bourgeoisie to fulfil their historical duty at their own leisure; Bolshevism could force the pace. Lenin's Will to Power and his belief in the power of the Idea to change reality made the difference between his success and the moderate socialists' failure.

Lenin's Imperialism, the Highest Stage of Capitalism

The second example of the power of the Idea concerns Soviet influence on the developing world.

Lenin wrote *Imperialism, the Highest Stage of Capitalism* in 1917, during the trials of the First World War and before the Bolshevik Revolution, to explain two crucial contradictions facing Marxists of the day. The first contradiction concerned the delayed outbreak of the promised world revolution. After all, it had already been sixty-nine years since Marx in the *Communist Manifesto* had proclaimed that "A Specter is haunting Europe—the specter of Communism." What had gone wrong?

The second failure of the Marxist promise involved the inability of the world's proletariat to prevent war and its rejection of internationalism for nationalism. It had been a common belief among those of all political stripes from the far right to the far left, that socialist influence on the proletariat had made a major European war impossible. One of the central socialist beliefs was that capitalists and capitalism fight wars for profits. Now, with the spread of democracy and the entry of powerful socialist parties into Europe's parliaments, the capitalists could try to provoke war to their heart's delight. They, however, would find it impossible to vote war credits through parliament or to mobilize soldiers who, following their socialist leadership, would refuse to fight. These ideas evoke memories of the anti-Vietnam War poster: "What if they gave a war and nobody came?"

Lenin's ingenious answer to both questions came in his book, *Imperialism: The Highest Stage of Capitalism.* In it, he argued that the concentration of production had transformed the capitalism of free competition into monopoly capitalism. The concentration of production also had dramatically increased the socialization of production. Big banks had changed from pure credit institutions into business banks and dominated whole sectors of industry. Together, the banks and industry built ties with government. This coalescence of bank capital with industrial capital with strong government ties had formed a financial oligarchy that controlled large sections of the national economy.

Share issues and state loans had increased the power and amount of surplus capital. This surplus flowed beyond political frontiers and extended the financial oligarchy's control to other countries. The capital exporting monopolies had divided the world among themselves. International cartels formed the basis for international relations, and the economic division of the world provided the ground for the struggle for colonies, spheres of influence, and world domination. But once the international cartels had divvied up the world, the struggle now became one for repartitioning the world. Because the economic development of individual countries is uneven and sporadic, some suffered a disadvantage in this repartitioning. Imperialism represented a special, highest, stage of capitalism.

An aggravation of contradictions, frictions, and conflicts accompanied this transition to a capitalism of this higher order with Monopolists assured profits by corrupting the upper stratum of the proletariat in the developed countries. The imperialist ideology permeated the working class. In other words, the burden of bourgeois oppression shifted from the shoulders of the domestic proletariat to those of the colonial peoples. In effect, the Monopolists bribed their domestic proletariat, who came to see that their material interests dependent on successful colonial enterprise. Now, successful war to repartition the world in the favour of a particular nation made fighting war against fellow proletarians in other countries worthwhile.

With his theory, Lenin seemingly had explained those two problems with Marx. The revolution had not yet swept the world because the potential revolutionaries, the proletariat, bribed by the illusion of short-term, material gains, had forgotten their true, long-term interests. They had rejected their class-based internationalism for nationalism because wars fought to expand colonial holdings seemed in their material self-interest. Hence, they did not prevent the outbreak of the Great War.

This theory held long-term importance because Lenin, unlike Marx and Engels, did not see the revolutionary perspectives as centred uniquely on advanced capitalist countries. After the Great War, in a period of "Capitalist Encirclement" the Soviets attacked "the weak link in the chain of imperialism," the colonies. Political influence went to where the oppression was—the colonies.

The colonial and post-colonial world after World War II lacked an entrepreneurial bourgeoisie with the will and capacity to transform existing conditions and to overcome the entrenched interests opposed to full-scale development. In this world, a gospel of competitive individualism seemed useless for modernization to those in the Third World. What seemed needed to get the underdeveloped country moving has been collective effort inspired by a national sense of political purpose. Only governments had enough capital, organizational skills, and commitment to make rapid development possible. Ideologically, therefore, the intelligentsia of such countries gravitated to one or another of the various socialist doctrines. Many have described this as state capitalism, that is, the state and not private individuals perform the entrepreneurial duties of gathering land, labor, and capital for productive enterprise. Socialist rhetoric disguised this crucial essence.

For most of the twentieth century, Soviet Russia provided the model for those in the Third World who wished to rapidly modernize their countries. And rapid modernization was necessary for the sake of national prestige and independence. Russia's success seemed obvious when we note that within forty short years Russia had risen from the ashes of World War I to defeat Hitler, to become one of the world's two superpowers, and to be the first in space. The vocabulary provided by Lenin was just as important as was this practical example. That Marx himself had had little to say to the underdeveloped world mattered little. I would argue that many Third World leaders—two contentious examples are Ho Chi-Minh and Fidel Castro—who led revolutions wanted to assert national pride, independence, and prosperity. They turned to Communism because Lenin had provided them with a vocabulary supplying a coherent explanation for colonial degradation and a means for asserting national regeneration. Additionally, of the major powers, the Soviet regime alone more-or-less consistently supported the aspirations of those wishing to throw off colonial and capitalist oppression. Of course, today, the Communist model no longer holds the same allure it once did.

Two Marxist Heresies: Leninism/Stalinism and Mussolini's Fascism

The final example of the power of ideas generated during World War I involves the intimate, kissing cousin-relationship between Stalinist Communism and Mussolini's Fascism.

Despite facile assumptions, Fascism and Communism were not antipodes. Although their exact relationship remains difficult to define, there exist commonalties, as one author has pointed out:

Fascism was the heir of a long intellectual tradition that found its origins in the ambiguous legacy left to revolutionaries in the work of Karl Marx and Friedrich Engels. Fascism was, in a clear and significant sense, a Marxist heresy. It was a Marxism creatively developed to respond to the specific needs of an economically retarded national community condemned, as a proletarian nation, to compete with the more advanced plutocracies of its time for space, resources, and international stature.

Was this self-awareness present as thinkers and politicians struggled to define these two ideologies as they co-developed earlier in this century? In fact, many did recognize that their common interests held much greater weight than did the Talmudic differences between Fascism and Communism.

Arturo Labriola's *Avanguardia Socialista* of Milan by 1903 had become the forum for Italy's Sorelian syndicalist revolutionaries, who were struggling to make Marx relevant and against reformist socialism. Such luminaries as Vilfredo Pareto and Benedetto Croce graced its pages, followed shortly by a second generation of Sorelian theoreticians, who came to dominate Italian radicalism for more than a generation. Together they constructed an alternative socialist orthodoxy, which they believed was the true heir to classical Marxism. Clearly, their ideas were no more heretical to those of Karl Marx and Friedrich Engels than was Lenin's Marxism.

By 1904 Mussolini, then a socialist agitator in Switzerland, had begun his collaboration with *Avanguardia Socialista,* a relationship he kept for the next five years. The syndicalist contributors to the journal affected the future Duce's intellectual and political development.

Radical syndicalists like A. O. Olivetti innovatively argued that, under retarded economic conditions, socialists must appeal to national sentiment if their ideas are to penetrate the masses. For him, both syndicalism and nationalism were dedicated to increasing production dramatically. As long as Italy remained underdeveloped, the bourgeoisie remained necessary to build the economic foundation requisite for a socialist revolution. Olivetti spoke of a national socialism, because in an underdeveloped economy, only the nation could pursue the economic development presupposed by classical Marxism. When Mussolini took over as editor of the socialist paper, *Avanti!*, in December 1912, he attracted anarchists and even some rigid Marxists like Angelica Balabanoff, whom he took on as his assistant editor. Paolo Orano, who served on the editorial staff of *Avanti!* with other syndicalists like Sergio Panunzio, set the tone of that socialist paper. Mussolini also founded and edited *Utopia* from November 1913 until December of the following year. This bi-monthly review attracted many of the most important young socialist and syndicalist theoreticians, who helped Mussolini to develop his own ideas.

In the final years before the First World War, many independent national syndicalists, including Panunzio and Ottavio Dinale saw war as progressive. Helping to put together the rationale for Fascism, they supported Italy's fight with the Ottomans over Libya in 1911, and, with Mussolini, they called for Italy's intervention in the First World War. Many socialists now passed into Mussolini's Fascist ranks, and syndicalists such as Panunzio, Olivetti, and Orano, became its principal ideologues.

As early as October 1914, Olivetti in *Pagine Libere* spoke of an Italian socialism infused with national sentiment, a socialism destined to complete Italy's unification, to accelerate production, and to place it among the world's advanced nations. Over the next three years in *L'Italia Nostra*, Olivetti spoke of the nation as uniting men of all classes in a common pursuit of historical tasks. Class membership did not align an individual against the nation, but united him with the nation. Patriotism was fully compatible with the revolutionary tradition of Italian socialism.

After Mussolini came to power, Fascism showed its commitment to industrialization and modernization of the economy. The Futurists, Nationalists, and National Syndicalists, the ideologies that composed Fascism, agreed that maximizing production was the first order of business. They also sought urban development, rationalized financial institutions, and bureaucracy reorganized by technical competence. They wanted to abolish "traditional" and nonfunctional agencies, to expand road, rail, waterways, and telephonic communications systems, to modernize secular control of the educational system, and to reduce illiteracy.

What does this mean for Fascism's relationship with Soviet Russia? Mussolini by 1919 was pointing out the absolute decline in economic productivity in Russia as proving its failure to recognize its historic obligations. He suspected the Bolsheviks eventually had to commit themselves to national reconstruction and national defence, that is, to some form of developmental national socialism as defined by Fascism's former Syndicalists. Speaking of the Bolshevik failure to understand their revolutionary necessities, Mussolini presciently predicted that Lenin had to appeal to bourgeois expertise to repair Russia's ravaged economy. Bolshevism, he said, must "domesticate" and mobilize labor to the task of intensive development. The Bolsheviks should have anticipated this, because Marxism had made it clear that socialism could be built only on a mature economic base. Russia, not having yet completed the capitalist stage of economic development, met none of the material preconditions for a classic Marxist revolution. Russia was no more ripe than was Italy for socialism.

Lenin, in the practical working out of his revolutionary government, did run headlong into many of these conundrums predicted by the Syndicalists. In the months following his takeover, he had expected that a revolution in Germany would bail Soviet Russia out of its difficulties. Thus, while the first Fascists were organizing for a national revolution, the Bolsheviks were still dreaming of an international insurrection. Lenin, changing horses, in 1921 proposed the New Economic Policy to replace the ideologically purer but failed War Communism. Like Fascists, Lenin now spoke of holding the entire fabric of society together with "a single iron will," and he began to see the withering away of the state as a long way away: "We need the state, we need coercion"—certainly a Fascist mantra.

After Lenin's death in 1924, this logic culminated in 1925 with Stalin's "creative development" of Marxism: "Socialism in One Country," a national socialism by any other name. Mussolini suspected that Stalin might be abandoning true Communism. This, it seemed, might provide economic advantages to Italy, and to Mussolini it made sense for his country to build ships and planes for the Soviets in exchange for one-third of Italy's oil supplies.

For him the even more interesting possibility was that Stalin might be the true heir to the tsars and an imperialist with whom Fascism could see eye-to-eye. In 1923, the Duce predicted,

"Tomorrow there will not be an imperialism with a socialist mark, but... [Russia] will return to the path of its old imperialism with a panslavic mark." Mussolini convinced himself that Russian Communism was proving to be less revolutionary than was Fascism. The Duce and some of his followers considered it possible that the two movements were moving together closely enough as to be no longer easily distinguishable.

Even dedicated Fascist party workers such as Dino Grandi, Mussolini's foreign minister from 1928 to 1932, early recognized Fascism's affinities with Lenin's Bolshevism. He had taken at least part of his own intellectual inspiration from revolutionary syndicalism, and in 1914 he had talked of the First World War as a class struggle between nations. Six years later, Grandi argued that socialists had failed to understand the simple reality of what was happening in revolutionary Russia. The Bolshevik Revolution had been nothing less than the struggle of an underdeveloped and proletarian nation against the more advanced capitalist states.

Not only Fascists made this analysis. Torquato Nanni, a revolutionary Marxist socialist and an early acquaintance of Mussolini, by 1922 had anticipated these developments. He analyzed the common economic foundations of Fascism and Bolshevism, which produced the related strategic, tactical, and institutional features of these two mass-mobilizing, developmental revolutions. Both, he wrote, had assumed the bourgeois responsibilities of industrializing backward economies and defending the nation-state, the necessary vehicle for progress.

2

The Bolshevik Revolution and its Impact on International Politics

A Defence of the Bolshevik Revolution

TEN YEARS ago Eric Hobsbawm presented his Deutscher Lecture on "Can we write the history of the Russian Revolution?" A lifelong Marxist and author of the groundbreaking series on capitalist development in the nineteenth century, Hobsbawm's credentials as the preeminent Marxist historian of our time are unrivalled. In the wake of the collapse of the Soviet Union, a balance-sheet appraisal on the definitive social movement of the twentieth century by Hobsbawm was quite appropriate. As we will argue tonight, however, some of the opinions that Hobsbawm articulated are less than convincing. The point here is not to concentrate on Hobsbawm the historian, but, rather, to reexamine a set of propositions that I believe reflected the somewhat inconsistent perspective on the Russian Revolution by a much wider audience on the Left after the fall of the Soviet Union. Indeed, many of these arguments still resonate today. Given that the archives of the former Soviet Union have now been open for some sixteen years, I would like to address some of the issues raised by Hobsbawm, to place this discussion within the much wider historiographical trends on the Russian Revolution, and also to engage in some unabashed self-promotion of my own work.

In framing his discussion on the Russian Revolution, Hobsbawm makes several points that I believe we can all agree on. First, his tribute to Isaac Deutscher's trilogy of *Trotsky* immediately answers the question yes, it is possible to write the history of the Russian Revolution, although any definitive history on such a politically charged subject is, as Hobsbawm suggests, problematic. I would add that other classic Marxist accounts of the Russian Revolution cannot go unmentioned. As a synthesis of the class forces involved in 1917, Leon Trotsky's epic masterpiece *The History of the Russian Revolution* remains unsurpassed. Victor Serge's Year One of the Russian Revolution is still the definitive work on the immediate counterrevolutionary attack on Soviet power. If we are to understand the Russian Revolution in its broader European context, then we must include Pierre Broué's masterful study of the German Revolution. Ernest Mandel's writings on Trotsky and Stalinism, and Tony Cliff's works on Lenin, Trotsky, and the class character of the Stalinist system remain essential reading for any student of the revolution.

The list of classic Marxist accounts on the Russian revolutionary era is obviously much longer than this, but the point here is that we are not starting from scratch. We stand on the shoulders of a very rich tradition that, in my opinion, despite sixteen years of archival access, has yet to be equaled by the academy. With all due respect to Eric Hobsbawm, I would also suggest that, were he more familiar with this tradition, he would have made fewer concessions to the renewed hostility to the Russian Revolution that again pervades the historiography.

Second, Hobsbawm argued that the opening of the archives of the former Soviet Union should recast our understanding of Soviet society. "Much of what actually happened can now be known," because information "previously hidden behind locked archive doors and barricades of official lies and half truths" is finally available. He logically asserts that when "better or more complete data are available, they must take the place of poor or incomplete ones." Unfortunately, the issue is much more complicated with the Russian Revolution. As I will argue tonight, if it were simply a question of sources, the standard textbook interpretation of the Russian Revolution would be moving to the left, towards the classical Marxist account, but, instead, we see just the opposite—a historiography shifting to the right and the repackaging of old arguments that often contradict the sources that they are based on.

The defects in the dominant academic interpretation of the Russian Revolution at any given time over the past half century or so have never been primarily due to a lack of access to sources; more important by far has been the question of political perspective. Revolutions inevitably invoke partisanship. Trotsky famously ridiculed historians who feigned neutrality by "climbing out on the wall dividing two camps." Hobsbawm, on the other hand, argues, "It is of course patent that it will take a long time before the passions of those who write the history of the USSR will have cooled down to the tepid temperature of those who nowadays write the history of the Protestant Reformation." This analogy with the Reformation, it seems to me, is quite faulty. Here Hobsbawm has underestimated the driving forces behind the standard academic interpretations of the Russian Revolution and the extent to which the Marxist interpretation, quite deliberately, has been marginalized.

Russian studies first emerged in the United States as a stepchild of the Cold War, and shared much in common with its Soviet state-sponsored counterpart. The Office of Strategic Services (the precursor to the CIA) helped set up the main academic research institutions. To construct a usable past, scholars simply redeployed the totalitarian paradigm, which had been popularized in the confrontation with the Nazi regime, against their former ally and new adversary—the Soviet Union. Cold War Western scholarship was dominated by what Stephen Cohen has aptly termed the "continuity thesis," which posited an uncomplicated, natural evolution from early Bolshevik organizational practice to the gulags. These accounts typically began by holding up Lenin's *What Is to Be Done?* as an embryonic dictatorial blueprint, fully developed well before the revolution. From here it was but a short step to the assertion that a conspiratorial minority of Bolsheviks seized power in 1917 through a military coup, monopolized the state for its own purposes, and, through brute force and terror, created the totalitarian party-state.

Now, of course, the Cold War textbook version of the "continuity thesis," that Lenin led to Stalin, did not go unchallenged. The social movements of the 1960s inspired a generation of historians to study history "from below," in which they attempted to reconstruct the actions and aspirations of those previously written out of history. In no area did this new social history produce a more thorough revision than in the contested field of Russian studies. Over the course of the decade, a talented group of historians proved beyond doubt what many Marxists had long argued—that the transfer of power to the soviets in 1917 was the culmination of a massive popular rebellion. The audacious scholarship of social historians of the Russian Revolution, such as Alexander Rabinowitch and Steve Smith, not only challenged, but ultimately dislodged the totalitarian school.

Western scholarship that challenged the Cold War interpretation of early Soviet society, however, was, for two reasons, much more speculative and problematic. First, primary source materials that were available for the revolutionary period remained largely inaccessible for the Soviet period. Second, the ideological outlook of some scholars accepted the dualistic framework imposed by the Cold War. Partially influenced by Stalinism in its various incarnations, but also as a simplistic response to the Western propaganda history, these scholars bent too far in the other direction, making absurd and unsubstantiated claims about the popular roots of Stalinism. Whatever shortcomings these academics might have exhibited as historians, however, they were quite skilled at marketing their scholarship. The notion that Stalinism was able to draw on considerable working-class support became, as one industrial expert asserted a decade ago, "an increasingly accepted view."

Several factors have shaped the academic study of the Russian Revolution since the fall of the Soviet Union and offset the advantages of unprecedented archival access. First, the emergence of the United States as the preeminent world power after the Cold War inevitably encouraged a shift to the right in the historiography as part of a broader political trend. For many Western scholars, the collapse of the Soviet Union acted as a catalyst for misplaced confidence and renewed strident anticommunism. If the political climate of the times influences the assessment of the most politically charged event of the twentieth century, as I believe it must, then the rightward shift of American politics also influenced the historiography. It was not that conservatives in the field managed to reassert themselves, but, rather, the political and moral collapse of American liberalism blurred the line between conservative and liberal experts on the Russian Revolution. When Richard Pipes published his magnum opus on the revolution just as the Soviet Union was collapsing, the American historian Peter Kenez spoke for a still very lively liberal tradition within the field when he ridiculed Pipes for "prosecuting" the Russian Revolution. A generation ago some of these liberal historians even toyed with Marxism, but they now lead the charge for the reemergence of the continuity thesis.

The other negative impact on the historiography can be attributed to the pervasive influence of postmodernism, which has served to provide a veneer of sophistication for the work of some extremely confused historians. As I detail in the introduction to *Revolution and Counterrevolution,* postmodernism has also encouraged a shortcut, smoke-and-mirrors approach to research over a systematic, comprehensive analysis of the sources. In short, what should be an exciting time for scholarly advancement of the study of the Russian Revolution has largely been squandered. Condemnation and prosecution of the Russian Revolution as an ill-fated endeavor has reasserted itself in the field over the past sixteen years. Yet what is striking in such studies as Orlando Figes' *The Russian Tragedy,* a book applauded by Hobsbawm as an excellent study, is the paucity of new evidence marshaled in support of such arguments.

Perhaps no book pinpoints the fundamental flaws in Western studies of the revolutionary era better than Lars Lih's recent *Lenin Rediscovered—What Is to Be Done? in Context.* As Lih argues, the standard textbook rendering of *What Is to Be Done?* presents it as the supposed first link in the repressive Bolshevik chain that eventually led to Stalinism. So widespread is this myth that even George Bush added it to his repertoire a few months ago when he argued:

> In the early 1900s, an exiled lawyer in Europe published a pamphlet called *What Is to Be Done?* in which he laid out his plan to launch a communist revolution in Russia. The world did not heed Lenin's words, and paid a terrible price.

Lih systematically debunks the standard textbook account of *What Is to Be Done?* and proves that the most steadfast champion of political liberty in the Russian revolutionary movement was none other than V.I. Lenin. Lih comments on the historiography,

"One sometimes gets the impression that the real split within the party was between the faction of Decent and Attractive Individuals vs. the faction of Amoral and Fanatical Thugs." For those with the perseverance to read through this groundbreaking book, there is only one explanation for the ubiquitous hatchet job on Lenin—the academic experts, a veritable who's who of heavyweights in the field, never even bothered to read Lenin systematically in their haste to demonize him.

Both the social historians of the 1970s and the Marxist tradition have rightly focused their attention on the mass revolts of 1905 and 1917: workers learning through conflict with their employers, the strike movements, the formation of soviets, factory committees, and so on. Where Marxists have differed with social historians is on the question of agency. As John Marot has convincingly argued, liberal social historians have tended to underestimate the role of revolutionaries, particularly the Bolsheviks, as an integral part of this radicalization. In fact, we now know that during the most prolonged political strike movement in world history, from 1912 to 1916, all of the contemporary protagonists recognized the role of revolutionaries in the thirty actions over such issues as the murder of Lena goldfield workers and the proroguing of the Duma. What I found is that the catalytic role of revolutionaries determined not just whether specific factories but even whether particular shops participated in these strikes. The argument for political industrial action had to be won on the shop floor. As one report to the Okhrana (the tsarist secret police) demanded, "Find the ones in the factory who are the worst scoundrels and set the tone for the others." The worst scoundrels turned out to be worker Bolsheviks and, after their arrest, the Socialist Revolutionaries.

But we should not just view militant workers as mere victims in this inspiring movement. The revolutionary ranks were constantly refreshed, despite regular rounds of Okhrana arrests and sending militant workers to the war front. The harsh measures enacted by management and the Okhrana actually fostered better labor organization—workers elected representatives and put forward demands in unison to avoid victimization. What I also found interesting in the Moscow metal works is that the various divisions in the workplace, based on skill, gender, and age, were overcome in this process, even before the 1917 revolt. Indeed, the issue that led to the ultimate confrontation with the factory owner, Iulii Guzhon, was the workers' demand to raise the minimum wage rates of the less skilled apprentices and female workers. This prompted the war-profiteering Guzhon to threaten to close the plant, as the demand for minimum pay in his view was "anti-state and anti-democratic because it creates a privileged class of people that is guaranteed its means of existence at the expense of other classes of the population."

Now, aside from a small and shrinking milieu of cold warriors, few historians today would attempt to turn the clock back and completely ignore the important contributions of the social historians. As Hobsbawm argues, "We can say, beyond serious doubt, that in the autumn of 1917 an enormous popular radicalization, of which the Bolsheviks were the main beneficiaries, swept the provisional government aside," and he goes on to say, "The idea that October was nothing more than some sort of conspiratorial coup simply won't stand up."

Yet Hobsbawm's own ambivalence over October is expressed in a series of "counterfactuals" or "what if?" questions. In this sense, he is very much in line with the prevailing historiography today when he asks "Could the October Revolution have been avoided? What might have happened if the Bolsheviks had not decided to take over, or had been willing to take over at the head of a broad coalition with the other socialist and socialist-revolutionary parties?" Hobsbawm argues, "That it would have been better if a democratic Russia had emerged from the revolution is something about which most people would agree."

This ambivalence about October continues to dominate the field—for many historians, October does not measure up to what they believe a genuine proletarian revolution should have looked like. That stridently anti-Marxist historians would have such a keen understanding of what a genuine revolution should look like might sound a bit odd; but let us suppose that this is the case. If you read Philip Foner's fascinating account of the immediate impact of the Russian Revolution on American politics, you find that, for anyone even slightly to the left of centre, the Russian Revolution was a fantastic beacon of hope and inspiration. For example, at a mass rally at Parkview Palace in New York City, 500 workers volunteered to join a Red Guard to defend the Soviet

Union against the German invasion, while hundreds of working women threw their jewellery on the stage to give their support to the revolution. But perhaps these workers had been deceived. When Lloyd George lamented that "the whole of Europe is filled with the spirit of revolution" maybe the European workers who were joining the communist parties in their hundreds of thousands should also have been better informed about the impure nature of the Russian Revolution. Perhaps the academic experts are correct, that they have a better understanding about what a genuine revolution should look like and why the Russian Revolution does not meet these standards. But, surely, if that were the case, they could enlighten us with some previously unknown details about October.

Actually, nothing new has been discovered to challenge what we know, or should know, about October. We do know that 507 of 670 delegates who arrived at the Second Congress of Soviets favoured a transfer of power to the soviets and that almost all of those who walked out were among the 163 minority delegates who were against soviet power in the first place. The argument about the use of force is a red herring today as it was in 1917. Nothing in the record of Right Socialist Revolutionaries and Mensheviks before, during, or after the Second Congress indicates that they were in any way inclined to support soviet power had only the Bolsheviks avoided the use of force—something the moderate socialists themselves were not averse to in their efforts to overthrow the Soviet regime. Obviously, a double standard is invoked here—the same historians who are so upset that the Bolsheviks used their dominant position in the Petrograd Soviet's Military Revolutionary Committee to overthrow the Provisional Government and hand political power to the Congress of Soviets are also conspicuously silent on the military machinations of the Mensheviks and Socialist Revolutionaries (SRs).

Given the liberal parties' strident antirevolutionary record throughout 1917, Hobsbawm rightly dismisses the Kadets as champions of democracy, noting that even liberal historians cannot argue with much conviction that a democratic parliamentary Russia was much of a possibility. That was undoubtedly true ten years ago, but Mark Steinberg, the current editor of *Slavic Review*, recently made an incredible attempt to resuscitate the long dead Kadets, arguing that the liberals, inspired by "noble political dreams and practical political courage," attempted "to construct a new democratic polity." Ultimately, these democratic efforts were thwarted by the authoritarianism of the Leninists, which "was little known or understood outside a small circle of activists."

Hobsbawm's notion of the possibility of "a broad coalition with other socialists" is a more serious but ultimately flawed proposition. Lenin and the Bolsheviks were not averse to conciliation with the Mensheviks and SRs, but on what basis? So disgraced were the Kadets by their compliance in the attempted Kornilov coup that Lenin proposed a peaceful transfer of power to the soviets—if the moderate socialists were willing to draw the lessons of the previous six months and break with the discredited ruling-class parties. In fact, the Second Congress of Soviets unanimously voted to form such a coalition government of parties represented in the soviets, but the minority socialists then immediately chose to ignore the resolution that they had just voted for, denounced the Bolsheviks for overthrowing the Provisional Government, and stormed out of the congress. Alexander Rabinowitch argues that, during the November discussions, the Mensheviks and Right SRs displayed little interest in coming to terms with the Bolshevik regime, or, as Victor Serge argues, they demanded total capitulation on the part of the victors.

In short, the class divide of 1917 emphasized in the Marxist classics by Trotsky, Serge, and others is simply ignored by Hobsbawm and by liberal historians today. In the United States a veritable academic cottage industry continues to perpetuate the myth of Mensheviks and SRs as advocates of socialist democracy. Here new archival sources are not necessary, but rather a simple reminder of the actions of the Mensheviks and SRs. Victor Serge recounts how, after walking out of the Second Congress of Soviets, the Right SRs and Mensheviks immediately united with the Kadets and industrial magnates to form the Committee of Public Safety, which openly appealed to troops to overthrow soviet power; but not one regiment heeded their call. The Right SRs, headed by Abraham Gotz and supported by the Mensheviks, then attempted to organize the failed "junker mutiny" in an unseemly alliance of monarchists, military officers, and anti-soviet socialists. A few weeks later the Right SRs offered military assistance to the Cossack warlord and future Nazi collaborator Petr Krasnov who was marching on Petrograd. The Menshevik Dan later admitted that they had hoped that the Bolsheviks could be "liquidated by force of arms." Serge comments, "Nothing is more tragic at this juncture than the moral collapse of the two great parties of democratic socialism." So no new sources will change the fact that, at one of the most decisive moments in working-class history, the Mensheviks and Right SRs walked out of the democratically elected assembly that represented the Russian masses, and joined the forces of reaction.

Indeed, the unprincipled tactics of the Right SRs and Mensheviks ultimately did lead to a socialist coalition government with the Bolsheviks and the Left SRs. The myth of the Right SR electoral victory could by now be put to rest, were it not for the role it plays in anti-Bolshevik propaganda. As Oliver Radkey, the historian of the Constituent Assembly election, shows, the election ballots unduly favoured the Right SRs, who were neither socialist nor revolutionary but had become "Kadets without admitting it." Additionally, we now know that, in the three areas that distinguished between Left and Right SRs, the Left SRs won overwhelming, by a margin of more than two to one in the Baltic Fleet, by nine to one in Kazan, and by thrity-two to one in Petrograd. A recent study of Saratov province has shown that peasants there complained that they had voted for the SRs under duress and wanted to have their votes changed to the Bolsheviks because of the party's land decree. Now, unless one wants to believe that the peasantry, in mass rebellion against the landlords, were actually simultaneously voting to hand power back to the Kadets in SR clothing, the conclusion, it seems to me, is inescapable: the Bolshevik 25 percent and Left SR majority of the SR 40 percent vote, combined to win the popular vote.

But, for Eric Hobsbawm, the October Revolution was a mistake. He asks, "What made the Bolsheviks decide to take power with an obviously unrealistic program of socialist revolution?" Why was the Bolshevik program unrealistic? He alludes to what he calls the "myth" of the German Revolution that failed to come to the aid of the Russian Revolution as the Bolsheviks had hoped. Hobsbawm recalls that, "My generation was brought up on the story of the betrayal of the German Revolution of 1918," but, according to Hobsbawm: Germany did not belong to the revolutionary sector of Europe.... A German October Revolution, or anything like it, was not seriously on and therefore didn't have to be betrayed. We believe that Pierre Broué's magnificent study of the German Revolution more than adequately refutes this notion of the German Revolution as "myth."

On the civil war, Hobsbawm agrees with Orlando Figes' claim that the Bolsheviks won because they fought under the red flag, however misleading, in the name of the soviets. Unfortunately, Hobsbawm does not address the issue of the origins of the civil war. For Marxists, the civil war was a continuation of the class war that had started in February. Throughout 1917 the far Right and liberals repeatedly made clear that brute force was their class solution to the rebellion. Yet the usual textbook version accuses the Bolsheviks of fighting dirty and asserts that the civil war started with the soviet seizure of power or the closing of the Constituent Assembly in January.

In my opinion, the most important revelation from the archives was found not in the former Soviet Union, but rather in the archives of President Wilson and his staff. David Foglesong's book, *America's Secret War Against Bolshevism,* shows that, just a few weeks after the October Revolution, the U.S. started funneling massive amounts of cash to White forces hostile to soviet power. While publicly claiming that the U.S. was attempting to promote democracy in Russia, privately Secretary of State Robert Lansing had convinced President Wilson that continuing the war efforts on the Eastern Front necessitated establishing a stable Russian government through a "military dictatorship." Over the course of the next several years the U.S. would funnel tens of millions of dollars to anti-Semitic Cossack warlords in an attempt to install such a military dictatorship amenable to U.S. interests. What has to be underscored here is that Russian experts know about all this—but I have yet to find a single reference in any academic study of the Russian Revolution that mentions it, even in a study that focuses exclusively on the Don Cossacks.

Marxists must insist that the massive U.S., British, and French military aid to the White armies is the starting point for any honest discussion about the degeneration of the Russian Revolution. Without such support, right from the beginning, the White armies would never have gotten off the ground. We now know that Trotsky's claim that the White armies were largely mercenary armies created by Western imperialism was quite accurate. Of course, we know that the U.S., Britain, France, and their allies also sent tens of thousands of soldiers into Soviet territory. Winston Churchill described these troops as the "lynchpin" that held the anti-Bolshevik forces together. We also know that, once Western aid to the Whites came to end in late 1919, the civil war also quickly came to an end.

In the aftermath of the civil war, Hobsbawm claims, "The Russian Revolution was destined to build socialism in one backward and soon utterly ruined country." It is indisputable that the economy was indeed ruined, but building socialism in such a context was problematic to say the least. For the Marxist tradition, this social and economic catastrophe, rather than ideologically-driven policies, provided the material basis for Stalinism to emerge.

There is no doubt that the New Economic Policy era, from 1921 to 1928, saw the demise of both soviet and party democracy. Yet this demise was not preordained or linear. Even after the SR trial in 1922, members of this organization, which had tried to organize a military coup and assassinate Lenin, spoke freely in the Hammer and Sickle factory and ran candidates for the Moscow soviet. In the 1923 faction fight, Bolshevik central committee members from both the majority and minority argued their respective positions in front of the factory cell. By 1926 party democracy, however, was a sham. The Hammer and Sickle vote was typical, with over 400 votes for the expulsion and only two votes against. Yet the hounding of oppositionists and anonymous notes to the speaker show that this was a stage-managed affair. Sixteen of seventeen anonymous notes at the expulsion meeting were either hostile to the Politburo line or wanted a hearing for the oppositionists.

The silencing of the opposition coincided with the attempt to convert the factory party organization into an institution that would impose economic concessions and attempt to discipline the workforce. Yet open dissent within the trade unions outlived that in the party. At a union conference in 1926 a Hammer and Sickle worker complained, "The trust administration drive around in automobiles, while cutting costs is done on the backs of workers.

They trick and screw the peasants and this is what is called the smychka [the union between workers and peasants]." Even in September 1927 the party could not silence dissent outside its own ranks. One report complained that the cell was in complete shambles, "The ideological situation in our cell is bad. There are incidents of drunken communists. Workers torment communists and their activity, but they remain silent. We have no group or individual agitation."

For historians intent on connecting the dots between 1917 and Stalinism, the NEP [New Economic Policy] presents a major problem. What I tried to illustrate in my study of the Hammer and Sickle factory is that the ideals of 1917 eventually clashed with ascending Stalinism on the shop floor. Yet there was also a very vibrant, active, and relatively tolerant life in the factories that was very different from the coercion of the first five-year plan. During the NEP dissident voices outside the party ranks could be heard; workers could and did practice religion in the shops. The majority of working women regularly attended women's meetings because these sessions provided a forum in which their grievances could be heard and acted upon. Most workers were active participants in the metal workers' union and rightfully expected their representatives to respond favorably to their concerns, submitting more than 13,000 grievances in 1924 and 1925, the majority resolved in favour of the workers. Far from being a state institution deployed against the working class, as it would later become, workers themselves viewed the union organization as an effective source of power. So strong was the union organization in 1925 that the factory director later wrote that trade-union deputies—rather than managers—held real power in the shops.

Despite the economic catastrophe of seven years of war, workers received real wage increases that approximated their prewar levels by 1926. In short, evidence from the archives now proves that, for much of the NEP, political considerations—a pro-working-class policy in industry—took precedence over economic expediency. Diane Koenker found similar evidence of strong union organization in her recent study of print workers. According to Koenker, print workers during the mid-NEP held control "in four key areas in relations with supervisors, issues of discipline, methods of pay, and consultation over the work process." I would suggest that this is a description of a system very different from capitalism. This is also a very different assessment of industrial relations during the NEP than what Koenker claimed a decade ago when she argued that the socialism that emerged from the civil war "relied on the power of the state agencies—the Cheka [Soviet secret police] and the concentration camp—to ensure adherence to its centrally defined goals and policies." As a litmus test for judging a society, incarceration rates, along with mass terror, might be useful barometers, but American scholars might want to think through the logic of using such a yardstick on a consistent basis. In point of fact, we know that the early Soviet state incarcerated very few workers and a relatively small number of its citizens. Recently published GPU [Soviet intelligence agency] summaries, from 1922 to 1928, report more than 3,000 strikes but mention only six incidents in which authorities arrested striking workers. The entire Soviet prison population only exceeded 100,000 in 1925, with a tiny minority imprisoned for political offences. In her Pulitzer Prize winning study of the gulags, Anne Applebaum reluctantly acknowledges that by the end of 1927 only 300,000 Soviet citizens were incarcerated and political prisoners received special privileged status until 1925. Only in the 1930s was their status reduced to one inferior to that of common criminals. Oleg Khlevniuk's more systematic study of the gulags begins in 1929, because, he notes, "the Stalinist penal system was formed and entrenched during the 1930s—more precisely between 1929 and 1941."

The most exciting area of scholarly research today on early Soviet society is the study of national minorities. Terry Martin makes the following bold comment: The Soviet Union was the world's first Affirmative Action Empire. Russia's new revolutionary government was the first of the old European multiethnic states to confront the rising tide of nationalism and respond by systematically promoting the national consciousness of ethnic minorities. Unfortunately, Martin fails to adequately delineate between the early Soviet support for non-Russian nationalities and Stalin's more ruthless national policies.

We know that the relative tolerance of the NEP was reversed during the first five-year plan. In the factories real wages were cut in half, while workers were forced to labor for much longer hours, factory committees that had previously defended their constituents were transformed into management productivity organs, and open dissent was ruthlessly silenced. While state agents did arrest workers, Stalinism's weapon of choice against the working class was, as the leading historian on Soviet labor, Donald Filtzer, argued long ago, the strategic use of food as a weapon to coerce workers into joining various productivity campaigns. Thanks to Jeffery Rossman's study of Ivanovo textile workers, we also know that there were areas of stiff resistance to the state offensive against the working class, but this was the exception rather than the norm. Recently published top-secret GPU reports show that smoldering but unorganized hatred against the draconian Stalinist labor policies reverberated throughout the Soviet Union. Lynne Viola's study of collectivization shows that the situation was even more volatile in the countryside. In 1930 alone there were 13,754 mass disturbances of armed resistance in which two-and-a-half million peasants fought pitched battles with state agents sent to organize collective farms.

So, if we look at evidence from what has emerged from the archives and from sources that were available long ago, we see a vast discrepancy between the data and the direction of the historiography. *What Is to Be Done?* was not an anti-democratic declaration for a hierarchal organization but a document that advocated political freedom and a practical way of attaining it. The Bolsheviks did not usurp power but provided leadership for a massive popular revolt that supported soviet power. The Civil War was not manufactured by the Bolsheviks but was a continuation of the class conflict of 1917 and only escalated because of the active intervention of the Western powers. Despite the utter devastation of seven years of war and civil war, Soviet citizens could openly criticize the regime; they had the right to practice their religion; workers continued to have considerable control in the factories; 700,000 women participated in the proletarian women's movement; the regime enacted favourable policies for national minorities, and the peasantry, for the most part, was left alone. All of this changed, of course, during the first five-year plan, when coercion and repression supplanted tolerance and persuasion in every aspect of Soviet society. Many historians might acknowledge some of the details on these issues, yet there persists, for ideological reasons, a profound resistance against drawing the conclusion that early Soviet society was fundamentally different from later Stalinism. The new *A History of Russia* textbook by Georgetown University scholars, for example, argues:

In terms of cultural flowering there was a notable divergence between the NEP and the following two and a half decades of blood-soaked Stalinism...yet, some of the horrors to come—show trials, camps, and executions of innocent people—were already in place. The structure of the Soviet system with its rule by party and ideology was well established before Stalin achieved full power, and that ideology looked forward to collectivization and the full realization of socialism and communism.

It should not shock us that Western historians are once again trying to connect the dots between 1917 and Stalinism. The ideologically selective recounting of the revolutionary era is no accident. But the rightward shift in the historiography could not have happened without the relative weakness of the Left that failed to meet the challenge. I would suggest that our isolation from the mainstream arguments is, in part, our own fault. The number of Marxist historians of the Russian Revolution is tiny—many of us are in this room tonight. I would propose that we take the initial steps to organize a Marxist historians' group on the Russian Revolution, to promote discussion on the problematic areas of the revolution but also to engage and challenge the prevailing trends in the field. A new generation of activists inevitably will start to ask questions about the Russian Revolution. We cannot concede this history to the anti-communists. But again we are not starting from scratch. We stand on the shoulders of a very rich tradition that, despite sixteen years of archival access, has yet to be equaled by the academy.

3

Rise of Fascism and Nazism in Europe and its Impact on International Relations

Fascism

Fascism, is a political ideology that seeks to combine radical and authoritarian nationalism with a corporatist economic system, and which is usually considered to be on the far right of the traditional left-right political spectrum.

Fascists advocate the creation of a single-party state, with the belief that the majority is unsuited to govern itself through democracy and by reaffirming the benefits of inequality. Fascist governments forbid and suppress openness and opposition to the fascist state and the fascist movement. Fascism opposes class conflict, blames capitalism and liberal democracies for its creation and communists for exploiting the concept. Fascism fashioned itself as the "Complete opposite of Marxian socialism..." by rejecting the economic and material conception of history, the fundamental belief of fascism being that human beings are motivated by glory and heroism rather than economic motives, in contrast to the worldview of capitalism and socialism.

In the economic sphere, many fascist leaders have claimed to support a "Third Way" in economic policy, which they believed superior to both the rampant individualism of unrestrained capitalism and the severe control of state socialism. This was to be achieved by establishing significant government control over business and labour (Mussolini called his nation's system "the corporate state"). No common and concise definition exists for fascism and historians and political scientists disagree on what should be in any concise definition. Following the defeat of the Axis powers in World War II and the publicity surrounding the atrocities committed during the period of fascist governments, the term *fascist* has been used as a pejorative word.

Etymology

The term *fascismo* is derived from the Italian word *fascio,* which means "bundle" or group, and from the Latin word *fasces;* a *fasces* was a bundle of sticks used symbolically for the power through unity. The fasces, which consisted of a bundle of rods that were tied around an axe, were an ancient Roman symbol of the authority of the civic magistrate; they were carried by his Lictors and could be used for corporal and capital punishment at his command. Furthermore, the symbolism of the fasces suggested *strength through unity*: a single rod is easily broken, while the bundle is difficult to break. This is a familiar theme throughout different forms of fascism; for example the Falange symbol is a bunch of arrows joined together by a yoke.

Definitions

Historians, political scientists, and other scholars have engaged in long debates concerning the exact nature of fascism. Since the 1990s, scholars like Stanley Payne, Roger Eatwell, Roger Griffin and Robert O. Paxton have begun to gather a rough consensus on the system's core tenets. Each form of fascism is distinct, leaving many definitions as too wide or too narrow.

Griffin wrote:

[Fascism is] a genuinely revolutionary, trans-class form of anti-liberal, and in the last analysis, anti-conservative nationalism. As such it is an ideology deeply bound up with modernization and modernity, one which has assumed a considerable variety of external forms to adapt itself to the particular historical and national context in which it appears, and has drawn a wide range of cultural and intellectual currents, both left and right, anti-modern and pro-modern, to articulate itself as a body of ideas, slogans, and doctrine. In the inter-war period it manifested itself primarily in the form of an elite-led "armed party" which attempted, mostly unsuccessfully, to generate a populist mass movement through a liturgical style of politics and a programme of radical policies which promised to overcome a threat posed by international socialism, to end the degeneration affecting the nation under liberalism, and to bring about a radical renewal of its social, political and cultural life as part of what was widely imagined to be the new era being inaugurated in Western civilization. The core mobilizing myth of fascism which conditions its ideology, propaganda, style of politics and actions is the vision of the nation's imminent rebirth from decadence.

Paxton wrote that fascism is:

a form of political behaviour marked by obsessive preoccupation with community decline, humiliation or victimhood and by compensatory cults of unity, energy and purity, in which a mass-based party of committed nationalist militants, working in uneasy but effective collaboration with traditional elites, abandons democratic liberties and pursues with redemptive violence and without ethical or legal restraints goals of internal cleansing and external expansion.

Position in the Political Spectrum

Fascism is normally described as "extreme right", but writers on the subject have often found placing fascism on a conventional left-right political spectrum difficult. There is a scholarly consensus that fascism was influenced by both the left and the right. A number of historians have regarded fascism either as a revolutionary centrist doctrine, as a doctrine which mixes philosophies of the left and the right, or as both of those things.

The historians Eugen Weber, David Renton, and Robert Soucy view fascism as on the ideological right. Rod Stackelberg argues that fascism opposes egalitarianism (particularly racial) and democracy, which according to him are characteristics that make it an extreme right-wing movement. Stanley Payne states that pre-war fascism found a coherent identity through alliances with right-wing movements Roger Griffin argues that since the end of World War II, fascist movements have become intertwined with the radical right, describing certain groups as part of a "fascist radical right".

Walter Laqueur says that historical fascism "did not belong to the extreme Left, yet defining it as part of the extreme Right is not very illuminating either", but that it "was always a coalition between radical, populist ('fascist') elements and others gravitating toward the extreme Right". Payne says "fascists were unique in their hostility to all the main established currents, left right and centre", noting that they allied with both left and right, but more often the right. However, he contends that German Nazism was closer to Russian communism than to any other non-communist system. The position that fascism is neither right nor left is regarded as credible by a number of contemporary historians and sociologists, including Seymour Martin Lipset and Roger Griffin. Griffin argued, "Not only does the location of fascism within the right pose taxonomic problems, there are good ground for cutting this particular Gordian knot altogether by placing it in a category of its own "beyond left and right."

On economic issues, fascists reject ideas of class conflict and internationalism, which are commonly held by Marxists and international socialists, in favour of class collaboration and statist nationalism. However, Italian fascism also declared its objection to excessive capitalism, which it called supercapitalism. Zeev Sternhell sees fascism as an anti-Marxist form of socialism.

A number of fascist movements described themselves as a "third force" that was outside the traditional political spectrum altogether. Mussolini promoted ambiguity about fascism's positions in order to rally as many people to it as possible, saying fascists can be "aristocrats or democrats, revolutionaries and reactionaries, proletarians and anti-proletarians, pacifists and anti-pacifists". Mussolini claimed that Italian Fascism's economic system of corporatism could be identified as either state capitalism or state socialism, which in either case involved "the bureaucratisation of the economic activities of the nation." Mussolini described fascism in any language he found useful. Spanish Falangist leader José Antonio Primo de Rivera was critical of both left-wing and right-wing politics, once saying that "basically the Right stands for the maintenance of an economic structure, albeit an unjust one, while the Left stands for the attempt to subvert that economic structure, even though the subversion thereof would entail the destruction of much that was worthwhile".

Roger Eatwell sees terminology associated with the traditional "left-right" political spectrum as failing to fully capture the complex nature of the ideology and many other political scientists have posited multi-dimensional alternatives to the traditional linear left-right spectrum. In some two dimensional political models, such as the Political Compass (where left and right are described in purely economic terms), fascism is ascribed to the economic centre, with its extremism expressing itself on the authoritarianism axis instead.

Fascist as Epithet

Following World War II, the word *fascist* has become a slur throughout the political spectrum. In contemporary political discourse, some adherents of political ideologies on both the left and right wings of the political spectrum associate fascism with their political enemies, or define it as the opposite of their own views. Some argue that the term *fascist* has become hopelessly vague over the years and that it is now little more than a pejorative epithet. George Orwell wrote in 1944:

The word 'Fascism' is almost entirely meaningless. In conversation, of course, it is used even more wildly than in print. I have heard it applied to farmers, shopkeepers, Social Credit, corporal punishment, fox-hunting, bull-fighting, the 1922 Committee, the 1941 Committee, Kipling, Gandhi, Chiang Kai-Shek, homosexuality, Priestley's broadcasts, Youth Hostels, astrology, women, dogs and I do not know what else... almost any English person would accept 'bully' as a synonym for 'Fascist'. – George Orwell, *What is Fascism?*. 1944.

Richard Griffiths argued in 2005 that the term fascism is the "most misused, and over-used word of our times".

Historical Causes of the Rise of Fascism

A variety of views exist on what led to the rise of fascism as an ideology. Common views include that fascism was a response to events during World War I that led to perceived failings of democracy, liberalism, and Marxism for each having favoured either individualism or internationalism at the expense of nations and nationalism. In Italy, the perceptions of failures of democratic government within the country, Italian liberalism, and the fears of Italian society having been torn apart by Marxism stimulated the creation and popularity of Italian Fascism.

Fascism presented itself as a radical nationalist alternative to rising Bolshevism that came in the Russian October Revolution of 1917 but it did incorporate government infrastructure aspects of Bolshevism into the ideology, such as the single-party state, the concept of rule by an elite group to represent the masses, and appeals to proletarian workers. With economic problems and unemployment facing recently returned veterans of World War I, fascism appealed to collectivism and honouring soldiers and the military by calling for the end of bourgeois individualism while calling for war on Marxism for its anti-nationalist and perceived anti-patriotic ways. The creation of the League of Nations after World War I aggravated nationalists in the world, as the League was seen as the imposition of an internationalist political order upon nations. Fascists saw the League of Nations as only benefiting the wealthy, capitalist democracies. Disillusionment with liberalism deepened with the Stock Market Crash of 1929 and the Great Depression and also created nationalist sentiment in opposition to internationalism.

Alfredo Rocco, Benito Mussolini, and Giovanni Gentile stressed that the primary justification for fascism was a need for purpose in a world that only provided absurdity. Mussolini wrote:

Therefore it is a spiritualized conception, itself the result of the general reaction of modern times against the flabby materialistic positivism of the nineteenth century. Anti-positivistic, but positive: not skeptical, nor agnostic, nor pessimistic, nor passively optimistic, as are, in general, the doctrines (all negative) that put the centre of life outside man, who with his free will can and must create his own world. Fascism desires an active man, one engaged in activity with all his energies: it desires a man virilely conscious of the difficulties that exist in action and ready to face them. It conceives of life as a struggle, considering that it behooves man to conquer for himself that life truly worthy of him, creating first of all in himself the instrument (physical, moral, intellectual) in order to construct it.

Core Tenets

Nationalism

Fascists see the struggle of nation and race as fundamental in society, in opposition to communism's perception of class struggle. In fascism, the nation is considered a single organic entity which binds people together by their ancestry, and is seen as a natural unifying force of peòple. Fascism seeks to solve existing economic, political, and social problems by achieving a millenarian national rebirth, exalting the nation or race above all else, and promoting cults of unity, strength and purity. Benito Mussolini stated in 1922, "For us the nation is not just territory but something spiritual... A nation is great when it translates into reality the force of its spirit."

Eoin O'Duffy, an Irish national corporatist, stated in 1934, We must lead the people always; nationally, socially and economically. We must clear up the economic mess and right the glaring social injustices of today by the corporative organization of Irish life; but before everything we must give a national lead to our people...The first essential is national unity. We can only have that when the Corporative system is accepted. We shall put our National programme to the people, and it is a programme in which even the most advanced Nationalist can find nothing to disturb him.

Joseph Goebbels described the Nazis as being affiliated with authoritarian nationalism: It enables us to see at once why democracy and Bolshevism, which in the eyes of the world are irrevocably opposed to one another, meet again and again on common ground in their joint hatred of and attacks on authoritarian nationalist concepts of State and State systems. For the authoritarian nationalist conception of the State represents something essentially new. In it the French Revolution is superseded.

Plínio Salgado, leader of the Brazilian Integralist Action party emphasized the role of the nation: The best governments in the world cannot succeed in pulling a country out of the quagmire, out of apathy, if they do not express themselves as national energies...Strong governments cannot result either from conspiracies or from military coups, just as they cannot come out of the machinations of parties or the Machiavellian game of political lobbying. They can only be born from the actual roots of the Nation.

Foreign Policy

Italian fascists described expansionist imperialism as a necessity. The 1932 *Italian Encyclopedia* stated: "For Fascism, the growth of empire, that is to say the expansion of the nation, is an essential manifestation of vitality, and its opposite a sign of decadence." Similarly, the Nazis promoted territorial expansionism to in their words provide "living space" to the German nation. Fascists oppose pacifism and believe that a nation must have a warrior mentality. Benito Mussolini spoke of war idealistically as a source of masculine pride, and spoke of pacifism in negative terms:

War alone brings up to their highest tension all human energies and puts the stamp of nobility upon the peoples who have the courage to meet it. Fascism carries this anti-pacifist struggle into the lives of individuals. It is education for combat...war is to man what maternity is to the woman. I do not believe in perpetual peace; not only do I not believe in it but I find it depressing and a negation of all the fundamental virtues of a man.

Joseph Goebbels of the Nazi Party compared World War II to childbirth, and described war as a positive transformative experience:

Every birth brings pain. But amid the pain there is already the joy of a new life. It is a sign of sterility to shy away from new life on the account of pain[...] Our age too is an act of historical birth, whose pangs carry with them the joy of richer life to come. The significance of the war has grown as its scale has increased. It is relentlessly at work, shattering old forms and ideas, and directing the eyes of human beings to new, greater objectives.

Authoritarianism

All fascist movements advocate the creation of an authoritarian government that is an autocratic single-party state led by a charismatic leader with the powers of a dictator. Many fascist movements support the creation of a totalitarian state. The Italian *Doctrine of Fascism* states: "The Fascist conception of the State is all-embracing; outside of it no human or spiritual values can exist, much less have value. Thus understood, Fascism is totalitarian, and the Fascist State—a synthesis and a unit inclusive of all values—interprets, develops, and potentiates the whole life of a people."

However Italian fascism didn't achieve full totalitarian features as in a case of German Nazism (and Soviet communism). Some have argued that in spite of Italian fascism's attempt to form a totalitarian state, fascism in Italy devolved rather to an authoritarian cult of personality around Mussolini. However, both proponents and opponents of fascism in Italy claimed that it had a clear intention to establish a totalitarian state. Only the Nazi regime in Germany has been described as totalitarian by most scholars and critics. Political theorist Carl Schmitt, as a Nazi party member, published *The Legal Basis of the Total State* in 1935, describing the Nazi regime's intention to form a totalitarian state:

The recognition of the plurality of autonomous life would, however, immediately lead back to a disastrous pluralism tearing the German people apart into discrete classes and religious, ethnic, social, and interest groups if it were not for a strong state which guarantees a totality of political unity transcending all diversity. Every political unity needs a coherent inner logic underlying its institutions and norms. It needs a unified concept which gives shape to every sphere of public life. In this sense there is no normal State which is not a total State.

Japanese fascist Nakano Seigo described the need for Japan to follow the Italian Fascist and German Nazi regimes as a model for Japanese government and declared that a totalitarian society was more democratic than democracies, saying:

Both Fascism and Nazism are clearly different from the despotism of the old period. They do not represent the conservatism which lags behind democracy, but are a form of more democratic government going beyond democracy. Democracy has lost its spirit and decayed into a mechanism which insists only on numerical superiority without considering the essence of human beings. It says the majority is all good. I do not agree, because it is the majority which is the precise cause of contemporary decadence. Totalitarianism must be based on essentials, superseding the rule of numbers.

Hungarian fascist leader Gyula Gömbös and his Hungarian National Defence Association also attempted to form a totalitarian state in Hungary, but that attempt failed after Gömbös' death in 1936.

A key authoritarian element of fascism is its endorsement of a prime national leader, who is often known simply as the "Leader" or a similar title, such as: *Duce* in Italian, *Führer* in German, *Caudillo* in Spanish, Poglavnik in Croatia, or *Conducător* in

Romanian. The fascist movement demands obedience to the leader, and may exhort people worship the leader as an infallible saviour of the people. Fascist leaders who ruled countries were not always heads of state, but heads of government, such as Benito Mussolini, who held power under the King of Italy, Victor Emmanuel III.

Social Darwinism

Fascist movements have commonly held social darwinist views of nations, races, and societies. Italian Fascist Alfredo Rocco shortly after World War I claimed that conflict was inevitable in society: Conflict is in fact the basic law of life in all social organisms, as it is of all biological ones; societies are formed, gain strength, and move forwards through conflict; the healthiest and most vital of them assert themselves against the weakest and less well adapted through conflict; the natural evolution of nations and races takes place through conflict. *Alfredo Rocco*

Italian Fascist philosopher Giovanni Gentile in *The Origins and Doctrine of Fascism* promoted the concept of conflict being an act of progress by stating that "mankind only progresses through division, and progress is achieved through the clash and victory of one side over another". Fascist movements commonly follow the social Darwinist view that in order for nations and races to survive in a world defined by perpetual national and racial conflict, nations and races must purge themselves of socially and biologically weak or degenerate people while simultaneously promoting the creation of strong people.

In Germany, the Nazis utilized social Darwinism to promote their racialist concept of the German nation as being part of the Aryan race and the need for the Aryan race to be strong in order to be victorious in what the Nazis believed was ongoing competition and conflict between different races. The Nazis attempted to strengthen the Aryan race in Germany by murdering those they regarded as weaker. To this end, the T4 project was introduced in the late 1930s and organized the murders of around roughly 275,000 handicapped and elderly German civilians using carbon monoxide gas.

Social Interventionism

Generally fascist movements endorse social interventionism

dedicated to influencing society to promote the state's interests. Some scholars say that one cannot speak of "fascist social policy" as a single concept with logical and internally consistent ideas and common identifiable goals. Different fascist movements have spoken of creating a "new man" and a "new civilization" as part of their intention to transform society. Mussolini promised a "social revolution" for "remaking" the Italian people. Adolf Hitler promised to purge Germany of non-Aryan influences on society and create a pure Aryan race through eugenics.

Indoctrination

Fascist states have pursued policies of indoctrination of society to their fascist movements such as through propaganda deliberately spread through education and media through regulation of the production of education and media material. Education was designed to glorify the fascist movement, inform students of it being of major historical and political importance to the nation, attempted to purge education of ideas that were not consistent with the beliefs of the fascist movement, and taught students to be obedient to the fascist movement. Thus fascism tends to be anti-intellectual. The Nazis in particular despised intellectuals and university professors. Hitler declared them unreliable, useless and even dangerous. Hitler said of them: "When I take a look at the intellectual classes we have-unfortunately, I suppose, they are necessary; otherwise one could one day, I don't know, exterminate them or something-but unfortunately they're necessary."

Abortion, Eugenics and Euthanasia

The Fascist government in Italy banned literature on birth control and increased penalties on abortion in 1926, declaring them both crimes against the state. The Nazis decriminalized abortion in cases where fetuses had hereditary defects or were of a race the government disapproved of, while the abortion of healthy "pure" German, "Aryan" fetuses remained strictly forbidden. For non-Aryans, abortion was not only allowed, but often compelled. Their eugenics program stemmed also from the "progressive biomedical model" of Weimar Germany. In 1935 Nazi Germany expanded the legality of abortion by amending its eugenics law, to promote abortion for women who have hereditary disorders. The law allowed abortion if a woman gave her permission, and if the fetus was not yet viable, and for purposes of so-called racial hygiene. The security chief of the neo-Nazi group Aryan Nations expressed similar views, stating: "I'm just against abortion for the pure white race. For blacks and other mongrelized races, abortion is a good idea."

Culture and Gender Roles

Fascism tends to promote principles of masculine heroism, militarism, and discipline; and rejects cultural pluralism and multiculturalism. Initially Italian Fascism officially stood in favour of expanding voting rights to women. In 1920 Mussolini declared that "Fascists do not belong to the crowd of the vain and skeptical who undervalue women's social and political importance. Who cares about voting? You will vote!". Women were briefly given the right to vote until 1925 when the Italian Fascist government abolished elections.

Benito Mussolini perceived women's primary role as childbearers while men should be warriors, once saying "war is to man what maternity is to the woman". The Italian Fascist government during the "Battle for Births" gave financial incentives to women who raised large families as well as policies designed to reduce the number of women employed to allow women to give birth to larger numbers of children.

In 1934, Benito Mussolini declared that employment of women was a "major aspect of the thorny problem of unemployment" which Italy was facing at the time and said that women having a habit of working was "incompatible with childbearing". Mussolini went on to say that the solution to unemployment for men was the "exodus of women from the work force". Italian Fascism called for women to be honoured as "reproducers of the nation" and the Italian Fascist government held ritual ceremonies to honour women's role within the Italian nation. In the 1920s, the Italian Fascist government's *Opera Nazionale Dopolavoro* (OND) allowed working women to attend various entertainment and recreation events including sports that in the past had traditionally been played by men. The Italian Fascist regime was criticized by the Roman Catholic Church that claimed that these activities were causing "masculinization" of women. The Italian Fascist regime responded to such criticism by restricting women to only being allowed to take part in "feminine" and "womanly" sports, while forbidding them to be part of sports that were played mostly by men.

The British Union of Fascists believed that it was unnatural for women to have more influence in a relationship with a man. After Oswald Mosley was arrested in 1940, during interrogation he declared that the British Fascists were committed to equality of the sexes and commended women's role in the British Fascist movement, claiming that the movement had "been largely built up by the fanaticism of women...Without the women I could not have got a quarter of the way...". It is believed that women accounted for 20 per cent to one-third of the British Union of Fascists' membership.

Nazi policies toward women strongly encouraged them to stay at home to bear children and keep house. This policy was reinforced by bestowing the Cross of Honour of the German Mother on women bearing four or more babies. The unemployment rate was cut substantially, mostly through arms production and sending women home so that men could take their jobs. Nazi propaganda sometimes promoted premarital and extramarital sexual relations, unwed motherhood, and divorce. At other times the Nazis opposed such behaviour. The growth of Nazi power, however, was accompanied by a breakdown of traditional sexual morals with regard to extramarital sex and licentiousness. Fascist movements and governments oppose homosexuality. The Italian Fascist government declared it illegal in Italy in 1931. The British Union of Fascists opposed homosexuality and pejoratively questioned their opponents' sexual orientation, especially of male anti-fascists. The Romanian Iron Guard opposed homosexuality as undermining society.

The Nazis thought homosexuality was degenerate, effeminate, perverted and undermined the masculinity which they promoted, because it did not produce children. Nevertheless the Nazis considered homosexuality curable through therapy. They explained it though modern scientism and the study of sexology which said that homosexuality could be felt by "normal" people and not just an abnormal minority. Critics have claimed that the Nazis' claim of scientific reasons for their promotion of racism, and hostility to homosexuals is pseudoscience, in that scientific findings were selectively picked that promoted their pre-existing views, while scientific findings opposing those views were rejected and not taken into account.

Economic Policies

Fascists explicitly promoted their ideology as a "Third Position" between capitalism and communism. Italian Fascism involved corporatism, a political system in which economy is collectively managed by employers, workers and state officials by formal mechanisms at national level. Fascists advocated a new national multi-class economic system that is labeled as either national corporatism, national socialism or national syndicalism. The common aim of all fascist movements was elimination of the autonomy or, in some cases, the existence of large-scale capitalism.

Fascist governments exercised influence over the economy differently than that of communist-led states, in that individual private property was controlled but not nationalized. Nevertheless, like the Soviet Union, fascist states pursued economic policies to strengthen state power and spread ideology, such as consolidating trade unions to be state or party-controlled. Attempts were made by both Fascist Italy and Nazi Germany to establish "autarky" (self-sufficiency) through significant economic planning, but both failed to make the two countries self-sufficient.

National Corporatism, National Socialism and National Syndicalism

While fascists support the unifying of proletariat workers to their cause along corporatistic, socialistic, or syndicalistic lines, fascists specify that they advocate a nationalized form of such economic systems such as corporatism, national socialism, or national syndicalism which promotes the creation of a strong proletarian nation, but not a proletarian class. Fascists also make clear that they have no hostility to the petite bourgeoisie (lower middle-class) or to small businesses and promise these groups protection alongside the proletariat from the upper-class bourgeoisie, big business, and Marxism. The promotion of these groups is the source of the term 'extremism of the centre' to describe fascism. Fascism blames capitalist liberal democracies for creating class conflict and in turn blames communists for exploiting class conflict. In Italy, the Fascist period presided over the creation of the largest number of state-owned enterprises in Western Europe such as the nationalization of petroleum companies in Italy into a single state enterprise called the Italian General Agency for Petroleum (*Azienda Generale Italiani Petroli*, AGIP). Fascists made populist appeals to the middle class (especially the lower middle class) by promising to protect small business and small property owners from communism, and by promising an economy based on competition and profit while pledging to oppose big business.

On economic issues, Benito Mussolini in 1933 declared Italian Fascism's opposition to "decadent capitalism" that he claimed prevailed in the world at the time, but did not denounce capitalism entirely. Mussolini claimed that capitalism had degenerated in three stages, starting with dynamic or heroic capitalism (1830–1870) followed by static capitalism (1870–1914) and then reaching its final form of decadent capitalism, also known as supercapitalism beginning in 1914. Mussolini argued that Italian Fascism was in favour of dynamic and heroic capitalism for its contribution to industrialism and technical developments but claimed that it did not favour supercapitalism, which he claimed was incompatible with Italy's agricultural sector.

Thus Mussolini claimed that Italy under Fascist rule was not capitalist in the modern use of the term which referred to supercapitalism. Mussolini denounced supercapitalism for causing the "standardization of humankind" and for causing excessive consumption. Mussolini claimed that at this stage of supercapitalism "[it] is then that a capitalist enterprise, when difficulties arise, throws itself like a dead weight into the state's arms. It is then that state intervention begins and becomes more necessary. It is then that those who once ignored the state now seek it out anxiously." Mussolini went on to claim that Fascism was the next logical step to solve the problems of supercapitalism and claimed that this step could be seen either as a form of capitalism or socialism which involved state intervention, saying "our path would lead inexorably into state capitalism, which is nothing more nor less than state socialism turned on its head. In either event, [whether the outcome be state capitalism or state socialism] the result is the bureaucratization of the economic activities of the nation."

Some fascists were indifferent or hostile to corporatism. The Nazis initially attempted to form a corporatist economic system like that in Fascist Italy, and created the National Socialist Institute for Corporatism in May 1933, which included many major economists who argued that corporatism was consistent with National Socialism.. In *Mein Kampf,* Hitler spoke enthusiastically about the "National Socialist corporative idea" as one which would eventually "take the place of ruinous class warfare" However, the Nazis later believed that corporatism was not beneficial to Germany because they deemed that it institutionalized and legitimized social differences within the German nation and instead the Nazis went on to promote economic organizations that emphasized the biological unity of the German national community.

Hitler had temporarily been interested in corporatism, but later just used it as a propaganda device, as corporatism was not put into place, even though a number of Nazi officials such as Walther Darré, Gottfried Feder, Alfred Rosenburg, and Gregor Strasser were in favour of a neo-medievalist form of corporatism, as corporations had been influential in German people's history in the medieval era. Spanish Falangist leader José Antonio Primo de Rivera did not believe that corporatism was effective and denounced it as a propaganda ploy, saying "This stuff about the corporative state is another piece of windbaggery".

Economic Planning

Fascists opposed laissez-faire economic policies dominant in the era prior to the Great Depression. After the Great Depression began, many people from across the political spectrum blamed laissez-faire capitalism for the Great Depression, and fascists promoted their ideology as a "third way" between capitalism and communism. Fascists declared their opposition to finance capitalism, interest charging, and profiteering. Nazis and other anti-Semitic fascists, considered finance capitalism a "parasitic" "Jewish conspiracy". Fascist governments nationalized some key industries, managed their currencies and made some massive state investments. Fascist governments introduced price controls, wage controls and other types of economic interventionist measures. Other than nationalization of certain industries, private property was allowed, but property rights and private initiative were contingent upon service to the state. For example, "an owner of agricultural land may be compelled to raise wheat instead of sheep and employ more labour than he would find profitable." According to historian Tibor Ivan Berend, *dirigisme* was an inherent aspect of fascist economies. The Labour Charter of 1927, promulgated by the Grand Council of Fascism, stated in article 7: "The corporative State considers private initiative, in the field of production, as the most efficient and useful instrument of the Nation", then goes on to say in article 9: "State intervention in economic production may take place only where private initiative is lacking or is insufficient, or when are at stakes the political interest of the State. This intervention may take the form of control, encouragement or direct management." Fascists thought that private property should be regulated to ensure that "benefit to the community precedes benefit to the individual." They also introduced price controls and other types of economic planning measures.

Fascism had Social Darwinist views of human relations and promoted "superior" individuals and saw people who were weak as being inferior. In terms of economic practice, this meant promoting the interests of successful businesses while banning trade unions and other workers' organizations. Benito Mussolini in his English autobiography in one section focused on the economy of the United States where he stated that he agreed with the capitalist notion held by Americans that profit should not be taken away from those who produced it from their own labour for any purpose, saying "I do not respect—I even hate—those men that leech a tenth of the riches produced by others".

Social Welfare

Benito Mussolini promised a "social revolution" that would "remake" the Italian people, which was only achieved in part. The people who primarily benefited from Italian fascist social policies were members of the middle and lower-middle classes, who filled jobs in the vastly expanding government workforce, which grew from about 500,000 to a million jobs in 1930. Health and welfare spending grew dramatically under Italian fascism, with welfare rising from seven percent of the budget in 1930 to 20% in 1940.

A major success in social welfare policy in Fascist Italy was the creation of the *Opera Nazionale Dopolavoro* (OND) or "National

After-work Program" in 1925. The OND was the state's largest recreational organizations for adults. The *Dopolavoro* was responsible for establishing and maintaining 11,000 sports grounds, over 6,400 libraries, 800 movie houses, 1,200 theatres, and over 2,000 orchestras.

Membership in the *Dopolavoro* was voluntary but had high participation because of its nonpolitical nature. It is estimated that by 1936 the OND had organized 80 percent of salaried workers. Nearly 40 percent of the industrial workforce had been recruited into the Dopolavoro by 1939 and the sports activities proved popular with large numbers of workers. The OND had the largest membership of any of the mass Fascist organizations in Italy.

The enormous success of the *Dopolavoro* in Fascist Italy was the key factor in Nazi Germany creating its own version of the *Dopolavoro*, the *Kraft durch Freude* (KdF) or "Strength through Joy" program of the Nazi government's German Labour Front, which was even more successful than the *Dopolavoro*.

KdF provided government-subsidized holidays for German workers. KdF was also responsible for the creation of the original Volkswagen ("People's Car") that was a state-made automobile that was meant to be cheap enough to allow all German citizens to be able to own one. While fascists promote social welfare for ameliorating negative economic conditions that are affecting their nation or race as whole, they do not support social welfare for egalitarian reasons. Fascists abhor egalitarianism for preserving the weak; they promote social Darwinist views and claim that nations and races must preserve and promote their strengths to ensure survival in a world that is in a perpetual state of national and/or racial conflict and competition.

Adolf Hitler was opposed to egalitarian and universal social welfare because, in his view, it encouraged the preservation of the degenerate and feeble. While in power, the Nazis created social welfare programs to deal with the large numbers of unemployed. However, those programs were neither egalitarian nor universal, but instead residual, as they excluded multiple minority groups and certain other people whom they felt were incapable of helping themselves, and who would pose a threat to the future health of the German people.

Racism and Racialism

Fascists are not unified on the issues of racism and racialism. Mussolini, in a 1919 speech to denounce Soviet Russia, claimed that Jewish bankers in London and New York City were bound by the chains of race to Moscow, and claimed that 80 percent of the Soviet leaders were Jews. In his 1920 autobiography, he said: "Race and soil are strong influences upon us all", and said of World War I: "There were seers who saw in the European conflict not only national advantages but the possibility of a supremacy of race". In a 1921 speech in Bologna, Mussolini stated that "Fascism was born... out of a profound, perennial need of this our Aryan and Mediterranean race". He said in 1928: [When the] city dies, the nation — deprived of the young life — blood of new generations— is now made up of people who are old and degenerate and cannot defend itself against a younger people which launches an attack on the now unguarded frontiers[...] This will happen, and not just to cities and nations, but on an infinitely greater scale: the whole White race, the Western race can be submerged by other coloured races which are multiplying at a rate unknown in our race. Many Italian fascists held anti-Slavist views, especially against neighbouring Yugoslav nations, whom the Italian fascists saw as being in competition with Italy, which had claims on territories of Yugoslavia, particularly Dalmatia. Mussolini claimed that Yugoslavs posed a threat after Italy did not receive the territory along the Adriatic coast at the end of World War I, as promised by the 1915 Treaty of London. He said: "The danger of seeing the Jugo-Slavians settle along the whole Adriatic shore had caused a bringing together in Rome of the cream of our unhappy regions. Students, professors, workmen, citizens—representative men—were entreating the ministers and the professional politicians. Italian fascists accused Serbs of having "atavistic impulses", and of being part of a "social democratic, masonic Jewish internationalist plot". The fascists accused Yugoslavs of conspiring together on behalf of "Grand Orient masonry and its funds".

In 1933, Mussolini contradicted his earlier statements on race, saying: "Race! It is a feeling, not a reality: ninety-five percent, at least, is a feeling. Nothing will ever make me believe that biologically pure races can be shown to exist today.... National pride has no need of the delirium of race."

Relation to Religion

The attitude of fascism toward religion has run the gamut from persecution, to denunciation, to cooperation, to embrace. Stanley Payne notes that fundamental to fascism was the foundation of a purely materialistic "civic religion" that would "displace preceding structures of belief and relegate supernatural religion to a secondary role, or to none at all", and that "though there were specific examples of religious or would-be 'Christian fascists,' fascism presupposed a post-Christian, post-religious, secular, and immanent frame of reference." According to Payne, such "would be" religious fascists only gain hold where traditional belief is weakened or absent, as fascism seeks to create new non-rationalist myth structures for those who no longer hold a traditional view. The rise of modern secularism in Europe and Latin America, and the incursion and large-scale adoption of western secular culture in the mid-east leave a void where this modern secular ideology, sometimes under a religious veneer, can take hold.

Many fascists were anti-clerical in both private and public life. Although both Hitler and Mussolini were anti-clerical, they both understood that it would be rash to begin their Kulturkampfs prematurely, such a clash, possibly inevitable in the future, being put off while they dealt with other enemies. Hitler had a general plan, even before the Nazis' rise to power, to destroy Christianity within the Reich. The leader of the Hitler Youth stated "the destruction of Christianity was explicitly recognized as a purpose of the National Socialist movement" from the start, but "considerations of expedience made it impossible" publicly to express this extreme position. In Mexico, the Red Shirts were vehemently atheist, renounced religion, killed priests, and on one occasion gunned down Catholics as they left Mass.

According to a biographer of Mussolini, "Initially, fascism was fiercely anti-Catholic" — the Church being a competitor for dominion of the people's hearts. Mussolini, originally an atheist, published anti-Catholic writings and planned for the confiscation of Church property, but eventually moved to accommodation. Mussolini endorsed the Roman Catholic Church for political legitimacy, as during the Lateran Treaty talks, Fascist Party officials engaged in bitter arguments with Vatican officials and put pressure on them to accept the terms that the regime deemed acceptable. Protestantism in Italy was not as significant as Catholicism, and the Protestant minority was persecuted. Mussolini's sub-secretary of Interior, Bufferini-Guidi issued a memo closing all houses of worship of the Italian Pentecostals and Jehovah's Witnesses, and imprisoned their leaders. In some instances, people were killed because of their faith.

The Ustaše in Croatia had strong Catholic overtones, with some clerics in positions of power. The fascist movement in Romania, known as the Iron Guard or the Legion of Archangel Michael, preceded its meetings with a church service, and their demonstrations were usually led by priests carrying icons and religious flags. The Romanian fascist movement promoted a cult of "suffering, sacrifice and martyrdom." In Latin America, the most notable fascist movement was Plinio Salgado's Brazilian Integralism. Built on a network of lay religious associations, its vision was of an integral state that "comes from Christ, is inspired in Christ, acts for Christ, and goes toward Christ." Salgado, however, criticised the "dangerous pagan tendencies of Hitlerism".

Hitler and the Nazi regime attempted to found their own version of Christianity called Positive Christianity which made major changes in its interpretation of the Bible which said that Jesus Christ was the son of God, but was not a Jew; they further claimed that Christ despised Jews, and that the Jews were the ones solely responsible for his death. By 1940, however, it was public knowledge that Hitler had abandoned even the syncretist idea of a positive Christianty.

The Catholic Church was particularly suppressed by Nazis in Poland. In addition to the deaths of some 3 million Polish Jews, 2 million Polish Catholics were killed. Between 1939 and 1945, an estimated 3,000 polish clergy (18 percent) were murdered; of these, 1,992 died in concentration camps. In the annexed territory of *Reichsgau Wartheland* it was even harsher than elsewhere. Churches were systematically closed, and most priests were either killed, imprisoned, or deported to the General Government.

The Germans also closed seminaries and convents persecuting monks and nuns throughout Poland. Eighty percent of the Catholic clergy and five of the bishops of Warthegau were sent to concentration camps in 1939; in Che³mno, 48 percent. Of those murdered by the Nazi regime, 108 are regarded as blessed martyrs. Among them, Maximilian Kolbe was canonized as a saint. Not only in Poland were Christians persecuted by the Nazis. In the Dachau concentration camp alone, 2,600 Catholic priests from 24 different countries were killed. One theory is that religion and fascism could never have a lasting connection because both are a "holistic weltanschauung" claiming the whole of the person. Along these lines, Yale political scientist, Juan Linz and others have noted that secularization had created a void which could be filled by a total ideology, making totalitarianism possible, and Roger Griffin has characterized fascism as a type of anti-religious political religion. Such political religions vie with existing religions, and try, if possible, to replace or eradicate them.

Variations and Subforms

Movements identified by scholars as fascist hold a variety of views, and what qualifies as fascism is often a hotly contested subject. The original movement which self-identified as Fascist was that of Benito Mussolini and his National Fascist Party. Intellectuals such as Giovanni Gentile produced The Doctrine of Fascism and founded the ideology. The majority of strains which emerged after the original fascism, but are sometimes placed under the wider usage of the term, self-identified their parties with different names. Major examples include; Falangism, Integralism, Iron Guard and Nazism as well as various other designations.

Italian Fascism

Fascism was born during a period of social and political unrest following World War I. The war had seen Italy begin to feel a sense of nationalism, rather than its historic regionalism. Despite being an Allied Power, Italy was given what nationalists considered an unfair deal at the Treaty of Versailles. When the other allies told Italy to hand over the city of Fiume at the Paris Peace Conference, war veteran Gabriele d'Annunzio declared the independent state there, the Italian Regency of Carnaro. He named himself *Duce* of the nation and declared a constitution, the *Charter of Carnaro*, which was highly influential to early Fascism, though he himself never became a fascist. Benito Mussolini founded Italian fascism as the Fasci italiani di combattimento after he returned from World War I, and published a Fascist manifesto. The birth of the Fascist movement can be traced to a meeting he held in the Piazza San Sepolcro in Milan on March 23, 1919, which declared the original principles of the Fascists through a series of declarations. These included a dedication to Italian war veterans, a declaration of the fascists' loyalty to Italy and its opposition to foreign aggressors, a pronouncment that the fascists would fight against other political factions and a declaration of opposition to bolshevism and socialism, particularly the socialism of the Italian Socialist Party. They also declared their intention to seize power and their opposition to the multiparty representative democracy in Italy.

The fascists took a moderate stance on the economy, effectively declaring that they favoured class collaboration while opposing excessive state intervention into the economy, and calling for pressure on industrialists and workers to be cooperative and constructive, saying: "As for economic democracy, we favour national syndicalism and reject State intervention whenever it aims at throttling the creation of wealth."

Mussolini and the fascists were simultaneously revolutionary and traditionalist. because this was vastly different from anything else in the political climate of the time, it is sometimes described as "The Third Way". The Fascisti, led by one of Mussolini's close confidants, Dino Grandi, formed armed squads of war veterans called Blackshirts (or *squadristi*) with the goal of restoring order. The blackshirts clashed with communists, socialists and anarchists at parades and demonstrations. The government rarely interfered with the blackshirts' actions, due in part to a widespread fear of a Communist revolution.

The Fascisti grew so rapidly that within two years, it transformed itself into the National Fascist Party at a congress in Rome. Also in 1921, Mussolini was elected to the Chamber of Deputies for the first time and was later appointed as Prime Minister by the King in 1922. He then went on to install a dictatorship after 10 June 1924 assassination of anti-fascist writer Giacomo Matteotti by agents of the Mussolini's *Ceka* secret police. Mussolini's colonialism reached further into Africa in an attempt to compete with British and French colonial empires. Mussolini spoke of making Italy a nation that was "great, respected and feared" throughout Europe, and indeed the world. An early example was his bombardment of Corfu in 1923. Soon after he succeeded in setting up a puppet regime in Albania and forcibly ended a rebellion in Libya, which had been a colony (loosely) since 1912. It was his dream to make the Mediterranean *mare nostrum* ("our sea" in Latin).

Nazism

Nazism, known officially in German as National Socialism (German: *Nationalsozialismus*), is the totalitarian ideology and practices of the Nazi Party or National Socialist German Workers' Party under Adolf Hitler, and the policies adopted by the dictatorial government of Nazi Germany from 1933 to 1945. Nazism is often considered by scholars to be a form of fascism. While it incorporated elements from both left and right-wing politics, the Nazis formed most of their alliances on the right. The Nazis were one of several historical groups that used the term National Socialism to describe themselves, and in the 1920s they became the largest such group. The Nazi Party presented its program in the 25 point National Socialist Program in 1920. Among the key elements of Nazism were anti-parliamentarism, Pan-Germanism, racism, collectivism, eugenics, antisemitism, anti-communism, totalitarianism and opposition to economic liberalism and political liberalism.

In the 1930s, Nazism was not a monolithic movement, but rather a (mainly German) combination of various ideologies and philosophies which centred around nationalism, anti-communism, traditionalism and the importance of the ethnostate. Groups such as Strasserism and Black Front were part of the early Nazi movement. Their motivations were triggered over anger about the Treaty of Versailles, and what they considered to have been a Jewish/communist conspiracy to humiliate Germany at the end of the World War I.

Germany's postwar ills were critical to the formation of the ideology and its criticisms of the postwar Weimar Republic. The Nazi Party came to power in Germany in 1933. In response to the instability created by the Great Depression, the Nazis sought a *Third Way* managed economy that was neither capitalism nor communism. Nazi rule effectively ended on May 7, 1945, V-E Day, when the Nazis unconditionally surrendered to the Allied

Powers, who took over Germany's administration until Germany could form its own democratic government.

Terminology

The term *Nazi* is derived from the first two syllables of *Nationalsozialistische Deutsche Arbeiterpartei,* the official German language name of the National Socialist German Workers' Party (commonly known in English as the Nazi Party). Party members rarely referred to themselves as *Nazis,* and instead used the official term, *Nationalsozialisten* (National Socialists). The word mirrors the term *Sozi,* a common and slightly derogatory term for members of the Social Democratic Party of Germany (*Sozialdemokratische Partei Deutschlands*). When Adolf Hitler took power, the use of the term *Nazi* almost disappeared from Germany, although it was still used by opponents in Austria.

History

National Socialist philosophy came together during a time of crisis in Germany; the nation had lost World War I in 1918, and had also been forced to sign the Treaty of Versailles, a devastating capitulation, and was in the midst of a period of great economic depression and instability. The *Dolchstosslegende* (or "stab in the back"), described by the National Socialists, featured a claim that the war effort was sabotaged internally, in large part by Germany's Jews. The National Socialists suggested that a lack of patriotism had led to Germany's defeat (for one, the front line was not on German soil at the time of the armistice). In politics, criticism was directed at the Social Democrats and the Weimar government (*Deutsches Reich* 1919–1933), which the National Socialists accused of selling out the country. The concept of *Dolchstosslegende* led many to look at Jews and other so-called "non-Germans" living in Germany as having extra-national loyalties, thereby raising antisemitic sentiments and the *Judenfrage* (German for "Jewish Question"), at a time when the Völkisch movement and a desire to create a Greater Germany were strong.

On January 5, 1919, the party that eventually became the Nazi Party was founded under the name German Workers' Party (DAP) by Anton Drexler, along with six other members. German intelligence authorities sent Hitler, a corporal at the time, to investigate the German Workers' Party. As a result, party members invited him to join after he impressed them with the speaking ability he displayed while arguing with party members. Hitler joined the party in September 1919, and he became the propaganda boss. The party was renamed the National Socialist German Workers' Party on February 24, 1920, against Hitler's choice of Social Revolutionary Party. Hitler ousted Drexler and became the party leader on July 29, 1921.

Although Adolf Hitler had joined the Nazi Party in September 1919, and published *Mein Kampf* ("My Struggle") in 1925 and 1926, the seminal ideas of National Socialism had their roots in groups and individuals of decades past. These include the Völkisch movement and its religious-occult counterpart, Ariosophy. Among the various Ariosophic lodge-like groups, only the Thule Society is related to the origins of the Nazi party.

The term *Nazism* refers to the ideology of the National Socialist German Workers' Party and its worldview which permeated German society (and to some degree European and American society) during the party's years as the German government (1933 to 1945). Free elections in 1932 under Germany's Weimar Republic made the NSDAP the largest parliamentary faction; no similar party in any country at that time had achieved comparable electoral success. Hitler's January 30, 1933 appointment as Chancellor of Germany and his subsequent consolidation of dictatorial power marked the beginning of Nazi Germany. During its first year in power, the NSDAP announced the *Tausendjähriges Reich* ("Thousand Years' Empire") or *Drittes Reich* ("Third Reich"), a putative successor to the Holy Roman Empire and the German Empire).

Post-1933 Developments

During the night of February 27, 1933, the Reichstag fire provided Hitler with a convenient excuse for suppressing his opponents. The following day, he persuaded President Paul von Hindenburg to sign an emergency decree suspending civil liberties and stripping the power of the federal German states. Opponents were imprisoned first in improvised camps (*wilde Lager*) and later in an organized system of Nazi concentration camps. On March 23, the Reichstag passed an "Enabling Law" which granted Hitler dictatorial powers. Unions were abolished and political parties, other than the National Socialists, forbidden.

Having dealt with his political enemies, Hitler moved against his rivals in the party, principally those allied with Ernst Röhm, leader of the Sturmabteilung (known as SA or "brownshirts") and Gregor Strasser, leader of the Nazi left wing. Between June 30 and July 2, 1934, these were purged in the so-called Night of the Long Knives. With this, Hitler assured the support of the powerful Reichswehr. After the death of President Paul von Hindenburg on August 2, there was no one left who could present an effective challenge to Nazi power.

The Nazi Party had been anti-Semitic from the beginning, and shortly after seizing power had attempted a boycott against the Jews (see Nazi boycott of Jewish businesses). Official measures against the Jews had been limited by the reluctance of President Hindenburg, but the Nuremberg Laws, proclaimed by Hitler at the 1935 Nazi rally in Nuremberg, provided a legal basis for systematic persecution. Visible signs of anti-Semitism were removed during the 1936 Summer Olympics, but replaced shortly thereafter.

Foreign Reaction

During the mid to late 1930s the British and French governments generally held a stance of appeasement for the Nazi regime and its breaching of Treaty of Versailles through rearmament. Though some figures in Britain and France they had begun to criticize this and Germany's embrace of totalitarianism and in Britain especially, Nazi Germany's policies towards the Jews. Important reasons behind this appeasement included the erroneous assumption that Hitler had no desire to precipitate another world war, even though in *Mein Kampf* he had outlined the party's program in detail, overtly and explicitly committing himself to another European-wide war. Later, when the rebirth of the German military could no longer be ignored, appeasement continued through the concern that neither Britain nor France was yet ready to fight an all-out war against Germany.

The latter line of argument, that the West was not ready for war with Germany, was, as Churchill pointed out, unsatisfactory, as the appeasement program in fact worsened the problem; for example by removing Czechoslovakia's resources from the anti-Nazi side, and adding them to the Nazi side. As Churchill said of appeasement: You were given the choice between war and dishonour. You chose dishonour, and you will have war. If you will not fight for the right when you can easily win without bloodshed; if you will not fight when your victory will be sure and not too costly, you may come to the moment when you will have to fight with all the odds are against you and only a precarious chance of survival. There may even be a worse case. You may have to fight when there is no hope of victory, because it is better to perish than live as slaves.

In 1936, Nazi Germany and Japan entered into the Anti-Comintern Pact, aimed directly at countering Soviet foreign policy. This alliance later became the basis for the Tripartite Pact with Italy, the foundation of the Axis Powers. The three nations united in their opposition to communism, as well as their militaristic, racist regimes, however they failed to coordinate their military efforts effectively.

World War II

The Nazis were determined to retrieve the territories that Germany had lost after the Versailles Treaty and create a powerful, German realm. They wanted this realm to include Danzig, towards which the state of Poland had had limited rights since the Versailles Treaty. When diplomacy failed to secure Danzig's return to Germany, the Nazis got lucky. The communist Soviet Union, an unlikely ally, wanted a non-aggression pact and promised to assist Germany if there was war with Poland. In 1939 Germany attacked Poland; France and the United Kingdom declared war on Germany in response. The Soviet Union then attacked Poland from the east as promised. Poland was defeated but the war between Germany, France and the United States continued.

In 1940, Germany attacked and defeated the French and British continental forces in France. France became an occupied country. The Battle of Britain followed, but Germany soon turned its attention to the East. Hitler believed that if the Soviet Union fell, the United Kingdom would come to terms with Germany.

In 1941, Germany and its allies launched Operation Barbarossa against the Soviet Union. In spite of its initial success, the Soviets were able to turn the tide. After the Battle of Stalingrad, the Soviets launched a powerful offensive and quickly advanced towards Germany from the East. In 1944, the United States and the United Kingdom landed in France as part of a major offensive against the Germans from the West. Within a year, Germany was occupied and defeated and World War II in Europe was over. The victors declared the Nazi Party (NSDAP) a criminal organization and the Nazi regime came to an end.

Today, in the Federal Republic of Germany, Nazism is outlawed as a political ideology, as are forms of iconography and propaganda from the Nazi era. Nevertheless, neo-Nazis continue to operate there and abroad. Following World War II and the Holocaust, the term *Nazi* and symbols associated with Nazism (such as the Swastika) have acquired overwhelmingly negative connotations in Europe and North America.

Ideology

Nazism has come to stand for a belief in the superiority of an Aryan race, an abstraction of the Germanic peoples. During Hitler's time, the Nazis advocated a strong, centralized government under the Führer and claimed to defend Germany and the German people (including those of German ethnicity abroad) against Communism and so-called Jewish subversion. Ultimately, the Nazis sought to create a largely homogeneous and autarkic ethnic state, absorbing the ideas of Pan-Germanism.

Historians often disagree on the principal interests of the Nazi Party and whether Nazism can be considered a coherent ideology. The original National Socialists claimed that there would be no program that would bind them, and that they wanted to reject any established world view. Still, as Hitler played a major role in the development of the Nazi Party from its early stages and rose to become the movement's indisputable iconographic figurehead, much of what is thought to be "Nazism" is in line with Hitler's own political beliefs – the ideology and the man remain largely interchangeable in the public eye. Some dispute whether Hitler's views relate directly to those surrounding the movement; the problem is exacerbated by the inability of various self-proclaimed Nazis and Nazi groups to decide on a universal ideology. But if Nazism is the world view promulgated in *Mein Kampf*, that world view is consistent and coherent, being characterized essentially by a conception of history as a race struggle; the Führerprinzip; anti-Semitism; and the need to acquire *Lebensraum* (living space) at the expense of the Soviet Union. The core concept of Nazism is that the German Volk is under attack from a judeo-bolshevist conspiracy, and must become united, disciplined and self-sacrificing (*id est* must submit to Nazi leadership) in order to win.

Hitler's political beliefs were formulated in *Mein Kampf*. His ideology had three main thoughts: a conception of history as a race struggle influenced by Social Darwinism; antisemitism; and the idea that Germany needed to acquire land from Russia. His antisemitism, coupled with his anti-Communism, gave the grounds of his conspiracy theory of "judeo-bolshevism". Hitler first began to develop his views through observations he made while living in Vienna from 1907 to 1913. He concluded that a racial, religious, and cultural hierarchy existed, and he placed "Aryans" at the top as the ultimate superior race, while Jews and "Gypsies" were people at the bottom. He vaguely examined and questioned the policies of the Austro-Hungarian Empire, where, as a citizen by birth, he had lived during the Empire's last throes. He believed that its ethnic and linguistic diversity had weakened the Empire and helped to create dissent. Furthermore, he saw democracy as a destabilizing force because it placed power in the hands of, amongst others, ethnic minorities who he claimed, "weakened and destabilized" the Empire by dividing it against itself. Hitler's political beliefs were affected by World War I and the 1917 October Revolution, and were further modified between 1920 and 1923. He formulated them definitively in *Mein Kampf*.

Fascism

In both popular thought and academic scholarship, Nazism is generally considered a form of fascism – a term whose definition is contentious. Both fascism and Nazism reject ideologies like democracy, liberalism and Marxism, but it is difficult to identify a perfect definition of the two terms. According to most scholars of fascism, there are both left and right influences on the ideology; it has historically attacked communism, conservatism and parliamentary liberalism, attracting support primarily from the far right.

Italian Fascists tended to believe that all elements in society should be unified through corporatism to form an "Organic State", and Italian fascists often had no strong opinion on race, since it was the state and nation that mattered. German Nazism, however, emphasized the Aryan race or "Volk" principle to the point where the state seemed to be simply a means to an end. Aryanism was not an attractive idea for Italians, who were not considered a Nordic population, but there was still strong racism and genocide in concentration camps in Italy, long before either was in place in Germany.

Some historians, such as Zeev Sternhell, see each movement as unique, however many historians argue that there is a stronger family resemblance between the Italian and the German fascist movements than there is between democracies in Europe or the communist states of the Cold War. Additionally, the crimes of the fascist movement can be compared, not only in numbers of casualties, but also in common developments, such as Benito Mussolini's March on Rome and Adolf Hitler's attempted coup d'etat in Munich.

Nationalism

Hitler founded the Nazi state upon a racially defined "German people" and principally rejected the idea of being bound by the limits of nationalism. That was only a means for attempting unlimited supremacy. In that sense, its hyper-nationalism was tolerated to reach a world-dominating Germanic-Aryan *Volksgemeinschaft*. This idea is a central concept of *Mein Kampf*, symbolized by the motto *Ein Volk, ein Reich, ein Führer* (one people, one empire, one leader). The Nazi relationship between the Volk and the state was called the *Volksgemeinschaft* (people's community), a late nineteenth or early twentieth century neologism that defined a communal duty of citizens in service to the Reich (as opposed to a simple society). The term "National Socialism" derives from this citizen-nation relationship, whereby the term *socialism* is invoked and is meant to be realized through the common duty of the individuals to the German people; all actions are to be in service of the Reich. The Nazis stated that their goal was to bring forth a nation-state as the locus and embodiment of the people's collective will, bound by the *Volksgemeinschaft*, as both an ideal and an operating instrument. In comparison, traditional socialist ideologies oppose the idea of nations.

Militarism

Nazi rationale invested heavily in the militarist belief that great nations grow from military power and maintained order, which in turn grow "naturally" from "rational, civilized cultures". The Nazi Party appealed to German nationalists and national pride, capitalizing on irredentist and revanchist sentiments as well as aversions to various aspects of modernist thinking (although at the same time embracing other modernist ideas, such as admiration for engine power). Many ethnic Germans felt deeply committed to the goal of creating the Greater Germany (the old dream to include German-speaking Austria), which some believe required the use of military force to achieve.

Racism and Discrimination

The Nazi racial philosophy was influenced by the works of Arthur de Gobineau, Houston Stewart Chamberlain, and Madison Grant, and was elaborated by Alfred Rosenberg in the Myth of the Twentieth Century.

Hitler also claimed that a nation was the highest creation of a "race", and "great nations" (literally *large* nations) were the creation of homogeneous populations of "great races" working together. These nations developed cultures that naturally grew from "races" with "natural good health, and aggressive, intelligent, courageous traits". The "weakest nations", Hitler said, were those of "impure" or "mongrel races", because they had divided, quarreling, and therefore weak cultures. Worst of all were seen to be the parasitic "Untermensch" ("subhumans"), mainly Jews, but also Gypsies and Jehovah's Witnesses, homosexuals, the disabled and so-called anti-socials, all of whom were considered "lebensunwertes Leben" ("life-unworthy life") owing to their perceived deficiency and inferiority, as well as their wandering, nationless invasions ("the International Jew"). The persecution of homosexuals as part of the Holocaust (with the *pink triangle*) has seen increasing scholarly attention since the 1990s, even though many homosexuals served in the Sturmabteilungen. According to Nazism, it is an obvious mistake to permit or encourage plurality within a nation. Fundamental to the Nazi goal was the unification of all German-speaking peoples, "unjustly" divided into different Nation States. The Nazis tried to recruit Dutch and Scandinavian men into the SS, considering them of superior "Germanic" stock, with only limited success.

Hitler claimed that nations that could not defend their territory did not deserve it. He thought "slave races", like the Slavic peoples, to be less worthy to exist than "leader races". In particular, if a master race should require room to live ("Lebensraum"), he thought such a race should have the right to displace the inferior indigenous races.

"Races without homelands", Hitler proclaimed, were "parasitic races", and the richer the members of a parasitic race were, the more virulent the parasitism was said to be. A master race could therefore, according to the Nazi doctrine, easily strengthen itself by eliminating parasitic races from its homeland. This idea was the given rationalization for the Nazis' later oppression and elimination of Jews, Gypsies, Czechs, Poles, the mentally and physically handicapped, homosexuals and others not belonging to these groups or categories that were part of the Holocaust. The Waffen-SS and other German soldiers (including parts of the Wehrmacht), as well as civilian paramilitary groups in occupied territories, were responsible for the deaths of an estimated eleven million men, women, and children in concentration camps, prisoner-of-war camps, labor camps, and death camps such as Auschwitz and Treblinka.

Eugenics

The belief in the need to purify the German race led them to eugenics; this effort culminated in the involuntary euthanasia of disabled people and the compulsory sterilization of people with mental deficiencies or illnesses perceived as hereditary. Adolf Hitler considered Sparta to be the first "Völkisch State", and praised its early eugenics treatment of deformed children.

Antisemitism

According to Nazi propaganda, the Jews thrived on fomenting division amongst Germans and amongst states. Nazi antisemitism was primarily racial: "The Jew is the enemy and destroyer of the purity of blood, the conscious destroyer of our race;" however, the Jews were also described as plutocrats exploiting the worker: "As socialists we are opponents of the Jews because we see in the Hebrews the incarnation of capitalism, of the misuse of the nation's goods." In addition, the Nazis articulated opposition to finance capitalism with an emphasis on antisemitic claims that this was manipulated by a conspiracy of Jewish bankers.

Homophobia

In late February 1933, as the moderating influence of Ernst Röhm weakened, the Nazi Party launched its purge of homosexual (gay, lesbian, and bisexual; then known as homophile) clubs in Berlin, outlawed sex publications, and banned organized gay groups. As a consequence, many fled Germany (e.g., Erika Mann, Richard Plaut). In March 1933, Kurt Hiller, the main organizer of Magnus Hirschfeld's Institute of Sex Research, was sent to a concentration camp.

An estimated 100,000 homosexuals were arrested after Hitler's rise to power in the 1930s. Of those, 50,000 were suspected to be incarcerated in concentration camps, making for 5,000 to 15,000 deaths.

On May 6, 1933, Nazi Youth of the Deutsche Studentenschaft made an organised attack on the Institute of Sex Research. A few days later the Institute's library and archives were publicly hauled out and burned in the streets of the Opernplatz. Around 20,000 books and journals, and 5,000 images, were destroyed. Also seized were the Institute's extensive lists of names and addresses of LGBT people. In the midst of the burning, Joseph Goebbels gave a political speech to a crowd of around 40,000 people.

Hitler initially protected Röhm from other elements of the Nazi Party which held his homosexuality to be a violation of the party's strong anti-gay policy. However, Hitler later changed course when he perceived Röhm to be a potential threat to his power. During the Night of the Long Knives in 1934, a purge of those who Hitler deemed threats to his power took place. He had Röhm murdered and used Röhm's homosexuality as a justification to suppress outrage within the ranks of the SA. After solidifying his power, Hitler would include gay men among those sent to concentration camps during the Holocaust.

Himmler had initially been a supporter of Röhm, arguing that the charges of homosexuality against him were manufactured by Jews. But after the purge, Hitler elevated Himmler's status and he became very active in the suppression of homosexuality. He exclaimed, "We must exterminate these people root and branch... the homosexual must be eliminated." (Plant, 1986, p. 99).

In 1936, Heinrich Himmler, Chief of the SS, created the "Reich Central Office for the Combating of Homosexuality and Abortion." Homosexuality was declared contrary to "wholesome popular sentiment," and gay men were regarded as "defilers of German blood." Homosexuals were persecuted for their sexuality. When they were prisoners in a concentration camp, they were forced to wear a pink triangle.

Lesbians were not widely persecuted under Nazi anti-gay laws, as it was considered easier to persuade or force them to comply with accepted heterosexual behaviour. However, they were viewed as a threat to state values and were often branded "anti-social."

Religion

Hitler extended his rationalizations into a religious doctrine, underpinned by his criticism of traditional Catholicism. In particular, and closely related to Positive Christianity, Hitler objected to Catholicism's ungrounded and international character – that is, it did not pertain to an exclusive race and national culture. At the same time, and somewhat contradictorily, the Nazis combined elements of Germany's Lutheran community tradition with its northern European, organic pagan past. Elements of militarism found their way into Hitler's own theology; he preached that his was a "true" or "master" religion, because it would "create mastery" and avoid comforting lies. Those who preached love and tolerance, "in contravention to the facts", were said to be "slave" or "false" religions. The man who recognized these "truths", Hitler continued, was said to be a "natural leader", and those who denied it were said to be "natural slaves". "Slaves" – especially intelligent ones, he claimed – were always attempting to hinder their masters by promoting false religious and political doctrines. Though the "National Socialist leaders and dogmas were basically uncompromisingly antireligious", the Nazi State primarily (but with exceptions) did not act officially in a directly anti-clerical manner except to those who refused to accommodate the new regime and yield to its power. As Martin Bormann put it, "Priests will be paid by us and, as a result, they will preach what we want. If we find a priest acting otherwise short work is to be made of him. The task of the priest consists in keeping the Poles quiet, stupid, and dull-witted." As a result almost 16% of the Catholic clergy in Poland were killed and many more including 13 out of the original 38 Bishops were sent to concentration camps in an attempt to demoralize the Polish population. These actions, combined with their closings of various religious instruction institutions and semininaries was successful in causing some great clergy shortages given Poland's highly Catholic populace. Within more loyal nations of the Reich, anti-clericism typically occurred in a more unofficial sense which took the form of arresting disliked clergy for non-religious offences such as immorality, as well as secret harassment by Nazi instigators and agents, especially those of the Gestapo and the SD. A particularly poignant example is seen in the life of Dietrich Bonhoeffer. However, the Nazis often used the church to justify their stance and included many Christian symbols in the Third Reich while in other cases, they replaced Christian symbols with those of the Third Reich.

Several of the founders and subsequent leadership of the Nazi Party had been associates – and very occasionally members – of the *Thule-Gesellschaft* (the Thule Society), which romanticized the Aryan race through theology and ritual. The Thule Society had been an offshoot of the Germanenorden. The racist-occult notions of Ariosophy were not uncommon within these groups; Rudolf von Sebottendorf and a certain Wilde gave two lectures on occultism for the Thule Society. In general, however, its lectures and excursions were devoted to such subjects as Germanic antiquity and antisemitism, and historically it is more notable for the role it played as a paramilitary group fighting against the Bavarian Soviet Republic.

Dietrich Eckart, a remote associate of the Thule Society (he gave a reading there once from his plays, on 30 May 1919) coached Hitler on his public speaking skills, and Hitler later dedicated *Mein Kampf* to him. However, Hitler himself has not been shown to have been a member of the Thule Society or even to have attended its meetings. The DAP initially received support from the group, but the Thulists were quickly sidelined because Hitler favoured a mass movement and denigrated the occult-conspiratorial approach.

Heinrich Himmler, by contrast, showed a strong interest in such matters, although as Steigmann-Gall points out, Hitler and many of his key associates attended Christian services.

Himmler's activities at the Wewelsburg, the Thule Society and several other remote connections of Nazism with the occult are commonly brought up in the modern mythology of Nazi occultism. This image of Nazism only vaguely corresponds to its historic reality.

One common scholarly view since the Second World War is that Martin Luther's 1543 treatise, *On the Jews and their Lies*, exercised a major and persistent influence on Germany's attitude toward its Jewish citizens in the centuries between the Reformation and the Holocaust. The National Socialists displayed *On the Jews and their Lies* during Nuremberg rallies, and the city of Nuremberg presented a first edition to Julius Streicher, editor of the Nazi newspaper *Der Stürmer*, the newspaper describing it as the most radically antisemitic tract ever published. Against this common view, theologian Johannes Wallmann writes that the treatise had no continuity of influence in Germany, and was in fact largely ignored during the eighteenth and nineteenth centuries.

According to Daniel Goldhagen, Bishop Martin Sasse, a leading Protestant churchman, published a compendium of Martin Luther's writings shortly after the Kristallnacht; Sasse applauded the burning of the synagogues and the coincidence of the day, writing in the introduction, "On November 10, 1938, on Luther's birthday, the synagogues are burning in Germany." The German people, he urged, ought to heed these words "of the greatest antisemite of his time, the warner of his people against the Jews." Diarmaid MacCulloch argued that *On the Jews and Their Lies* was a "blueprint" for the Kristallnacht.

There was a Persecution of Jehovah's Witnesses in Nazi Germany as well as of members of some other small Christian communities. Those groups were forced to wear a purple triangle in Nazi concentration camps.

Anticapitalist Rhetoric

Nazi publications and speeches included anticapitalist (especially anti-finance capitalist) rhetoric. Hitler attacked what he called "pluto-democracy," which he claimed to be a Jewish conspiracy to favour democratic parties in order to keep capitalism intact. The "corporation" was attacked by orthodox Nazis as being the leading instrument of finance capitalism, with the role of Jews emphasized. The National Socialist party described itself as socialist, and, at the time, conservative opponents such as the Industrial Employers Association described it as "totalitarian, terrorist, conspiratorial, and socialist." The Nazi Party's 1920 "Twenty-Five Point Programme" demanded:

...that the State shall make it its primary duty to provide a livelihood for its citizens... the abolition of all incomes unearned by work... the ruthless confiscation of all war profits... the nationalization of all businesses which have been formed into corporations... profit-sharing in large enterprises... extensive development of insurance for old-age... land reform suitable to our national requirements...

Nazi Party officials made several attempts in the 1920s to change some of the program or replace it entirely. In 1924, Gottfried Feder proposed a new 39-point program that kept some of the old planks, replaced others and added many completely new ones. Hitler did not mention any of the planks of the programme in his book, *Mein Kampf,* and he only mentioned it in passing as "the so-called programme of the movement".

Hitler said in 1927, "We are socialists, we are enemies of today's capitalistic economic system for the exploitation of the economically weak, with its unfair salaries, with its unseemly evaluation of a human being according to wealth and property instead of responsibility and performance." However, In 1929, Hitler called socialism "an unfortunate word altogether" and said that "if people have something to eat and their pleasures, then they have their socialism". According to Henry A. Turner, Hitler expressed regret for having integrated the word *socialism* into his party's name. Hitler wrote in 1930, "Our adopted term 'Socialist' has nothing to do with Marxian Socialism. Marxism is anti-property; true Socialism is not."

In a confidential 1931 interview, Hitler told the influential editor of a pro-business newspaper, "I want everyone to keep what he has earned subject to the principle that the good of the community takes priority over that of the individual. But the State should retain control; every owner should feel himself to be an agent of the State... The Third Reich will always retain the right to control property owners." Party spokesman Joseph Goebbels claimed in 1932 that the Nazi Party was a "workers' party" and "on the side of labor and against finance". According to Friedrich Hayek, writing in 1944, "whatever may have been his reasons, Hitler thought it expedient to declare in one of his public speeches as late as February 1941 that 'basically National Socialism and Marxism are the same.' "

Working Class Appeal

Hitler attempted to ensure that the Nazis were seen as a unique movement by discredting other nationalist and racialist political parties as being out of touch with the masses, especially lower-class youth, saying in 1922:

The racialists were not capable of drawing the practical conclusions from correct theoretical judgements, especially in the Jewish Question. In this way the German racialist movement developed a similar pattern to that of the 1880s and 1890s. As in those days, its leadership gradually fell into the hands of highly honourable but fantastically naive men of learning, professors, district counsellors, schoolmasters, and lawyers-in short a bourgeois, idealistic and refined class. It lacked the warm breath of the nation's youthful vigour.

Many scholars have discredited the Nazis' appeal to the working-class as neither being effective nor true in intent, and say that the Nazis were largely a movement of the middle-class. Other scholars like Michael Burleigh have challenged this notion, claiming that there was a sizable number of working-class supporters of the Nazis. Burleigh also claims that the financial situation of middle-class supporters must be considered, in that the economic situation of hyperinflation of currency in the 1920s smashed the financial situation of middle-class and caused high unemployment of middle-class people who previously held white-collar jobs. Therefore, a larger percentage of declared middle-class support for the Nazis does not necessarily mean that a financially-stable middle-class supported the Nazis, but rather a financially-unstable middle-class. In the early 1930s amid high unemployment and poverty in Germany, the Nazis emphasized their socialist policies by providing shelter and food to unemployed or homeless recruits to the SA.

Ideological Roots and Variants

The ideological roots that became German National Socialism were based on numerous sources in European history, drawing especially from Romantic nineteenth century idealism, and from a biological reading of Friedrich Nietzsche's thoughts on "breeding upwards" toward the goal of an *Übermensch* ("superhuman"). Hitler was an avid reader and received ideas that later influenced Nazism from traceable publications, such as those of the Germanenorden or the Thule society. He also adopted many populist ideas such as limiting profits, abolishing rents and generously increasing social benefits—but only for Germans.

The Nordic myth has been attributed to an inferiority complex. Phillip Wayne Powell claimed that the Nordic myth began to arise "in the fifteenth and early sixteenth centuries, a powerful surge of German patriotism was stimulated by the disdain of Italians for German cultural inferiority and barbarism, which lead to a counterattempt by German humanists to laud German qualities." M. W. Fodor claimed in *The Nation* in 1936, "No race has suffered so much from an inferiority complex as has the German. National Socialism was a kind of Coué method of converting the inferiority complex, at least temporarily, into a feeling of superiority".

Nazism as a doctrine is far from homogeneous, and can be divided into at least two sub-ideologies. During the 1920s and 1930s, there were two dominant Nazi factions; the followers of Otto Strasser and the followers of Adolf Hitler. The Strasserite faction eventually fell afoul of Hitler, when Otto Strasser was expelled from the party in 1930, and his attempt to create an oppositional left-block in the form of the Black Front failed. The remainder of the faction, which was to be found mainly in the ranks of the SA, was purged in the Night of the Long Knives, which included the murder of Gregor Strasser, Otto's brother. Afterwards, the Hitlerite faction became dominant. In the post-

World War II era, Strasserism has enjoyed something of a revival among many neo-Nazi groups.

Ideological Competition

Nazism and communism emerged as two serious contenders for power in Germany after the First World War, particularly as the Weimar Republic became increasingly unstable. What became the Nazi movement arose out of resistance to the Bolshevik-inspired insurgencies that occurred in Germany in the aftermath of the First World War. The Russian Revolution of 1917 caused a great deal of excitement and interest in the Leninist version of Marxism and caused many socialists to adopt revolutionary principles. The Spartacist uprising in Berlin and the Bavarian Soviet Republic in 1919 were both manifestations of this. The Freikorps, a loosely organized paramilitary group (essentially a militia of former World War I soldiers) was used to crush both these uprisings and many leaders of the Freikorps, including Ernst Röhm, later became leaders in the Nazi Party. After Mussolini's fascists took power in Italy in 1922, fascism presented itself as a realistic option for opposing communism, particularly given Mussolini's success in crushing the communist and anarchist movements that had destabilized Italy with a wave of strikes and factory occupations after the First World War. Fascist parties formed in numerous European countries.

Many historians, such as Ian Kershaw and Joachim Fest, argue that Hitler's Nazis were one of numerous nationalist and increasingly fascistic groups that existed in Germany and contended for leadership of the anti-communist movement and, eventually, of the German state. Further, they assert that fascism and its German variant, *National Socialism*, became the successful challengers to communism because they were able to both appeal to the establishment as a bulwark against Bolshevism and appeal to the working class base, particularly the growing underclass of unemployed and unemployable and growingly impoverished middle class elements who were becoming declassed (denounced as the *lumpenproletariat*). The Nazis' use of pro-labor rhetoric appealed to those disaffected with capitalism by promoting the limiting of profits, the abolishing of rents and the increasing of social benefits (only for Germans) while simultaneously presenting a political and economic model that divested "Soviet socialism" of elements that were dangerous to capitalism, such as the concept of class struggle, "the dictatorship of the proletariat" or worker control of the means of production. Thus, Nazism's populism, anti-communism and anti-capitalism helped it become more powerful and popular than traditional conservative parties, like the DNVP. For the above reasons, particularly the fact that Nazis and communists fought each other (often violently) during most of their existence, nazism and communism are commonly seen as opposite extremes on the political spectrum. Nevertheless, this view is not without its challengers. Several political theorists and economists, primarily those associated with the Austrian school, argue that Nazism, Soviet communism and other totalitarian ideologies share a common underpinning in socialism and collectivism.

The simplicity of Nazi rhetoric, campaigns, and ideology also made its conservative allies underestimate its strength, and its ability to govern or even to last as a political party. Michael Mann defined fascism as a "transcendent and cleansing nation statism through paramilitarism", with "transcendent" meaning that the all classes were to be abolished in order for a new, organic and pure people: all classes are abolished by transition, all "others" (an estimated two-thirds of the German population alone).

World War II Europe: The Road to War

Moving Towards Conflict

Effects of the Treaty of Versailles

Many of the seeds of World War II in Europe were sown by the Treaty of Versailles that ended World War I. In its final form, the treaty placed full blame for the war on Germany and Austria-Hungary, as well as exacted harsh financial reparations and led to territorial dismemberment. For the German people, who had believed that the armistice had been agreed to based on US President Woodrow Wilson's lenient Fourteen Points, the treaty caused resentment and a deep mistrust of their new government, the Weimar Republic. The need to pay war reparations, coupled with the instability of the government, contributed to massive hyperinflation which crippled the German economy. This situation was made worse by the onset of the Great Depression. In addition to the economic ramifications of the treaty, Germany was required to demilitarize the Rhineland and had severe limitations placed on the size of its military, including the abolishment of its air force. Territorially, Germany was stripped of its colonies and forfeited land for the formation the country of Poland. To ensure that Germany would not expand, the treaty forbade the annexation of Austria, Poland, and Czechoslovakia.

Rise of Fascism & the Nazi Party

In 1922, Benito Mussolini and the Fascist Party rose to power in Italy. Believing in a strong central government and strict control of industry and the people, Fascism was a reaction to the perceived failure of free market economics and a deep fear of communism. Highly militaristic, Fascism also was driven by a sense of belligerent nationalism that encouraged conflict as a means of social improvement. By 1935, Mussolini was able to make himself the dictator of Italy and transformed the country into a police state.

To the north in Germany, Fascism was embraced by the National Socialist German Workers Party, also known as the Nazis. Swiftly rising to power in the late 1920s, the Nazis and their charismatic leader, Adolf Hitler, followed the central tenets of Fascism while also advocating for the racial purity of the German people and additional German *Lebensraum* (living space). Playing on the economic distress in Weimar Germany and backed by their "Brown Shirts" militia, the Nazis became a political force. On January 30, 1933, Hitler was placed in position to take power when he was appointed Reich Chancellor by President Paul von Hindenburg

The Nazis Assume Power

A month after Hitler assumed the Chancellorship, the Reichstag building burned. Blaming the fire on the Communist Party of Germany, Hitler used the incident as an excuse to ban those political parties that opposed Nazi policies. On March 23, 1933, the Nazis essentially took control of the government by passing the Enabling Acts. Meant to be an emergency measure, the acts gave the cabinet (and Hitler) the power to pass legislation without the approval of the Reichstag. Hitler next moved to consolidate his power and executed a purge of the party (The Night of the Long Knives) to eliminate those who could threaten his position. With his internal foes in check, Hitler began the persecution of those who were deemed racial enemies of the state. In September 1935, he passed the Nuremburg Laws which stripped Jews of their citizenship and forbade marriage or sexual relations between a Jew and an "Aryan." Three years later the first pogrom began (Night of Broken Glass) in which over one hundred Jews were killed and 30,000 arrested and sent to concentration camps.

Germany Remilitarizes

On March 16, 1935, in clear violation of the Treaty of Versailles, Hitler ordered the remilitarization of Germany, including the reactivation of the *Luftwaffe* (air force). As the German army grew through conscription, the other European powers voiced minimal protest as they were more concerned with enforcing the economic aspects of the treaty. In a move that tacitly endorsed Hitler's violation of the treaty, Great Britain signed the Anglo-German Naval Agreement in 1935, which allowed Germany to build a fleet one third the size of the Royal Navy and ended British naval operations in the Baltic.Two years after beginning the expansion of the military, Hitler further violated the treaty by ordering the reoccupation of the Rhineland by the German Army. Proceeding cautiously, Hitler issued orders that the German troops should withdrawal if the French intervened. Not wanting to become involved in another major war, Britain and France avoided intervening and sought a resolution, with little success, through the League of Nations. After the war several German officers indicated that if the reoccupation of the Rhineland had been opposed, it would have meant the end of Hitler's regime.

The Anschluss

Emboldened by Great Britain and France's reaction to the Rhineland, Hitler began to move forward with a plan to unite all German-speaking peoples under one "Greater German" regime. Again operating in violation of the Treaty of Versailles, Hitler made overtures regarding the annexation of Austria. While these were generally rebuffed by the government in Vienna, Hitler was able to orchestrate a coup by the Austrian Nazi Party on March 11, 1938, one day before a planned plebiscite on the issue. The next day, German troops crossed the border to enforce the *Anschluss* (annexation). A month later the Nazis held a plebiscite on the issue and received 99.73% of the vote. International reaction was again mild, with Great Britain and France issuing protests, but still showing that they were unwilling to take military action.

The Rise of Fascism in Europe

Some political commentators have suggested that the European Elections indicate that the economic depression has resulted in a rise in the support of fascist political parties. Some have even gone onto to say that what we are seeing is a repeat of what happened in Europe following the Wall Street Crash. I strongly disagree that this is a re-run of the 1930s. It is often forgotten that the fascists took power in Italy long before the Depression. Even in Germany most of the unemployed voted for the left. It was the Catholics and the middle-classes that allowed Hitler to take power.

It is true that the BNP in the UK won two seats in the European Parliament. Nearly all the extra votes they obtained this time came from former Labour voters who wanted to register a protest against Gordon Brown and his government. The BNP will not be able to hold onto these votes as long as Brown is ousted from power and we introduce a sensible housing policy.

It would have been worrying if the BNP had picked up the votes of UKIP. However, people have preferred to vote for UKIP instead of the BNP. Large sections of the population are hostile to the idea of immigration (both black and white) and during a recession will vote for nationalist parties. However, our history makes it highly unlikely that fascists will ever get close to power.

We suspect this is also true of Western Europe. However, I am much more concerned about the Baltic states and the new democracies in Eastern Europe. These countries have been hit by severe economic problems and they have little experience of democracy and might be tempted to support strong leaders who promise to solve their problems.

Nazism and the Rise of Hitler

In the spring of 1945, a little eleven-year-old German boy called Helmuth was lying in bed when he overheard his parents discussing something in serious tones. His father, a prominent physician, deliberated with his wife whether the time had come to kill the entire family, or if he should commit suicide alone. His father spoke about his fear of revenge, saying, 'Now the Allies will do to us what we did to the crippled and Jews.' The next day, he took Helmuth to the woods, where they spent their last happy time together, and singing old children's songs. Later, Helmuth's father shot himself in his office. Helmuth remembers that he saw his father's bloody uniform being burnt in the family fireplace. So traumatized was he by what he had overheard and what had happened, that he reacted by refusing to eat at home for the following nine years! He was afraid that his mother might poison him.

Although Helmuth may not have realized all that it meant, his father had been a Nazi and a supporter of Adolf Hitler. Many of you will know something about the Nazis and Hitler. You probably know of Hitler's determination to make Germany into a mighty power and his ambition of conquering all of Europe. You may have heard that he killed Jews. But Nazism was not one or two isolated acts. It was a system, a structure of ideas about the world and politics. Let us try and understand what Nazism was all about. Let us see why Helmuth's father killed himself and what the basis of his fear was.

In May 1945, Germany surrendered to the Allies. Anticipating what was coming, Hitler, his propaganda minister Goebbels and his entire family committed suicide 'collectively in his Berlin bunker in April. At the end of the war, an International Military Tribunal at Nuremberg was set up to prosecute Nazi war criminals for Crimes against Peace, for War Crimes and Crimes against Humanity. Germany's conduct during the war, especially those actions which came to be called Crimes against Humanity, raised serious moral and ethical questions and invited worldwide condemnation. What were these acts?

Under the shadow of the Second World War, Germany had waged a genocidal war, which resulted in the mass murder of selected groups of innocent civilians of Europe. The number of people killed included 6 million Jews, 200,000 Gypsies, and 1 million Polish civilians, 70,000 Germans who were considered mentally and physically disabled, besides innumerable political opponents. Nazis devised an unprecedented means of killing people, that is, by gassing them in various killing centres like Auschwitz. The Nuremberg Tribunal sentenced only eleven leading Nazis to death. Many others were imprisoned for life. The retribution did come, yet the punishment of the Nazis was far short of the brutality and extent of their crimes. The Allies did not want to be as harsh on defeated Germany as they had been after the First World War.

Everyone came to feel that the rise of Nazi Germany could be partly traced back to the German experience at the end of the First World War.

Birth of the Weimar Republic

Germany, a powerful empire in the early years of the twentieth century, fought the First World War (1914-1918) alongside the Austrian empire and against the Allies (England, France and Russia.) All joined the war enthusiastically hoping to gain from a quick victory. Little did they realize that the war would stretch on, eventually draining Europe of all its resources. Germany made initial gains by occupying France and Belgium. However the Allies, strengthened by the US entry in 1917, won, defeating Germany and the Central Powers in November 1918. The defeat of Imperial Germany and the abdication of the emperor gave an opportunity to parliamentary parties to recast German polity. A National Assembly met at Weimar and established a democratic constitution with a federal structure. Deputies were now elected to the German Parliament or Reichstag, on the basis of equal and universal votes cast by all adults including women.

This republic, however, was not received well by its own people largely because of the terms it was forced to accept after Germany's defeat at the end of the First World War. The peace treaty at Versailles with the Allies was a harsh and humiliating peace. Germany lost its overseas colonies, a tenth of its population, 13 per cent of its territories, 75 per cent of its iron and 26 per cent of its coal to France, Poland, Denmark and Lithuania. The Allied Powers demilitarized Germany to weaken its power. The War Guilt Clause held Germany responsible for the war and damages the Allied countries suffered. Germany was forced to pay compensation amounting to 6 billion. The Allied armies also occupied the resource-rich Rhineland for much of the 1920s. Many Germans held the new Weimar Republic responsible for not only the defeat in the war but the disgrace at Versailles.

The Effects of the War

The war had a devastating impact on the entire continent both psychologically and financially. From a continent of creditors, Europe turned into one of debtors. Unfortunately, the infant Weimar Republic was being made to pay for the sins of the old empire. The republic carried the burden of war guilt and national humiliation and was financially crippled by being forced to pay compensation. Those who supported the Weimar Republic, mainly Socialists, Catholics and Democrats, became easy targets of attack in the conservative nationalist circles. They were mockingly called the 'November criminals'. This mindset had a major impact on the political developments of the early 1930s, as we will soon see.

The First World War left a deep imprint on European society and polity. Soldiers came to be placed above civilians. Politicians and publicists laid great stress on the need for men to be aggressive, strong and masculine. The media glorified trench life. The truth, however, was that soldiers lived miserable lives in these trenches, trapped with rats feeding on corpses. They faced poisonous gas and enemy shelling, and witnessed their ranks reduce rapidly. Aggressive war propaganda and national honour occupied centre stage in the public sphere, while popular support grew for conservative dictatorships that had recently come into being. Democracy was indeed a young and fragile idea, which could not survive the instabilities of interwar Europe.

Political Puritanism and Economic Crises

The birth of the Weimar Republic coincided with the revolutionary uprising of the Sparta cist League on the pattern of the Bolshevik Revolution in Russia. Soviets of workers and sailors were established in many cities. The political atmosphere in Berlin was charged with demands for Soviet-style governance. Those opposed to this-such as the socialists, Democrats' and Catholics-met in Weimar to give shape to the democratic republic. The Weimar Republic crushed the uprising with the help of a war veterans organization called Free Corps. The anguished Spartacists later founded the Communist Party of Germany. Communists and Socialists henceforth became irreconcilable enemies and could not make common cause against Hitler. Both revolutionaries and militant nationalists craved for radical solutions.

Political radicalization was only heightened by the economic crisis of 1923. Germany had fought the war largely on loans and had to pay war reparations in gold. This depleted gold reserves at a time resources were scarce. In 1923 Germany refused to pay, and the French occupied its leading industrial area, Ruhr, to claim their coal. Germany retaliated with passive resistance and printed paper currency recklessly. With too much printed money in circulation, the value of the German mark fell. In April the US dollar was equal to 24,000 marks, in July 353,000 marks, in August 4,621,000 marks and at 98,860,000 marks by December, the figure had run into trillions. As the value of the mark collapsed, prices of goods soared. The image of Germans carrying cartloads of currency notes to buy a loaf of bread was widely publicized evoking worldwide sympathy. This crisis came to be known as hyperinflation, a situation when prices rise phenomenally high.

Eventually, the Americans intervened and bailed Germany out of the crisis by introducing the Dawes Plan, which reworked the terms of reparation to ease the financial burden on Germans.

The Years of Depression

The years between 1924 and 1928 saw some stability. Yet this was built on sand. German investments and industrial recovery were totally dependent on short-term loans, largely from the USA. This support was withdrawn when the Wall Street Exchange crashed in 1929. Fearing a fall in prices, people made frantic efforts to sell their shares. On one single day, 24 October, 13 million shares were sold. This was the start of the Great Economic Depression. Over the next three years, between 1929 and 1932, the national income of the USA fell by half. Factories shut down, exports fell, farmers were badly hit and speculators withdrew their money from the market. The effects of this recession in the US economy were felt worldwide.

The German economy was the worst hit by the economic crisis. By 1932, industrial production was reduced to 40 per cent of the 1929 level. Workers lost their jobs or were paid reduced wages. The number of unemployed touched an unprecedented 6 million. On the streets of Germany you could see men with placards around their necks saying, 'Willing to do any work'. Unemployed youths played cards or simply sat at street corners, or desperately queued up at the local employment exchange. As jobs disappeared, the youth took to criminal activities and total despair became commonplace.

The economic crisis created deep anxieties and fears in people. The middle classes, especially salaried employees and pensioners, saw their savings diminish when the currency lost its value. Small businessmen, the self-employed and retailers suffered as their businesses got ruined.

These sections of society were filled with the fear of proletarianization, an anxiety of being reduced to the ranks of the working class, or worse still, the unemployed. Only organized workers could manage to keep their heads above water, but unemployment weakened their bargaining power. Big business was in crisis. The large mass of peasantry was affected by a sharp fall in agricultural prices and women, unable to fill their children's stomachs, were filled with a sense of deep despair.

Politically too the Weimar Republic was fragile. The Weimar constitution had some inherent defects, which made it unstable and vulnerable to dictatorship. One was proportional representation. This made achieving a majority by anyone party a near impossible task, leading to a rule by coalitions. Another defect was Article 48, which gave the President the powers to impose emergency, suspend civil rights and rule by decree. Within its short life, the Weimar Republic saw twenty different cabinets lasting on an average 239 days, and a liberal use of Article 48. Yet the crisis could not be managed. People lost confidence in the democratic parliamentary system, which seemed to offer no solutions.

Hitler's Rise to Power

This crisis in the economy, polity and society formed the background to Hitler's rise to power. Born in 1889 in Austria, Hitler spent his youth in poverty. When the First World War broke out, he enrolled for the army, acted as a messenger in the front, became a corporal, and earned medals for bravery. The German defeat horrified him and the Versailles Treaty made him furious. In 1919, he joined a small group called the German Workers' Party. He subsequently took over the organization and renamed it the National Socialist German Workers' Party. This party came to be known as the Nazi Party.

In 1923, Hitler planned to seize control of Bavaria, march to Berlin and capture power. He failed, was arrested, tried for treason, and later released. The Nazis could not effectively mobilize popular support till the early 1930s.

It was during the Great Depression that Nazism became a mass movement. As we have seen, after 1929, banks collapsed and businesses shut down, workers lost their jobs and the middle classes were threatened with destitution. In such a situation Nazi propaganda stirred hopes of a better future. In 1928, the Nazi Party got no more than 2. 6 per cent votes in the Reichstag-the German parliament. By 1932, it had become the largest party with 37 per cent votes.

Hitler was a powerful speaker. His passion and his words moved people. He promised to build a strong nation, undo the injustice of the Versailles Treaty and restore the dignity of the German people. He promised employment for those looking for work, and a secure future for the youth. He promised to weed out all foreign influences and resist all foreign 'conspiracies' against Germany.

Hitler devised a new style of politics. He understood the significance of rituals and spectacle in mass mobilization. Nazis held massive rallies and public meetings to demonstrate the support for Hitler and instill a sense of unity among the people. The Red banners with the Swastika, the Nazi salute, and the ritualized rounds of applause after the speeches were all part of this spectacle of power.

Nazi propaganda skillfully projected Hitler as a messiah, a savior, as someone who had arrived to deliver people from their distress. It is an image that captured the imagination of a people whose sense of dignity and pride had been shattered, and who were living in a time of acute economic and political crises.

The Destruction of Democracy

On 30 January 1933, President Hindenburg offered the Chancellorship, the highest position in the cabinet of ministers, to Hitler. By now the Nazis had managed to rally the conservatives to their cause. Having acquired power, Hitler set out to dismantle the, structures of democratic rule.

A mysterious fire that broke out in the German Parliament building in February facilitated his move. The Fire Decree of 28 February 1933 indefinitely suspended civic rights like freedom of speech, Press and assembly that had been guaranteed by the Weimar constitution.

Then he turned on his archenemies, the Communists, most of who were hurriedly packed off to the newly established concentration camps. The repression of the Communists was severe. Out of the surviving 6,808 arrest files of Duesseldorf, a small city of half a million population, 1,440 were those of Communists alone. They were. However,only one among the 52 types of victims persecuted by the Nazis across the country.

On 3 March 1933, the famous Enabling Act was passed. This Act established dictatorship in Germany. It gave Hitler all powers to sideline Parliament and rule by decree. All political parties and trade unions were banned except for the Nazi Party and its affiliates. The state established complete control over the economy, media, army and judiciary.

Special surveillance and security forces were created to control and order society in ways that the Nazis wanted. Apart from the already existing regular police in green uniform and the SA or the Storm Troopers, these included the Gestapo (secret state police), the SS (the protection squads), criminal police and the Security Service (SD).

It was the extra-constitutional powers of these newly organized forces that gave the Nazi state its reputation as the most dreaded criminal stat. People could now be detained in Gestapo torture chambers, rounded up and sent to concentration camps. Deported at will or arrested without any legal procedures. The police forces acquired powers to rule with impunity.

Neo-Nazism on the rise in Eastern Europe

Seventy-five years after Hitler came to power in Germany the baleful influence of his ideology lives on with increasing numbers of racist attacks reported, particularly in the countries of the former Soviet Union. In Russia, one of the main hotspots for neo-Nazi activity, human rights activists estimate there are roughly 70,000 skinheads. Galina Kozhevnikova, deputy head of the Sova centre, an organization which tracks xenophobia and hate crime, said right-wing extremist organizations in Russia were 'growing stronger.'

According to data from the Sova centre, 68 people were killed last year in racist crimes and 565 were injured in attacks. The number of attacks has increased by 20 to 25 per cent in recent years, the centre said.

African and other foreign students in Russia are regularly warned not to leave their dormitories on key danger dates such as the eve of Hitler's birthday. Rights advocates complain that the legal penalties are not severe enough to deter hate crimes. They charge that Russian authorities often obfuscate the real motives behind attacks by prosecuting on charges such as hooliganism or alcohol-fulled homicide, which carry much more lenient sentences.

Russia's Interior Ministry released a report on January 19, warning about 'an increase in ultranationalist sentiment' in Russia. The report said that over 15 per cent of Russian youth identify with ultranationalist sentiment. Human rights campaigners accuse the state of tolerating, if not encouraging, extremist nationalists movements. Right-wing extremist groups feel supported by the state and law enforcement bodies, Kozhevnikova said. 'It is not perhaps direct support, but a clear emphasis on patriotic and nationalist rhetoric, which is in fashion right now,' she said.

In the Baltic republics of Estonia, Lithuania and Latvia, neo-Nazi groups are largely marginalized from mainstream politics. They make themselves known at events and parades, such as in March when Latvian right-wingers commemorate Latvian Waffen SS soldiers who fought against the Soviets in World War II.

Right-wingers in the three Baltic countries-EU member states since 2004-also target gay rights parades. In 2007 skinheads attacked with sticks and stones such a parade in the Estonian capital Tallinn, wounding several.

Ukraine, too, has seen its share of right-wing activity. In November neo-Nazi skinheads and Indian engineering students battled in a mass fist-fight involving hundreds in Zaporizhia in the heart of the country's industrial east.

Racial and xenophobic tensions in Ukraine generally are low. However, extremist nationalist groups are active in most cities of the former Soviet republic. Most members of such groups are unemployed teenagers or young men from low-income families.

Actual violence against ethnic minorities in Ukraine is an infrequent but recurring event. The most common targets are Jews and Muslim Tartars, but in recent years attacks against foreigners from Asia and Africa have increased. Other new member countries of the European Union have also seen a rising level of right-wing activity and violence.

Last November in the eastern Slovak city of Kosice three right-wing extremists beat up a 16-year-old dark-skinned girl of Slovak and Cuban origin while yelling Nazi slogans. Racist attacks, mostly against the Roma and foreign students, are not unusual in Slovakia. The police registered 188 racially-motivated crimes, including violent attacks, in 2006, an increase from 121 cases in 2005. Activists add that not all victims report attacks.

The Czech Republic's estimated 3,000 to 5,000 right-wing radicals remain an insignificant fringe group without a strong centralized leadership and political backing, according to Czech counter-intelligence. 'What makes the Czechs different is that they lack a party cover. They are politically isolated,' political scientist Miroslav Mares told Deutsche Presse-Agentur dpa.

He added that the Czech right-wing scene is 'very weak' compared to Germany precisely because there is no National Democratic Party (NPD) in the Czech Republic. A small National Party is still insignificant and unpopular despite attempts to make headlines by provocative populist actions. However, Czech right-wingers have recently begun trying to gain visibility and promote their political ideas by organizing marches and protests in Czech towns. 'They wanted to get favour with the street following the

German example of the NPD as someone who can establish order,' Mares said.

'We are against this system. We are against this establishment,' one 28-year-old ultra-nationalist said of the reasons for protests.

Such activities, though, have been met with outrage not only from Jewish groups and human-rights activists but also from politicians of all stripes, and the public.

When some 400 Czech, German and Slovak neo-Nazis unsuccessfully tried to gather in Prague for a banned march through the city's historic Jewish district on November 10-the anniversary of the so-called Kristallnacht (Night of Broken Glass) pogrom-at least 1,000 people convened in the chilly drizzle in protest.

'The far right does not have a strong historical tradition in the Czech ethnic environment,' Mares explained. 'Nationalist parties do not impress the public. They do not have a bigger chance to enter real power structures. Most people disapprove of them.'

In Poland, the all-Poland Youth, the youth wing of the Catholic-nationalist League of Polish Families (LPR) party, has been accused of having neo-Nazi sympathies. The group is known for its sometimes violent anti-gay protests.

Hungary, too, has seen a significant rise in the far right since the riots that hit Budapest in September 2006 when football hooligans and extreme-right activists attacked the headquarters of Hungarian Television following the leaking of a tape on which the prime minister admitted lying. While the violence only continued sporadically for around five weeks, right-wing groups have been far more prominent since then. There have been isolated attacks, particularly one on a gay rights parade that saw skinheads pelt marchers with rotten eggs, but the most worrying development for many was the formation last August of the Magyar Garda, a uniformed wing of extreme-right party Jobbik.

Jewish organisations and government officials have expressed concern over the group, which wears black uniforms Jewish groups say are similar to those worn by Hungarian fascists in the 1940s. The guard has chosen as its coat of arms a variation of the medieval flag associated with Hungary's Nazi-aligned Arrow Cross party-in power for a brief period during World War II and responsible for the slaughter of hundreds of thousands of Jews. Moves have been made to disband the group, which now numbers over six hundred, but they have made themselves very visible, particularly with regard to their attitudes to Hungary's Roma minority. Some 260 members of the guard marched through a Roma-majority town near Budapest in their uniforms in December, claiming they were simply protesting against violent crimes by Roma against Hungarians.

The long-established democracies of Western Europe have also not been immune to the neo-Nazi scourge with attacks and far-right movements in countries such as Spain and Greece. Across the continent the picture looks broadly the same-the far right attracts unemployed, undereducated youth and those who oppose immigration. But there's little evidence that extreme right-wing parties will ever be able to attract significant popular support.

4

League of Nations

League of Nations

The League of Nations (LoN) was an inter-governmental organization founded as a result of the Treaty of Versailles in 1919–1920. At its greatest extent from 28 September 1934 to 23 February 1935, it had 58 members. The League's goals included upholding the new found Rights of Man such as right of non whites, rights of women, rights of soldiers, disarmament, preventing war through collective security, settling disputes between countries through negotiation, diplomacy and improving global quality of life. The diplomatic philosophy behind the League represented a fundamental shift in thought from the preceding hundred years. The League lacked its own armed force and so depended on the Great Powers to enforce its resolutions, keep to economic sanctions which the League ordered, or provide an army, when needed, for the League to use. However, they were often reluctant to do so. Sanctions could also hurt the League members, so they were reluctant to comply with them. When, during the Second Italo-Abyssinian War, the League accused Benito Mussolini's soldiers of targeting Red Cross medical tents, Mussolini responded that Ethiopians were not fully human, therefore the human rights laws did not apply. Benito Mussolini stated that "The League is very well when sparrows shout, but no good at all when eagles fall out."

After a number of notable successes and some early failures in the 1920s, the League ultimately proved incapable of preventing aggression by the Axis powers in the 1930s. In May 1933, the League was powerless to convince Adolf Hitler that Franz

Bernheim, a Jew, was protected under the minority clauses established by the League in 1919 (that all minorities were fully human and held equal rights among all men). Hitler claimed these clauses violated Germany's sovereignty. Germany withdrew from the League, soon to be followed by many other totalitarian and militaristic nations. The onset of World War II showed that the League had failed its primary purpose, which was to avoid any future world war. The United Nations replaced it after the end of the war and inherited a number of agencies and organizations founded by the League.

Origins of the League

The concept of a peaceful community of nations had been outlined as far back as 1795, when Immanuel Kant's *Perpetual Peace: A Philosophical Sketch* outlined the idea of a league of nations that would control conflict and promote peace between states. There, Kant argues for establishment of a peaceful world community not in a sense that there be a global government but in the hope that each state would declare itself as a free state that respects its citizens and welcomes foreign visitors as fellow rational beings. It is in this rationalization that a union of free states would promote peaceful society worldwide, therefore there can be a perpetual peace bound by the international community. International cooperation to promote collective security originated in the Concert of Europe that developed after the Napoleonic Wars in the nineteenth century in an attempt to maintain the status quo between European states and so avoid war. This period also saw the development of international law with the first Geneva conventions establishing laws about humanitarian relief during war and the international Hague Conventions of 1899 and 1907 governing rules of war and the peaceful settlement of international disputes. The forerunner of the League of Nations, the Inter-Parliamentary Union (IPU), was formed by peace activists William Randal Cremer and Frederic Passy in 1889. The organization was international in scope with a third of the members of parliament, in the 24 countries with parliaments, serving as members of the IPU by 1914. Its aims were to encourage governments to solve international disputes by peaceful means and arbitration and annual conferences were held to help governments refine the process of international arbitration. The IPU's structure consisted of a Council headed by a President which would later be reflected in the structure of the League.

At the start of the twentieth century two power blocs emerged through alliances between the European Great Powers. It was these alliances that came into effect at the start of the First World War in 1914, drawing all the major European powers into the war. This was the first major war in Europe between industrialized countries and the first time in Western Europe the results of industrialization (for example mass production) had been dedicated to war. The result of this industrial warfare was an unprecedented casualty level with eight and a half million members of armed services dead, an estimated 21 million wounded, and approximately 10 million civilian deaths. By the time the fighting ended in November 1918, the war had had a profound impact, affecting the social, political and economic systems of Europe and inflicting psychological and physical damage on the continent. Anti-war sentiment rose across the world; the First World War was described as "the war to end all wars", and its possible causes were vigorously investigated. The causes identified included arms races, alliances, secret diplomacy, and the freedom of sovereign states to enter into war for their own benefit. The perceived remedies to these were seen as the creation of an international organisation whose aim was to prevent future war through disarmament, open diplomacy, international cooperation, restrictions on the right to wage wars, and penalties that made war unattractive to nations.

While the First World War was still underway, a number of governments and groups had already started developing plans to change the way international relations were carried out in order to prevent a repetition of the war. United States President Woodrow Wilson and his advisor Colonel Edward M. House enthusiastically promoted the idea of the League as a means of avoiding any repetition of the bloodshed seen in World War I, and the creation of the League was a centerpiece of Wilson's Fourteen Points for Peace. Specifically the final point provided: "A general association of nations must be formed under specific covenants for the purpose of affording mutual guarantees of political independence and territorial integrity to great and small states alike."

Before drafting the specific terms of his peace deal, Wilson recruited a team led by Colonel House to compile whatever information deemed pertinent in assessing Europe's geopolitical situation. In early January, 1918, Wilson summoned House to Washington and the two began hammering out, in complete secrecy, the President's first address on the League of Nations which was delivered to an unsuspecting Congress on January 8, 1918.

Wilson's final plans for the League were strongly influenced by the South African Prime Minister, Jan Christiaan Smuts. In 1918 Smuts had published a treatise entitled *The League of Nations: A Practical Suggestion*. According to F.S. Crafford's biography on Smuts, Wilson adopted "both the ideas and the style" of Smuts.

On July 8, 1919, Woodrow Wilson returned to the United States and embarked on a nation-wide campaign to secure the support of the American people for their country's entry into the League. On July 10, Wilson addressed the Senate declaring that "a new role and a new responsibility have come to this great nation that we honour and which we would all wish to lift to yet higher levels of service and achievement." Positive reception, particularly from Republicans, was scarce at best.

The Paris Peace Conference, convened to build a lasting peace after World War I, approved the proposal to create the League of Nations (French: *Société des Nations*, German: *Völkerbund*) on 25 January 1919. The Covenant of the League of Nations was drafted by a special commission, and the League was established by Part I of the Treaty of Versailles. On 28 June 1919, 44 states signed the Covenant, including 31 states which had taken part in the war on the side of the Triple Entente or joined it during the conflict. Despite Wilson's efforts to establish and promote the League, for which he was awarded the Nobel Peace Prize in October 1919, the United States did not join the League. Opposition in the U.S. Senate, particularly from Republican politicians Henry Cabot Lodge and William E. Borah, together with Wilson's refusal to compromise, ensured that the United States would not ratify the Covenant.

The League held its first council meeting in Paris on 16 January 1920, six days after the Versailles Treaty came into force. In November, the headquarters of the League moved to Geneva, where the first General Assembly was held on 15 November 1920 with representatives from 41 nations in attendance.

Languages and Symbols

The official languages of the League of Nations were French, English and Spanish (from 1920). The League considered adopting Esperanto as their working language and actively encouraging its use but neither option was ever adopted. In 1921, there was a proposal by Lord Robert Cecil to introduce Esperanto into state schools of member nations and a report was commissioned to investigate this. When the report was presented two years later it recommended the teaching of Esperanto in schools, a proposal that 11 delegates accepted.

The strongest opposition came from the French delegate, Gabriel Hanotaux, partially in order to protect the French Language which he argued was already the international language. This opposition meant the report was accepted apart from the section that approved Esperanto in schools.

The League of Nations had neither an official flag nor logo. Proposals for adopting an official symbol were made during the League's beginning in 1920, but the member states never reached agreement. However, League of Nations organizations used varying logos and flags (or none at all) in their own operations. An international contest was held in 1929 to find a design, which again failed to produce a symbol.

One of the reasons for this failure may have been the fear by the member states that the power of the supranational organization might supersede their own. Finally, in 1939, a semi-official emblem emerged: two five-pointed stars within a blue pentagon. The pentagon and the five-pointed stars were supposed to symbolize the five continents and the five races of mankind.

In a bow on top and at the bottom, the flag had the names in English (*League of Nations*) and French (*Société des Nations*). This flag was used on the building of the New York World's Fair in 1939 and 1940. The League did have a very active postal department. Large numbers of mailings were made from headquarters, the specialized agencies, and at international conferences. In many cases special envelopes or overprinted postage stamps were used.

Principal organs

The League had four principal organs, a secretariat (headed by the General Secretary and based in Geneva), a Council, an Assembly and a Permanent Court of International Justice. The League also had numerous agencies and commissions. Authorization for any action required both a unanimous vote by the Council and a majority vote in the Assembly.

Secretariat and Assembly

The staff of the League's secretariat was responsible for preparing the agenda for the Council and Assembly and publishing reports of the meetings and other routine matters, effectively acting as the civil service for the League. The secretariat was often considered to be too small to handle all of the league administrative affairs. The League of Nations' Assembly was a meeting of all the member states, with each state allowed up to three representatives and one vote. The Assembly met in Geneva and, after its initial sessions in 1920, sessions were held once a year in September.

Council

The League Council acted as a type of executive body directing the Assembly's business. The Council began with four permanent members (Great Britain, France, Italy, Japan) and four non-permanent members which were elected by the Assembly for a three year period. The first four non-permanent members were Belgium, Brazil, Greece and Spain. The United States was meant to be the fifth permanent member, but the US Senate voted on 19 March 1920 against the ratification of the Treaty of Versailles, thus preventing American participation in the League. The composition of the Council was subsequently changed a number of times. The number of non-permanent members was first increased to six on 22 September 1922, and then to nine on 8 September 1926. Werner Dankwort of Germany pushed for his home country to join the league which they eventually did in 1926. Germany became the fifth permanent member of the Council, giving the Council a total of fifteen members. Later, after Germany and Japan both left the League, the number of non-permanent seats was increased from nine to eleven. The Council met, on average, five times a year and in extraordinary sessions when required. In total, 107 public sessions were held between 1920 and 1939.

Commission for Refugees

Led by Fridtjof Nansen, the Commission for Refugees looked after the interests of refugees including overseeing their repatriation and, when necessary resettlement. At the end of the First World War there were two to three million ex-prisoners of war dispersed throughout Russia, within two years of the commission's foundation, in 1920, it had helped 425,000 of them return home. It established camps in Turkey in 1922 to aid the country with a refugee crisis it was dealing with, helping to prevent disease and hunger. It also established the Nansen passport as a means of identification for stateless peoples.

Committee for the Study of the Legal Status of Women

The Committee for the Study of the Legal Status of Women sought to make an inquiry into the status of women all over the world. It was formed in April 1938, and dissolved in early 1939. Committee members included Mme. P. Bastid (France), M. de Ruelle (Belgium), Mme. Anka Godjevac (Yugoslavia), Mr. H. C. Gutteridge (Great Britain), Mlle. Kerstin Hesselgren (Sweden), Ms. Dorothy Kenyon (United States), M. Paul Sebastyen (Hungary) and Secretariat Mr. Hugh McKinnon Wood (Great Britain).

Members

Of the League's 42 founding members, 23 (or 24, counting Free France) remained members until it was dissolved in 1946. In the founding year, six other states joined, only two of which remained members throughout the League's existence. An additional 15 countries joined in later years. The largest number of member states was 58, between 28 September 1934 (when Ecuador joined) and 23 February 1935 (when Paraguay withdrew). At this time, only Costa Rica (22 January 1925), Brazil (14 June 1926), the Empire of Japan (27 March 1933), and Germany (19 September 1933) had withdrawn citing a diplomatic disadvantage due to inferior powers.

The Soviet Union only became a member on 18 September 1934, when it joined to antagonise Germany (which had left the year before), and was expelled from the League on 14 December 1939 for aggression against Finland. In expelling the Soviet Union, the League broke its own norms; only 7 of 15 members of the Council voted for the expulsion (Great Britain, France, Belgium, Bolivia, Egypt, South Africa, and the Dominican Republic), which was not the majority of votes required by the Covenant to do so. Three of these members were chosen as members of the Council the day before the voting (South Africa, Bolivia, and Egypt). This was one of the League's final acts before it practically ceased functioning due to the Second World War.

Egypt was the last state to join the League (26 May 1937). The first member to withdraw from the League after its founding was Costa Rica on 22 January 1925; having joined on 16 December 1920, this also makes it the member to have most quickly withdrawn from the League after joining. The last member to withdraw from the League before its dissolution was Luxembourg on 30 August 1942. Brazil was the first founding member to leave (14 June 1926) and Haiti was the last (April 1942). Iraq, which joined in 1932, was the first member of the league that had previously been a League of Nations Mandate.

Mandates

League of Nations Mandates were established under Article 22 of the Covenant of the League of Nations. These territories were former colonies of the German Empire and the Ottoman Empire that were placed under the supervision of the League following World War I. The Permanent Mandates Commission supervised League of Nations mandates, and also organised plebiscites in disputed territories so that residents could decide which country they would join. There were three Mandate classifications.

"A" Mandates

The "A" Mandates (applied to parts of the old Ottoman Empire) were 'certain communities' that had...reached a stage of development where their existence as independent nations can be provisionally recognised subject to the rendering of administrative advice and assistance by a Mandatory until such time as they are able to stand alone. The wishes of these communities must be a principal consideration in the selection of the Mandatory. – *Article 22, The Covenant of the League of Nations*

"B" Mandates

The "B" Mandates were applied to the former German Colonies that the League took responsibility for after the First World War. These were described as 'peoples' that the League said were...at such a stage that the Mandatory must be responsible for the administration of the territory under conditions which will guarantee freedom of conscience and religion, subject only to the maintenance of public order and morals, the prohibition of abuses such as the slave trade, the arms traffic and the liquor traffic, and the prevention of the establishment of fortifications or military and naval bases and of military training of the natives for other than police purposes and the defence of territory, and will also secure equal opportunities for the trade and commerce of other Members of the League. – *Article 22, The Covenant of the League of Nations*

"C" Mandates

South-West Africa and certain of the South Pacific Islands were administrated by League members under a C Mandate. These were classified as 'territories'...which, owing to the sparseness of their population, or their small size, or their remoteness from the centres of civilisation, or their geographical contiguity to the territory of the Mandatory, and other circumstances, can be best administered under the laws of the Mandatory as integral portions of its territory, subject to the safeguards above mentioned in the interests of the indigenous population." – *Article 22, The Covenant of the League of Nations*

Mandatory Powers

The territories were governed by "Mandatory Powers", such as the United Kingdom in the case of the Mandate of Palestine and the Union of South Africa in the case of South-West Africa, until the territories were deemed capable of self-government. There were fourteen mandate territories divided up among the six Mandatory Powers of the United Kingdom, France, Belgium, New Zealand, Australia and Japan. With the exception of the Kingdom of Iraq, which joined the League on 3 October 1932, these territories did not begin to gain their independence until after the Second World War, a process that did not end until 1990. Following the demise of the League, most of the remaining mandates became United Nations Trust Territories. In addition to the Mandates, the League itself governed the Saarland for 15 years, before it was returned to Germany following a plebiscite, and the free city of Danzig (now Gdańsk, Poland) from 15 November 1920 to 1 September 1939.

Resolving territorial disputes

The aftermath of World War I left many issues to be settled between nations, including the exact position of national boundaries and which country particular regions would join. Most of these questions were handled by the victorious Allied Powers in bodies such as the Allied Supreme Council. The Allies tended to refer only particularly difficult matters to the League. This meant that, during the first three years of the 1920s, the League played little part in resolving the turmoil that resulted from the war. The questions the League considered in its early years included those designated by the Paris Peace treaties.

As the League developed, its role expanded, and by the middle of the 1920s, it became the centre of international activity. This change can be seen in the relationship between the League and non-members. The United States and Russia, for example, increasingly worked with the League. During the second half of the 1920s, France, Britain and Germany were all using the League of Nations as the focus of their diplomatic activity and each of their foreign secretaries attended League meetings at Geneva during this period. They also used the League's machinery to try to improve relations and settle their differences.

Upper Silesia

The Allied Powers referred the problem of Upper Silesia to the League after they had been unable to resolve the territorial dispute. After the First World War, Poland laid claim to Upper Silesia, which had been part of Prussia. The Treaty of Versailles had recommended a plebiscite in Upper Silesia to determine whether the territory should be part of Germany or Poland. Complaints about the attitude of the German authorities led to rioting and eventually to the first two Silesian Uprisings (1919 and 1920). A plebiscite took place on 20 March 1921 with 59.6% (around 500,000) of the votes cast in favour of joining Germany, but Poland claimed the conditions surrounding it had been unfair. This result led to the Third Silesian Uprising in 1921. On 12 August 1921, the League was asked to settle the matter, and the Council created a commission with representatives from Belgium, Brazil, China and Spain to study the situation. The committee recommended that Upper Silesia should be divided between Poland and Germany according to the preferences shown in the plebiscite and that the two sides should decide the details of the interaction between the two areas. For example, whether goods should pass freely over the border due to the economic and industrial interdependency of the two areas. In November 1921 a conference was held in Geneva to negotiate a convention between Germany and Poland. A final settlement was reached, after five meetings, in which most of the area was given to Germany but with the Polish section containing the majority of the region's mineral resources and much of its industry. When this agreement became public in May 1922, bitter resentment was expressed in Germany, but the treaty was still ratified by both countries. The settlement produced peace in the area lasting until the run up to the Second World War.

Albania

The frontiers of Albania had not been set during the Paris Peace Conference in 1919, being left to the League to be decided, but had not yet been determined by September 1921. This created an unstable situation with Greek troops repeatedly crossing into Albanian territory on military operations in the south and Yugoslavian forces engaged, after clashes with Albanian tribesmen, far into the northern part of the country. The League sent a commission of representatives from various powers to the region and in November 1921, the League decided that the frontiers of Albania should be the same as they had been in 1913 with three minor changes that favoured Yugoslavia. Yugoslav forces withdrew a few weeks later, albeit under protest.

The borders of Albania again become the cause of international conflict when Italian General Enrico Tellini and four of his assistants were ambushed and killed on 24 August 1923 while marking out the new newly decided border between Greece and Albania. Italian leader Benito Mussolini was incensed, and demanded that a commission should be set up to investigate the incident and that its enquires should be completed within five days. Whatever the results of the enquiry, Mussolini insisted that the Greek government should pay Italy fifty million lira reparations. The Greeks said they would not pay unless it was proved that the crime was committed by Greeks.

Mussolini sent a warship to shell the Greek island of Corfu and Italian forces occupied Corfu on 31 August 1923. This contravened the League's covenant so Greece appealed to the League to deal with the situation. The Allies, however, agreed (under Mussolini's insistence) that the Conference of Ambassadors should be responsible for resolving the dispute because it was the conference that had appointed General Tellini. The League Council examined the dispute but then passed their findings to the Council of Ambassadors to make the final decision. The conference accepted most of the League's recommendations forcing Greece to pay fifty million lira to Italy even though those who committed the crime were never discovered. Mussolini was able to leave Corfu in triumph.

Åland Islands

Åland is a collection of around 6,500 islands midway between Sweden and Finland. The islands are exclusively Swedish speaking, but in 1809, Sweden had lost both Finland and the Åland Islands to Imperial Russia. In December 1917, during the turmoil of the Russian October Revolution, Finland declared independence, and most of the Ålanders wished the islands to become part of Sweden again; the Finnish government, however, felt that the islands were part of their new nation, as the Russians had included Åland in the Grand Duchy of Finland formed in 1809. By 1920, the dispute had escalated to such a level that there was a danger of war. The British government referred the problem to the League's Council, but Finland did not let the League intervene as they considered it an internal matter. The League created a small panel to decide if the League should investigate the matter and, with an affirmative response, a neutral commission was created. In June 1921, the League announced its decision; the islands should remain a part of Finland but with guaranteed protection of the islanders, including demilitarization. With Sweden's reluctant agreement, this became the first European international agreement concluded directly through the League.

Hatay

The Republic of Hatay was a transitional political entity that formally existed from September 7, 1938 to June 29, 1939 in the territory of the Sanjak of Alexandretta of the French Mandate of Syria. With League of Nations oversight, the state was annexed by the Republic of Turkey on June 29, 1939 and transformed into the Turkish Hatay Province (excluding districts of Erzin, Dörtyol, Hassa).

Memel

The port city of Memel (now Klaipėda) and the surrounding area, with a predominantly German population, were under Allied control after the end of the World War I. The area had been awarded to Lithuania by Article 99 of the Treaty of Versailles but the French and Polish governments favoured turning Memel into an international city. By 1923, control of the area had still not been transferred to Lithuania, prompting Lithuanian forces to invade in January 1923 and seize the port. After the Allies failed to reach an agreement with Lithuania, they referred the matter to the League of Nations. In December 1923, the League Council appointed a Commission of Inquiry to investigate. The Commission chose to cede Memel to Lithuania and give the area autonomous rights. This decision was approved by the League Council on 14 March 1924 and then by the Allied Powers and Lithuania.

Mosul

The League resolved a dispute between the Kingdom of Iraq and the Republic of Turkey over the control of the former Ottoman province of Mosul in 1926. According to the British, who were awarded a League of Nations A-mandate over Iraq in 1920 and therefore represented Iraq in its foreign affairs, Mosul belonged to Iraq; on the other hand, the new Turkish republic claimed the province as part of its historic heartland. A League of Nations' Commission of Inquiry with Belgian, Hungarian and Swedish members was sent to the region in 1924 to study the case and found that the people of Mosul did not want to be part of Turkey or Iraq but if they had to choose would pick Iraq. In 1925, the commission recommended that the region stay part of Iraq, under the condition that the British would hold the mandate over Iraq for another 25 years, to assure the autonomous rights of the Kurdish population. The League Council adopted the recommendation and it decided on 16 December 1925 to award Mosul to Iraq. Although Turkey had accepted the League of Nations' arbitration in the Treaty of Lausanne in 1923, it rejected the League's decision questioning the Council's authority. The matter was referred to the Permanent Court of International Justice which ruled that when the Council made a unanimous decision it must be accepted. Nonetheless, Britain, Iraq and Turkey ratified a separate treaty on 5 June 1926, that mostly followed the decision of the League Council and also assigned Mosul to Iraq. It was agreed, however, that Iraq could still apply for League membership within 25 years and that the mandate would end upon its admittance.

Vilnius

After World War I, Poland and Lithuania both regained their independence but there was disagreement about the frontiers between the countries. During the Polish-Soviet War, Lithuania signed a peace treaty with the Soviet Union that laid out Lithuania's frontiers. This agreement gave control of the city of Vilnius (Lithuanian: *Vilnius*, Polish: *Wilno*), the old Lithuanian capital, to Lithuania which became the country's seat of government. This heightened tension between Lithuania and Poland led to fears that they would go to war, and on 7 October 1920 the League negotiated a short-lived armistice The majority of the population of the city of Vilnius during the inter-war era were Polish and on 9 October 1920 General Zeligowski with a Polish military force took the city and claimed that the Government of Central Lithuania was now under their protection.

Lithuania requested the League's assistance and in response, the League Council called for Poland's withdrawal from the area. The Polish Government indicated they would comply with the League, but rather than leaving, it reinforced the city with more Polish troops. This prompted the League to decide that the future of Vilnius should be determined by its residents in a plebiscite and that the Polish forces should withdraw and be replaced by an international force organised by the League. Several League nations, included France and Britain, started preparing troops to be sent to the area as part of the international force. At the end of 1920, hostilities between Poland and Lithuania increased again but early in 1921, the Polish government began to seek a peaceful settlement. It agreed to support the League's plan for the area, withdraw Polish troops and cooperate with the plebiscite. The League, however, now faced opposition from Lithuania and the Soviet Union, who opposed any international force in Lithuania. In March 1921, the League abandoned plans for the plebiscite and the international force, and returned to attempting to facilitate a negotiated settlement between the two sides. Vilnius and the surrounding area were formally annexed by Poland in March 1922, and on 14 March 1923, the Allied Conference set the frontier between Lithuania and Poland leaving Vilnius within Poland. Lithuanian authorities refused to accept the decision, and officially remained in a state of war with Poland until 1927. It was not until the 1938 Polish ultimatum that Lithuania restored diplomatic relations with Poland, ending the war, and thus *de facto* accepted the borders of its neighbour.

Colombia and Peru

There were several border conflicts between Colombia and Peru in the early part of the 20th century, and in 1922, their governments signed the Salomón-Lozano Treaty to try and resolve these conflicts. As part of this treaty, the border town Leticia and its surrounding area were ceded from Peru to Colombia, giving Colombia access to the Amazon River. On 1 September 1932, business leaders from the Peruvian rubber and sugar industries who had lost land when the area was given to Colombia organised an armed takeover of Leticia. At first, the Peruvian government did not recognise the military takeover but Peru's President Luis Sánchez Cerro decided to resist a Colombian re-occupation. The Peruvian army occupied Leticia, resulting in an armed conflict between the two nations. After months of diplomatic wrangling, the governments accepted mediation by the League of Nations, and their representatives presented their cases before the League's Council. A provisional peace agreement, signed by both parties in May 1933, provided for the League to assume control of the disputed territory while bilateral negotiations proceeded. In May 1934, a final peace agreement was signed, resulting in the return of Leticia to Colombia, a formal apology from Peru for the 1932 invasion, demilitarization of the area around Leticia, free navigation on the Amazon and Putumayo Rivers, and a pledge of non-aggression.

Saar

Saar was a province, formed from parts of Prussia and the Rhenish Palatinate, that was established and placed under League control by the Treaty of Versailles. A plebiscite was to be held after fifteen years of League rule to determine whether the region should belong to Germany or France. When the referendum was held in 1935, 90.3% of votes supported becoming part of Germany On 17 January 1935, the territory's re-integration with Germany was approved by the League Council.

Peace and security

In addition to territorial disputes, the League also tried to intervene in other conflicts between (and even within) nations. Among its successes were its attempts to combat the international trade in opium and sexual slavery, and its work to alleviate the plight of refugees, particularly in Turkey in the period to 1926. One of its innovations in this latter area was the 1922 introduction of the Nansen passport, which was the first internationally recognized identity card for stateless refugees. Many of the League's successes were accomplished by its various agencies and commissions.

Greece and Bulgaria

After an incident between sentries on the border between Greece and Bulgaria in October 1925, fighting began between the two countries. Three days after the initial incident, Greek troops invaded Bulgaria. The Bulgarian government ordered its troops to provide only token resistance, and evacuated between ten thousand and fifteen thousand people from the border region, trusting the League to settle the dispute.

The League did indeed condemn the Greek invasion, and called for both Greek withdrawal and compensation to Bulgaria.

Greece complied, but complained about the disparity between their treatment and that of Italy after the Corfu incident.

Liberia

Following accusations of forced labor on the massive American-owned Firestone rubber plantation and American accusations of slave trading, the Liberian government asked the League to launch an investigation. The commission created to investigate was jointly appointed by the League, the United States of America, and Liberia. In 1930, a report by the League confirmed slavery and forced labor was taking place. The report implicated many government officials in the selling of contract labor and recommended that they be replaced by Europeans or Americans. The Liberian government outlawed forced labor and slavery and asked for American help, this created anger within Liberia and led to the resignation of President Charles D.B. King and his vice-president. The League then threatened to establish a trusteeship over Liberia unless reforms were carried out, enacting these reforms then became the central focus of President Edwin Barclay.

Mukden Incident

The Mukden Incident, also known as the "Manchurian Incident" or the "Far Eastern Crisis", was one of the League's major setbacks and acted as the catalyst for Japan's withdrawal from the organization. Under the terms of an agreed lease, the Japanese government had the right to station its troops in the area around the South Manchurian Railway, a major trade route between the two countries, in the Chinese region of Manchuria. In September 1931, a section of the railway was lightly damaged by officers and troops of the Japanese Kwantung Army as a pretext for an invasion of Manchuria. The Japanese army, however, claimed that Chinese soldiers had sabotaged the railway and in apparent retaliation (acting contrary to the civilian government's orders) occupied the entire region of Manchuria. They renamed the area Manchukuo, and on 9 March 1932 set up a puppet government with Pu Yi, the former emperor of China, as its executive head. Internationally, this new country was recognised only by the governments of Italy and Germany; the rest of the world still considered Manchuria legally part of China. In 1932, Japanese air and sea forces bombarded the Chinese city of

Shanghai, sparking the January 28 Incident. The League of Nations agreed to a request for help from the Chinese government, but the long voyage by ship delayed League officials from investigating the matter. When they arrived, the officials were confronted with Chinese assertions that the Japanese had invaded unlawfully, while the Japanese claimed they were acting to keep peace in the area. Despite Japan's high standing in the League, the subsequent Lytton Report declared Japan to be the aggressor and demanded Manchuria be returned to the Chinese. Before the report could be voted on by the Assembly, Japan announced its intention to push further into China. The report passed 42-1 in the Assembly in 1933 (only Japan voted against), but instead of withdrawing its troops from China, Japan withdrew its membership from the League.

According to the Covenant, the League should have responded by placing economic sanctions on Japan, or gathered an army and declared war. Neither of these actions was undertaken, however. The threat of economic sanctions would have been almost useless because the United States was not a League member. Any economic sanctions the League had placed on its member states would have been ineffective, as a country barred from trading with other member states could simply turn and trade with the United States. The League could have assembled an army, but major powers like Britain and France were too preoccupied with their own affairs, such as keeping control of their extensive colonies, especially after the turmoil of World War I. Japan was therefore left in control of Manchuria, until the Soviet Union's Red Army took over the area and returned it to China at the end of World War II.

Chaco War

The League failed to prevent the 1932 war between Bolivia and Paraguay over the arid Gran Chaco region of South America. Although the region was sparsely populated, it contained the Paraguay River which would have given one of the two landlocked countries access to the Atlantic Ocean, and there was also speculation, later proved incorrect, that the Chaco would be a rich source of petroleum. Border skirmishes throughout the late 1920s culminated in an all-out war in 1932, when the Bolivian army attacked the Paraguayans at Fort Carlos Antonio López at Lake Pitiantuta. Paraguay appealed to the League of Nations, but the

League did not take action when the Pan-American conference offered to mediate instead. The war was a disaster for both sides, causing 57,000 casualties for Bolivia, whose population was around three million, and 36,000 dead for Paraguay, whose population was approximately one million. It also brought both countries to the brink of economic disaster. By the time a ceasefire was negotiated on 12 June 1935, Paraguay had seized control over most of the region. This was recognized in a 1938 truce by which Paraguay was awarded three-quarters of the Chaco Boreal.

Italian invasion of Abyssinia

In October 1935, Italian dictator Benito Mussolini sent 400,000 troops to invade Abyssinia (Ethiopia). Marshal Pietro Badoglio led the campaign from November 1935, ordering bombing, the use of chemical weapons like mustard gas, and the poisoning of water supplies, against targets which included undefended villages and medical facilities. The modern Italian Army defeated the poorly armed Abyssinians, and captured Addis Ababa in May 1936, forcing Emperor Haile Selassie to flee.

The League of Nations condemned Italy's aggression and imposed economic sanctions in November 1935, but the sanctions were largely ineffective since they did not ban the sale of oil or close the Suez Canal (controlled by Britain). As Stanley Baldwin, the British Prime Minister, later observed, this was ultimately because no one had the military forces on hand to withstand an Italian attack. In October 1935, U.S. President Franklin D. Roosevelt invoked the recently-passed Neutrality Act and placed an embargo on arms and ammunition with both sides, but extended a further "moral embargo" to the belligerent Italians, including other trade items. On 5 October and later on 29 February 1936 the United States endeavoured, with uncertain success, to limit its exports of oil and other materials to normal peacetime levels. The League sanctions were lifted on 4 July 1936, but by that point Italy had already gained control of the urban areas of Abyssinia.

In December 1935, the Hoare-Laval Pact was an attempt by British Foreign Secretary Samuel Hoare and French Prime Minister Pierre Laval to end the conflict in Abyssinia by drawing up a plan to partition the country into two parts, an Italian sector and an Abyssinian sector. Mussolini was prepared to agree to the Pact, but news of the deal was leaked and both the British and French public venomously protested against it, describing it as a sell-out of Abyssinia. Hoare and Laval were forced to resign their positions, and both the British and French governments dissociated themselves from their respective men. In June 1936, although there was no precedent for a head of state addressing the Assembly of the League of Nations in person, the Emperor of Ethiopia Haile Selassie I spoke to the Assembly to appeal for its help in protecting his country.

As was the case with Japan, the vigour of the major powers in responding to the crisis in Abyssinia was tempered by their perception that the fate of this poor and far-off country, inhabited by non-Europeans, was not a central interest of theirs. In addition, it showed how the League could be influenced by the self-interest of its members; one of the reasons why the sanctions were not very harsh was that both Britain and France feared the prospect of driving Mussolini and German dictator Adolf Hitler into an alliance.

Spanish Civil War

On 17 July 1936, the Spanish Army launched a coup d'état, leading to a prolonged armed conflict between Spanish Republicans (the leftist government of Spain) and the Nationalists (conservative, anti-communist rebels who included most officers of the Spanish Army). Alvarez del Vayo, the Spanish Minister of Foreign Affairs, appealed to the League in September 1936 for arms to defend its territorial integrity and political independence. The League members, however, would not intervene in the Spanish Civil War nor prevent foreign intervention in the conflict. Hitler and Mussolini continued to aid General Francisco Franco's Nationalist insurrectionists, and the Soviet Union aided the Spanish Republic. In February 1937, the League did launch a ban on the intervention of foreign national volunteers.

Second Sino-Japanese War

Following a long record of instigating localised conflicts throughout the 1930s, Japan began a full scale invasion of China on 7 July 1937. On 12 September, the Chinese representative, Wellington Koo, appealed to the League for an international intervention. Western countries were sympathetic to the Chinese in their struggle against Japan, particularly in their stubborn defence of Shanghai, a city with a substantial number of foreigners. However, the League was unable to provide any practical measure other than a final statement that gave China "spiritual support." On 4 October, the League adjourned and turned the case over to the Nine Power Treaty Conference.

Disarmament and failures en route to World War II

Article eight of the League's covenant gave the League the task of reducing "armaments to the lowest point consistent with national safety and the enforcement by common action of international obligations" A significant amount of the League's time and energy was devoted to disarmament even though many member governments were uncertain that such extensive disarmament could be achieved or was even desirable. The Allied Powers were also under obligation from the Treaty of Versailles to attempt to disarm and the armament restrictions imposed on the defeated countries had been described as the first step toward world wide disarmament. The League Covenant assigned the League the task of creating a disarmament plan for each state but the Council devolved this responsibility to a special commission set-up in 1926 to prepare for the 1932-34 World Disarmament Conference. Members of the League held different views towards disarmament. The French were reluctant to reduce their armaments without a guarantee of military help if they were attacked, Poland and Czechoslovakia felt vulnerable to attack from the west and wanted the League's response to aggression against its members to be strengthened before they disarmed. Without this guarantee they would not reduce armaments because they felt the risk of attack from Germany was too great. Fear of attack increased as Germany regained strength after the First World War especially after Hitler gained power and became German Chancellor in 1933. In particular Germany's attempts to overturn the Treaty of Versailles and the reconstruction of the German military made France increasingly unwilling to disarm.

The World Disarmament Conference was convened by the League of Nations in Geneva in 1932 with representatives from 60 states. A one year truce on the expansion of armaments, later extended by a few months, was proposed at the start of the conference. The Disarmament Commission obtained initial agreement from France, Italy, Japan, and Britain to limit the size of their navies. The Kellogg-Briand Pact, facilitated by the commission in 1928, failed in its objective of outlawing war. Ultimately, the Commission failed to halt the military build-up by Germany, Italy and Japan during the 1930s. The League was mostly silent in the face of major events leading to World War II such as Hitler's re-militarisation of the Rhineland, occupation of the Sudetenland and Anschluss of Austria, which had been forbidden by the Treaty of Versailles. In fact, League members themselves re-armed. In 1933, Japan simply withdrew from the League rather than submit to its judgement, as did Germany in 1933 (using the failure of the World Disarmament Conference to agree to arms parity between France and Germany as a pretext), and Italy in 1937. The League commissioner in Danzig was unable to deal with German claims on the city, a significant contributing factor in the outbreak of World War II in 1939. The final significant act of the League was to expel the Soviet Union in December 1939 after it invaded Finland.

General Weaknesses

The onset of the Second World War demonstrated that the League had failed in its primary purpose, which was to avoid any future world war. There were a variety of reasons for this failure, many connected to general weaknesses within the organization.

Origins and Structure

The origins of the League as an organization created by the Allied Powers as part of the peace settlement to end the First World War led to it being viewed as a "League of Victors". It also tied the League to the Treaty of Versailles, so that when the Treaty became discredited and unpopular, this reflected on the League of Nations.

The League's supposed neutrality tended to manifest itself as indecision. It required a unanimous vote of its nine-, later fifteen-, member Council to enact a resolution; hence, conclusive and effective action was difficult, if not impossible. It was also slow in coming to its decisions as certain decisions required the unanimous consent of the entire Assembly. This problem mainly stemmed from the fact that the main members of the League of Nations were not willing to accept the possibility that their fate would be decided by other countries and had therefore, in effect, by enforcing unanimous voting given themselves the power of veto.

Global Representation

Representation at the League was often a problem. Though it was intended to encompass all nations, many never joined, or their time as part of the League was short. Most notably missing was the position that the United States of America was supposed to play in the League, not only in terms of helping to ensure world peace and security but also in financing the League. The U.S. President Woodrow Wilson had been a driving force behind the League's formation and strongly influenced the form it took but the United States Senate voted not to join on 19 November 1919. Ruth Henig has suggested that, had the United States been a member of the League, it would have also provided backup to France and Britain, possibly making France feel more secure and so encouraging France and Britain to cooperate more regarding Germany and so made the rise to power of the Nazi party less likely. On the contrary, Henig acknowledges that if America had been a member of the League, its reluctance to engage in war with European states and to enact economic sanctions may have hampered the ability of the League to deal with international incidents. The structure of government in America may also have made its membership problematic as its representatives at the League could not have made decisions on behalf of the United States executive branch without this having already been approved by the legislative branches.

In January 1920, when the League began, Germany was not permitted to join because it was seen as the aggressor in World War I. Soviet Russia was also initially excluded from the League, as communist views were not welcomed by the victors of World War I. The League was further weakened when critical powers left in the 1930s. Japan began as a permanent member of the Council, but withdrew in 1933 after the League voiced opposition to its invasion of the Chinese territory of Manchuria. Italy also began as a permanent member of the Council but withdrew in 1937. The League had accepted Germany as a member in 1926, deeming it a "peace-loving country", but Adolf Hitler pulled Germany out when he came to power in 1933.

Collective Security

Another important weakness grew from the contradiction between the idea of collective security, that formed the basis of the League, and international relations between individual states. The collective security system the League used meant that nations were required to act against states they considered friends, and in a way that might endanger their national interests, to support states that they had no normal affinity with. This weakness was exposed during the Abyssinia Crisis when Britain and France had to balance attempts to maintain the security they had attempted to create for themselves in Europe "in order to defend against the enemies of internal order", in which Italy's support played a pivotal role, with their obligations to Abyssinia as a member of the League.

On 23 June 1936, in the wake of the collapse of League efforts to restrain Italy's war of conquest against Abyssinia, British Prime Minister Stanley Baldwin told the House of Commons that collective security had

"failed ultimately because of the reluctance of nearly all the nations in Europe to proceed to what I might call military sanctions... The real reason, or the main reason, was that we discovered in the process of weeks that there was no country except the aggressor country which was ready for war... [I]f collective action is to be a reality and not merely a thing to be talked about, it means not only that every country is to be ready for war; but must be ready to go to war at once. That is a terrible thing, but it is an essential part of collective security."

Ultimately, Britain and France both abandoned the concept of collective security in favour of appeasement in the face of growing German militarism under Adolf Hitler.

Pacifism and Disarmament

The League of Nations lacked an armed force of its own and depended on the Great Powers to enforce its resolutions, which they were very reluctant to do. The League's two most important members, Britain and France, were reluctant to use sanctions and even more reluctant to resort to military action on behalf of the League. Immediately after World War I, pacifism was a strong force both in the populations and the governments of the two countries. The British Conservatives were especially tepid on the League and preferred, when in government, to negotiate treaties without the involvement of the organization.

Moreover, the League's advocacy of disarmament for Britain, France and its other members while at the same time advocating collective security meant that the League was unwittingly depriving itself of the only forceful means by which its authority would be upheld. If the League was to force countries to abide by international law, it would require the Royal Navy and the French Army to do the enforcing.

When the British Cabinet discussed the concept of the League during the First World War, Maurice Hankey, the Cabinet Secretary, circulated a memorandum on the subject. He started by saying: "Generally it appears to me that any such scheme is dangerous to us, because it will create a sense of security which is wholly fictitious". He attacked the British pre-war faith in the sanctity of treaties as delusional and concluded by claiming:

"It [a League of Nations] will only result in failure and the longer that failure is postponed the more certain it is that this country will have been lulled to sleep. It will put a very strong lever into the hands of the well-meaning idealists who are to be found in almost every Government, who deprecate expenditure on armaments, and, in the course of time, it will almost certainly result in this country being caught at a disadvantage".

The Foreign Office minister Sir Eyre Crowe also wrote a memorandum to the British Cabinet claiming that "a solemn league and covenant" would just be "a treaty, like other treaties": "What is there to ensure that it will not, like other treaties, be broken?". Crowe went on to express scepticism of the planned "pledge of common action" against aggressors because he believed the actions of individual states would still be determined by national interests and the balance of power. He also criticised the proposal for League economic sanctions because it would ineffectual and that "It is all a question of real military preponderance". Universal disarmament was a practical impossibility, Crowe warned.

Demise and Legacy

As the situation in Europe deteriorated into war, the Assembly transferred enough power to the Secretary General on 30 September 1938 and 14 December 1939 to allow the League to continue to legally exist and to carry on reduced operations. The headquarters of the League, the Palace of Peace, remained unoccupied for nearly six years until the Second World War ended. At the 1943 Tehran Conference, the Allied Powers agreed to create a new body to replace the League: the United Nations. Many League bodies, such as the International Labour Organization, continued to function and eventually became affiliated with the UN. The structure of the United Nations was intended to make it more effective than the League.

The final meeting of the League of Nations was held in April 1946 in Geneva. Delegates from 34 nations attended the assembly. This session concerned itself with liquidating the League: assets worth approximately $22,000,000 in 1946, including the Palace of Peace and the League's archives, were given to the UN, reserve funds were returned to the nations that had supplied them, and the debts of the League were settled. Robert Cecil is said to have summed up the feeling of the gathering during a speech to the final assembly when he said: Let us boldly state that aggression wherever it occurs and however it may be defended, is an international crime, that it is the duty of every peace-loving state to resent it and employ whatever force is necessary to crush it, that the machinery of the Charter, no less than the machinery of the Covenant, is sufficient for this purpose if properly used, and that every well-disposed citizen of every state should be ready to undergo any sacrifice in order to maintain peace... I venture to impress upon my hearers that the great work of peace is resting not only on the narrow interests of our own nations, but even more on those great principles of right and wrong which nations, like individuals, depend.

The League is Dead. Long live the United Nations

The motion that dissolved the League passed unanimously: "The League of Nations shall cease to exist except for the purpose of the liquidation of its affairs." The motion also set the date for the end of the League as the day after the session was closed. On 19 April 1946, the President of the Assembly, Carl J. Hambro of Norway, declared "the twenty-first and last session of the General Assembly of the League of Nations closed." As a result, the League of Nations ceased to exist on 20 April 1946.

Professor David Kennedy has suggested that the League is a unique moment when international affairs were "institutionalized" as opposed to the pre-World War I methods of law and politics. The principal Allies in World War II (the UK, the USSR, France, the U.S., and Republic of China) became permanent members of the UN Security Council; these new "Great Powers" gained significant international influence, mirroring the League Council. Decisions of the UN Security Council are binding on all members of the UN; however, unanimous decisions are not required, unlike the League Council. Permanent members of the UN Security Council are also given a shield to protect their vital interests, which has prevented the UN acting decisively in many cases. Similarly, the UN does not have its own standing armed forces, but the UN has been more successful than the League in calling for its members to contribute to armed interventions, such as during the Korean War and the peacekeeping mission in the former Yugoslavia. The UN has in some cases been forced to rely on economic sanctions. The UN has also been more successful than the League in attracting members from the nations of the world, making it more representative.

League of Nations

The League of Nations came into being after the end of World War One. The League of Nation's task was simple-to ensure that war never broke out again. After the turmoil caused by the Versailles Treaty, many looked to the League to bring stability to the world. America entered World War One in 1917. The country as a whole and the president-Woodrow Wilson in particular-was horrified by the slaughter that had taken place in what was meant to be a civilised part of the world. The only way to avoid a repetition of such a disaster, was to create an international body whose sole purpose was to maintain world peace and which would sort out international disputes as and when they occurred.

This would be the task of the League of Nations. After the devastation of the war, support for such a good idea was great (except in America where isolationism was taking root).

The Organisation of the League of Nations

The League of Nations was to be based in Geneva, Switzerland. This choice was natural as Switzerland was a neutral country and had not fought in World War One. No one could dispute this choice especially as an international organisation such as the Red Cross was already based in Switzerland. If a dispute did occur, the League, under its Covenant, could do three things-these were known as its sanctions:

It could call on the states in dispute to sit down and discuss the problem in an orderly and peaceful manner. This would be done in the League's Assembly-which was essentially the League's parliament which would listen to disputes and come to a decision on how to proceed. If one nation was seen to be the offender, the League could introduce verbal sanctions-warning an aggressor nation that she would need to leave another nation's territory or face the consequences.

If the states in dispute failed to listen to the Assembly's decision, the League could introduce economic sanctions. This would be arranged by the League's Council. The purpose of this sanction was to financially hit the aggressor nation so that she would have to do as the League required. The logic behind it was to push an aggressor nation towards bankruptcy, so that the people in that state would take out their anger on their government forcing them to accept the League's decision. The League could order League members not to do any trade with an aggressor nation in an effort to bring that aggressor nation to heel.

if this failed, the League could introduce physical sanctions. This meant that military force would be used to put into place the League's decision. However, the League did not have a military force at its disposal and no member of the League had to provide one under the terms of joining-unlike the current United Nations. Therefore, it could not carry out any threats and any country defying its authority would have been very aware of this weakness. The only two countries in the League that could have provided any military might were Britain and France and both had been severely depleted strength-wise in World War One and could not provide the League with the backing it needed. Also both Britain and France were not in a position to use their finances to pay for an expanded army as both were financially hit very hard by World War One.

The League also had other weaknesses: The country, whose president, Woodrow Wilson, had dreamt up the idea of the League-America-refused to join it. As America was the world's most powerful nation, this was a serious blow to the prestige of the League. However, America's refusal to join the League, fitted in with her desire to have an isolationist policy throughout the world.

Germany was not allowed to join the League in 1919. As Germany had started the war, according to the Treaty of Versailles, one of her punishments was that she was not considered to be a member of the international community and, therefore, she was not invited to join. This was a great blow to Germany but it also meant that the League could not use whatever strength Germany had to support its campaign against aggressor nations.

Russia was also not allowed to join as in 1917, she had a communist government that generated fear in western Europe, and in 1918, the Russian royal family-the Romanovs-was murdered. Such a country could not be allowed to take its place in the League. Therefore, three of the world's most powerful nations (potentially for Russia and Germany) played no part in supporting the League. The two most powerful members were Britain and France-both had suffered financially and militarily during the war-and neither was enthusiastic to get involved in disputes that did not affect western Europe. Therefore, the League had a fine ideal-to end war for good. However, if an aggressor nation was determined enough to ignore the League's verbal warnings, all the League could do was enforce economic sanctions and hope that these worked as it had no chance or enforcing its decisions using military might.

The Successes of the League of Nations

In view of the League's desire to end war, the only criteria that can be used to classify a success, was whether war was avoided and a peaceful settlement formulated after a crisis between two nations. The League experienced success in:

The Aaland Islands (1921)

These islands are near enough equal distant between Finland and Sweden. They had traditionally belonged to Finland but most of the islanders wanted to be governed by Sweden. Neither Sweden nor Finland could come to a decision as to who owned the islands and in 1921 they asked the League to adjudicate. The League's decision was that they should remain with Finland but that no weapons should ever be kept there. Both countries accepted the decision and it remains in force to this day.

Upper Silesia (1921)

The Treaty of Versailles had given the people of Upper Silesia the right to have a referendum on whether they wanted to be part of Germany or part of Poland. In this referendum, 700,000 voted for Germany and 500,000 for Poland. This close result resulted in rioting between those who expected Silesia to be made part of Germany and those who wanted to be part of Poland. The League was asked to settle this dispute. After a six-week inquiry, the League decided to split Upper Silesia between Germany and Poland. The League's decision was accepted y both countries and by the people in Upper Silesia.

Memel (1923)

Memel was/is a port in Lithuania. Most people who lived in Memel were Lithuanians and, therefore, the government of Lithuania believed that the port should be governed by it. However, the Treaty of Versailles had put Memel and the land surrounding the port under the control of the League. For three years, a French general acted as a governor of the port but in 1923 the Lithuanians invaded the port. The League intervened and gave the area surrounding Memel to Lithuania but they made the port an "international zone". Lithuania agreed to this decision. Though this can be seen as a League success – as the issue was settled – a counter argument is that what happened was the result of the use of force and that the League responded in a positive manner to those (the Lithuanians) who had used force.

Turkey (1923)

The League failed to stop a bloody war in Turkey but it did

respond to the humanitarian crisis caused by this war. 1,400,000 refugees had been created by this war with 80% of them being women and children. Typhoid and cholera were rampant. The League sent doctors from the Health Organisation to check the spread of disease and it spent £10 million on building farms, homes etc. for the refugees. Money was also invested in seeds, wells and digging tools and by 1926, work was found for 600,000 people. A member of the League called this work "the greatest work of mercy which mankind has undertaken."

Greece and Bulgaria (1925)

Both these nations have a common border. In 1925, sentries patrolling this border fired on one another and a Greek soldier was killed. The Greek army invaded Bulgaria as a result. The Bulgarians asked the League for help and the League ordered both armies to stop fighting and that the Greeks should pull out of Bulgaria. The League then sent experts to the area and decided that Greece was to blame and fined her £45,000. Both nations accepted the decision.

The failures of the League of Nations

Article 11 of the League's Covenant stated: "Any war of threat of war is a matter of concern to the whole League and the League shall take action that may safe guard peace." Therefore, any conflict between nations which ended in war and the victor of one over the other must be considered a League failure.

Italy (1919)

In 1919, Italian nationalists, angered that the "Big Three" had, in their opinion, broken promises to Italy at the Treaty of Versailles, captured the small port of Fiume. This port had been given to Yugoslavia by the Treaty of Versailles. For 15 months, Fiume was governed by an Italian nationalist called d'Annunzio. The newly created League did nothing. The situation was solved by the Italian government who could not accept that d'Annunzio was seemingly more popular than they were – so they bombarded the port of Fiume and enforced a surrender. In all this the League played no part despite the fact that it had just been set up with the specific task of maintaining peace.

Teschen (1919)

Teschen was a small town between Poland and Czechoslovakia. Its main importance was that it had valuable coal mines there which both the Poles and the Czechs wanted. As both were newly created nations, both wanted to make their respective economies as strong as possible and the acquisition of rich coal mines would certainly help in this respect. In January 1919, Polish and Czech troops fought in the streets of Teschen. Many died. The League was called on to help and decided that the bulk of the town should go to Poland while Czechoslovakia should have one of Teschen's suburbs. This suburb contained the most valuable coal mines and the Poles refused to accept this decision. Though no more wholesale violence took place, the two countries continued to argue over the issue for the next twenty years.

Vilna (1920)

Many years before 1920, Vilna had been taken over by Russia. Historically, Vilna had been the capital of Lithuania when the state had existed in the Middle Ages. After World War One, Lithuania had been re-established and Vilna seemed the natural choice for its capital. However, by 1920, 30% of the population was from Poland with Lithuanians only making up 2% of the city's population. In 1920, the Poles seized Vilna. Lithuania asked for League help but the Poles could not be persuaded to leave the city. Vilna stayed in Polish hands until the outbreak of World War Two. The use of force by the Poles had won.

War between Russia and Poland (1920 to 1921)

In 1920, Poland invaded land held by the Russians. The Poles quickly overwhelmed the Russian army and made a swift advance into Russia. By 1921, the Russians had no choice but to sign the Treaty of Riga which handed over to Poland nearly 80,000 square kilometres of Russian land. This one treaty all but doubled the size of Poland. What did the League do about this violation of another country by Poland? The answer is simple – nothing. Russia by 1919 was communist and this "plague from the East" was greatly feared by the West. In fact, Britain, France and America sent troops to attack Russia after the League had been set up. Winston Churchill, the British War Minister, stated openly that the plan was to strangle Communist Russia at birth. Once again, to outsiders, it seemed as if League members were selecting which countries were acceptable and ones which were not. The Allied invasion of Russia was a failure and it only served to make Communist Russia even more antagonistic to the West.

The invasion of the Ruhr (1923)

The Treaty of Versailles had ordered Weimar Germany to pay reparations for war damages. These could either be paid in money or in kind (goods to the value of a set amount) In 1922, the Germans failed to pay an installment. They claimed that they simply could not rather than did not want to. The Allies refused to accept this and the anti-German feeling at this time was still strong. Both the French and the Belgium's believed that some form of strong action was needed to 'teach Germany a lesson'.

In 1923, contrary to League rules, the French and the Belgium's invaded the Ruhr – Germany's most important industrial zone. Within Europe, France was seen as a senior League member – like Britain – and the anti-German feeling that was felt throughout Europe allowed both France and Belgium to break their own rules as were introduced by the League. Here were two League members clearly breaking League rules and nothing was done about it. For the League to enforce its will, it needed the support of its major backers in Europe, Britain and France. Yet France was one of the invaders and Britain was a major supporter of her. To other nations, it seemed that if you wanted to break League rules, you could. Few countries criticised what France and Belgium did. But the example they set for others in future years was obvious. The League clearly failed on this occasion, primarily because it was seen to be involved in breaking its own rules.

Italy and Albania (1923)

The border between Italy and Albania was far from clear and the Treaty of Versailles had never really addressed this issue. It was a constant source of irritation between both nations. In 1923, a mixed nationality survey team was sent out to settle the issue. Whilst travelling to the disputed area, the Italian section of the survey team, became separated from the main party. The five Italians were shot by gunmen who had been in hiding.

Italy accused Greece of planning the whole incident and demanded payment of a large fine. Greece refused to pay up. In response, the Italians sent its navy to the Greek island of Corfu and bombarded the coastline. Greece appealed to the League for help but Italy, lead by Benito Mussolini, persuaded the League via the Conference of Ambassadors, to fine Greece 50 million lire. To follow up this success, Mussolini invited the Yugoslavian government to discuss ownership of Fiume. The Treaty of Versailles had given Fiume to Yugoslavia but with the evidence of a bombarded Corfu, the Yugoslavs handed over the port to Italy with little argument

The Social Successes of the League of Nations

At a social level the League did have success and most of this is easily forgotten with its failure at a political level. Many of the groups that work for the United Nations now, grew out of what was established by the League. Teams were sent to the Third World to dig fresh water wells, the Health Organisation started a campaign to wipe out leprosy. This idea-of wiping out from the world a disease-was taken up by the United Nations with its smallpox campaign. Work was done in the Third World to improve the status of women there and child slave labour was also targeted. Drug addiction and drug smuggling were also attacked.

These problems are still with us in the C21st-so it would be wrong to criticise the League for failing to eradicate them. If we cannot do this now, the League had a far more difficult task then with more limited resources. The greatest success the League had involving these social issues, was simply informing the world at large that these problems did exist and that they should be tackled. No organisation had done this before the League. These social problems may have continued but the fact that they were now being actively investigated by the League and were then taken onboard by the United Nations must be viewed as a success.

The Failure of the League of Nations

The League of Nations, a former international organization, was formed after World War I to promote international peace and security. The basis of the League, also called the Covenant, was written into the Treaty of Versailles and other peace treaties and provided for an assembly, a council, and a secretariat. Because the peace treaties had created the League of Nations, the League was bound to uphold their principles. but however, it became apparent that some of the terms of the treaties were harsh and unjust and needed amending. This undermined the league. Woodrow Wilson hoped however, by including it in the treaties that this would ensure that the League was accepted by all nations. However, from the start, the League shared many of the weaknesses of the treaties themselves. The defeated powers were not consulted about the league and were not invited to join. The victorious powers did not really agree among themselves about the League.

A system of colonial commands was also set up. Based in Geneva, the League proved useful in settling minor international disputes, but they had a hard time stopping aggression involving major powers such as, Japan's occupation of Manchuria in 1931, Italy's invasion of Ethiopia in 1935-36, and Germany's seizure of Austria in 1938. It collapsed early in World War II and ended in 1946.

Its ending in 1946 was because it had some basic and fundamental problems such as dealing with aggression involving major powers. Countries like Japan and Italy were able to just walk over the League of Nations because it had no armed forces of its own and it relied upon the cooperation of its members. This problem was inter-linked with the fact that the League was very slow at making decisions. With no armed forces this made it difficult to impose decisions. Therefore when a crisis occurred the league was supposed to act fast with resoluteness. Although, often the League met too infrequently and took far too long to make critical decisions. This need for all members to agree on a course of action undermined the strength of the League. The League was too indecisive they needed some influential countries. The absence of the powerful USA and, until 1934, the USSR were felt, this could have been the answer to the League's problems. However these countries did not join and again this contributed the failure of the league, as non-members, they could and did trade with countries facing League sanctions and therefore to a certain extent it was in their own interests to remain detached from such a commitment as the League. Another problem for the League however, was that it was being too closely linked to the victors of the First World War and the Peace Treaties. Another reason why the league failed was that because one their aims, 'To keep collective security...' failed. Britain and France along with other members were more concerned about their own interests. As a result they were reluctant to get involved in collective security (one of the reasons why Britain and France were reluctant to commit troops to fight for the League of Nations) and their League could not make powerful countries obey their rulings.

The League also failed because there was a lack of unity between Britain and France. They often disagreed and they did not trust each other. With this and the fact decisions had to be unanimous made it almost impossible for the League to make a decision.

The League was also weakened by the Great Depression that hit the world in the years following the Wall Street Crash. At a time of economic crises it meant that the League had trouble imposing sanctions especially at this time. This meant that countries like Japan and Italy were able to annex other countries without effective punishment.

All these reasons did not fear the likes of Hitler and Mussolini; in fact they gained in confidence. Therefore the failure of the League was really a vicious circle as the basic problems led to other problems and encouraged the rise of powerful nationalist dictators and militaristic governments prepared to ignore the League and to use force.

5

Factors Leading to the Second World War and Post-War Settlement

Overview: World War Two in Europe

It's known as the 'good war', the struggle against fascism and genocide by the free democracies, the triumph of good over an evil which had infused Germany and Japan. But, as you might expect of the single largest conflict in history, World War Two wasn't so simple.

Dates and Belligerents of World War Two

For a start, there's disagreement on when the war started and two common dates for when it finished. In terms of Europe, Russia generally holds that the 'Great Patriotic War' began on June 22nd 1941 with Operation Barbarossa (the German invasion of Russia) while Western Europe uses September 1st 1939, the German invasion of Poland. Both use the date of Germany's unconditional surrender as the end in Europe, but the Western Allies accepted the surrender on May 8th and the Russian May 9th 1945.

Despite featuring Nazi Germany, the media's most famous 'baddies', the opposing alliances aren't clear either thanks to some fluid politics. The bulk of the European war was fought by the fascist 'Axis' of Germany and Italy against the uneasy alliance of France, the British Empire, the United States and Communist Russia with numerous small contributors on both sides. However, Russia began the war by seizing and suppressing Poland in allegiance with Germany in 1939-albeit having first tried to find support against Germany from the western nations – until Germany invaded Russia in 1941, while an Italy freed from fascist rulers joined the Allies in 1943. All across Europe over fifty million combatants fought, with over ten million causalities and equal that number of civilian deaths.

The Causes of World War Two

The immediate trigger for war was the Nazi invasion of Poland, a conquest too far for the allied nations who had seen Austrian and Czech lands subsumed into the Reich already. The driving force was unquestionably Hitler, who wanted war and racial domination. But argument rages about the wider background, the political, cultural and economic climate which allowed Hitler into power to begin with.

Many start in 1918 with the end of World War One and the Treaty of Versailles, whose 'war guilt' and rampant anti-German clauses has led some to say another war was inevitable, or even that world wars one and two are part of the same conflict, albeit with a large ceasefire in the middle. Hitler certainly played on German beliefs that they had been betrayed and treated unfairly at the war's end. The Allied Occupation of Germany which ended World War Two prevented a repeat.

Studies of the 'causes' often examine the creation and fall of the Weimer Republic (Germany's fragile inter-war democracy), the world depression which began in 1929, the latent racism of European culture, the rise of fascism in Germany and Italy, the intransigence of Britain and France in the face of growing central European militarism and the successful application of German might in the Spanish Civil War. These factors are usually tied together to present a picture which, at its simplest, involves desperate citizens turning from weak democracies to martial dictatorships which played on people's basest fears and appeared able to solve their problems.

World War Two Itself

World War Two in Europe was fought on three main fronts: East, West and Italian. The most decisive and bloody was the East, where Axis troops reached Stalingrad in the south and almost Moscow in the north before being pushed all the way back to

Berlin by a Soviet army of over twenty million combatants. The Western Front was temporarily dominated by Germany after their swift conquest of France in 1940, but on June 6th 1944 it was reopened by successful allied landings in Normandy. The Italian front, often called the 'forgotten front' saw Allied troops fight their way up the peninsular, allowing a non-fascist Italy to join the Allies. European troops also fought in North Africa, Asia and Australasia.

Unlike many previous conflicts, World War Two was also a battle of racial and individual survival. Nazi Germany was actively trying to enslave the Slavic groups and exterminate Jews, Gypsies and the physically or mentally handicapped, leading to the deployment of mass execution and the development of death camps which murdered twelve million people, the most infamous being Auschwiz-Birkenau. At the same time the Soviet Gulag system imprisoned millions, while the ideology/cruelty of Communist high command, which considered people as just another national resource to be spent, led to millions of civilian deaths. The Soviets, just like the Nazis, also purged the Polish population of 'enemies'.

The Aftermath of World War Two

You cannot overstate the consequences of World War Two; every facet of human life was change, often permanently. The borders of Europe were redrawn again and the Cold War developed from a Europe divided between democratic western Allies and a newly dominant Soviet Union. Science advanced as code-breakers invented computers, synthetic materials and vaccines were developed and the atomic age began. Culture was radically altered as class and race systems broke down and humanity began to face the horror of what had occurred.

Key Themes of World War Two

Battles

A number of battles/events have earnt considerable attention. In the west the aerial battle of Britain, the D-Day landings and Operation Market Garden, in the East the siege of Stalingrad, the Battle for Moscow, Kursk (the largest tank battle ever fought) and the Warsaw Uprising.

Tanks and Blitzkrieg

In terms of studying weapons and tactics the tanks – or 'panzers'-are particularly prominent, each side racing to develop improved types, as are the 'blitzkrieg' tactics of German armies.

The Holocaust

There are people around the world who try to deny the Holocaust, Nazi Germany's attempt (with considerable assistance from other nations) to kill every single Jew.

Let me be clear: there is absolutely no doubt whatsoever that the Holocaust occurred and that it killed six million people. However, the figure of six million is sometimes misleading: Nazi executions at concentration and death camps, as well as elsewhere, actually killed twelve million people of all races and creeds.

Appeasement

The governments of Europe were slow to tackle Nazi aggression, with the British Prime Minister Neville Chamberlain believing he had negotiated 'Peace in Our Time' with a man whose ideology demanded war.

Key Debates

Did We Really Win?

The Allied West went to war in 1939 to free Poland from Nazi tyranny, but when the war closed in 1945 Poland was under Soviet tyranny. Debate still rages about the consequences of removing the Nazis but leaving the Soviets in Eastern Europe. Did World War Two only really end once democracy had replaced Soviet rule?

Who Really Won World War Two

Were Allied Carpet Bombings War Crimes?

As the war raged Allied air crews bombed Germany, not just to destroy armies and production, but to leave such terror in German hearts that there would be no World War Three caused by them. Today some historians and politicians look back and call these actions war crimes.

Who Won the War?

The question of who did the most to won the war, although pathetic, is still raised every day in chats across the world as national pride rears an ugly head. No single nation was the sole cause of victory, and perhaps the best you can say is Soviet manpower, American supplies and British (Empire) bombing won the day.

Timeline for World War Two: Contributing Factors in the Early Days

While the second World War officially began on September 3, 1939, the timeline for WWII traces all the way back to the end of the First World War. After Germany's first overwhelming defeat, the Treaty of Versailles was signed to officially end the War. Because of the extensive damage caused at least partially by the German army, and the high cost of rebuilding, Germany was made to provide significant financial compensation to France for the havoc they had caused. Having to pay out so much money soon resulted in extreme poverty for Germany. Their poor economic state, along with a naval blockade enforced by the British-which prevented much-needed supplies from reaching German shores-resulted in the German public strongly resenting those that enforced the Treaty.

Most German citizens were left in complete destitution, and a high number of deaths occurred due to abject poverty. The worldwide stock market crash of 1929 created a global economic depression, which made their particular situation that much worse. These factors, combined with distrust for the weak postwar democratic rule, left Germany primed for the uprising of Adolf Hitler.

When Hitler was appointed to the position of Chancellor on January 30, 1933, he quickly transferred legislative power to his own cabinet. Anyone with different political ideas were banned from expressing them, and some individuals were later murdered for trying to oppose him. Hitler appointed himself Furher (Leader) in August 1934, and Germany's armed forces swore absolute obedience to him. One of his first acts was to re-introduce military conscription to quickly rebuild the German regime; he also reconstructed the German navy, soon producing a fleet one-third the size of the British navy. Hitler's fleet re-secured the Baltic Sea, taking back control from the British Royal Navy.

One major factor that allowed World War II to occur was that while the United Kingdom and France officially protested against Hitler's actions, they did nothing to rein him in. Many Britons believed that the Treaty had been too harsh on Germany and that Hitler was just attempting to relieve some of the pressures on his country. Hitler's early conquests-such as the German annexation of Austria in March 1938-succeeded mainly because no other country stood up to him.

World War II

World War II, or the Second World War (often abbreviated WWII or WW2), was a global military conflict which involved most of the world's nations, including all great powers, organised into two opposing military alliances: the Allies and the Axis. The war involved the mobilisation of over 100 million military personnel, making it the most widespread war in history. In a state of "total war," the major participants placed their entire economic, industrial, and scientific capabilities at the service of the war effort, erasing the distinction between civilian and military resources. Over seventy million people, the majority civilians, were killed, making it the deadliest conflict in human history.

The start of the war is generally held to be September 1, 1939, with the invasion of Poland by Nazi Germany and subsequent declarations of war on Germany by most of the countries in the British Empire and Commonwealth, and by France. Many countries were already at war before this date, such as Ethiopia and Italy in the Second Italo-Abyssinian War and China and Japan in the Second Sino-Japanese War. Many who were not initially involved joined the war later, as a result of events such as the German invasion of the Soviet Union, the attacks on Pearl Harbour and British colonies, and subsequent declarations of war on Japan by the United States, the Netherlands, and British Commonwealth.

In 1945, the war ended in a victory for the Allies. The Soviet Union and the United States subsequently emerged as the world's superpowers, setting the stage for the Cold War. This cold war would last for the next 46 years. The United Nations was formed in the hope of preventing another world conflict. The acceptance of the principle of self-determination accelerated decolonization movements in Asia and Africa, while Western Europe itself began moving toward integration.

Chronology

The start of the war is generally held to be September 1, 1939 with the German invasion of Poland; Britain and France declared war on Germany two days later. Other dates for the beginning of war include the Japanese invasion of Manchuria September 13, 1931; the start of the Second Sino-Japanese War on July 7, 1937; or one of several other events. Others follow A. J. P. Taylor, who holds that there was a simultaneous Sino-Japanese War in East Asia, and a Second European War in Europe and her colonies. Neither war became a global conflict until they merged in 1941, at which point the war continued until 1945. This article uses the conventional dating. Other important events that happened at the dawn of the war include the Second Italo-Abyssinian War between Ethiopia and Italy on October 1935 that led to the collapse of the League of Nations. The exact date of the war's end is not universally agreed upon. It has been suggested that the war ended at the armistice of August 14, 1945, rather than the formal surrender of Japan (September 2, 1945); in some European histories, it ended on V-E Day (May 8, 1945). The Treaty of Peace with Japan was not signed until 1951.

Background

A variety of events led to the escalation of hostilities between the Axis and Allied powers prior to the start of the war. In the aftermath of World War I, a defeated Germany signed the Treaty of Versailles. This caused Germany to lose around 13 percent of its territory, stripped it of its colonies, prohibited German annexation of other states, imposed massive reparations and limited the size and makeup of Germany's armed forces. The Russian Civil War led to the creation of the Soviet Union, which soon was under the control of Joseph Stalin. In Italy, Benito Mussolini seized power as a fascist dictator promising to create a "New Roman Empire."

The Kuomintang (KMT) party in China launched a unification campaign against regional warlords and nominally unified China in the mid-1920s, but was soon embroiled in a civil war against its former Chinese communist allies. In 1931, an increasingly militaristic Japanese Empire, which had long sought influence in China as the first step of its right to rule Asia, used the Mukden Incident as justification to invade Manchuria and anex two Chinese provinces. The two nations then fought several small conflicts, in Shanghai, Rehe and Hebei, until the Tanggu Truce in 1933. Thereafter, Chinese volunteer forces continued the resistance to Japanese aggression in Manchuria, and Chahar and Suiyuan.

Adolf Hitler, after an unsuccessful attempt to overthrow the German government in 1923, became the Chancellor of Germany in 1933. He abolished democracy, espousing a radical, racially-motivated revision of the world order, and soon began a massive rearmament campaign. Meanwhile, France, to secure its alliance, allowed Italy a free hand in Ethiopia, which Italy desired as a colonial possession. The situation was aggravated in early 1935 when the Saarland was legally reunited with Germany and Hitler repudiated the Treaty of Versailles, speeding up his rearmament programme and introducing conscription. Hoping to contain Germany, the United Kingdom, France and Italy formed the Stresa Front. The Soviet Union, concerned due to Germany's goals of capturing vast areas of eastern Europe, wrote a treaty of mutual assistance with France. Before taking effect though, the Franco-Soviet pact was required to go through the bureaucracy of the League of Nations, which rendered it essentially toothless. In June 1935, the United Kingdom made an independent naval agreement with Germany, easing prior restrictions. The United States, concerned with events in Europe and Asia, passed the Neutrality Act in August. In October, Italy invaded Ethiopia, with Germany the only major European nation supporting her invasion. Italy then revoked objections to Germany's goal of absorbing Austria.

Hitler defied the Versailles and Locarno treaties by remilitarizing the Rhineland in March 1936. He received little response from other European powers. When the Spanish Civil War broke out in July, Hitler and Mussolini supported fascist Generalissimo Francisco Franco's nationalist forces in his civil war against the Soviet-supported Spanish Republic. Both sides used the conflict to test new weapons and methods of warfare, and the nationalists won the war in early 1939. Mounting tensions led to several efforts to strengthen or consolidate power. In October 1936 Germany and Italy formed the Rome-Berlin Axis and a month later Germany and Japan, each believing communism and the Soviet Union to be a threat, signed the Anti-Comintern Pact, which Italy would join in the following year. In China, the Kuomintang and communist forces agreed on a ceasefire in order to present a united front to oppose Japan.

Pre-war Events

Invasion of Ethiopia

The Second Italo–Abyssinian War was a brief colonial war that started in October 1935 and ended in May 1936. The war was fought between the armed forces of the Kingdom of Italy (*Regno d'Italia*) and the armed forces of the Ethiopian Empire (also known as Abyssinia). The war resulted in the military occupation of Ethiopia and its annexation into the newly created colony of Italian East Africa (*Africa Orientale Italiana*, or AOI).

Politically, the war is best remembered for exposing the inherent weakness of the League of Nations. Like the Mukden Incident in 1931, the Abyssinia Crisis in 1934 is often seen as a clear example of the ineffectiveness of the League. Both Italy and Ethiopia were member nations and yet the League was unable to control Italy or to protect Ethiopia when Italy clearly violated the League's own Article X. The war is also remembered for the Italian armed forces' illegal use of mustard gas and phosgene.

Invasion of China

In mid-1937, following the Marco Polo Bridge Incident, the Second Sino-Japanese War culminated in the Japanese campaign to invade all of China. The Soviets quickly signed a non-aggression pact with China, effectively ending China's prior cooperation with Germany. Starting at Shanghai, the Japanese pushed the Chinese forces back, capturing the capital Nanjing in December. In June 1938, Chinese forces stalled the Japanese advance by flooding the Yellow River; although this manoeuvre bought time for the Chinese to prepare their defences at Wuhan, the city was taken by October. During this time, Japanese and Soviet forces engaged in a skirmish at Lake Khasan; in May 1939, they became involved in a more serious border war that ended with their signing a cease-fire agreement on September 15 and restoring the *status quo*. On April 13, 1941, Japan and the Soviet Union signed the Soviet–Japanese Neutrality Pact, pledging to respect the territorial integrity and inviolability of Manchukuo and Mongolian People's Republic.

European Occupations and Agreements

In Europe, Germany and Italy were becoming bolder. In March 1938 Germany annexed Austria, again provoking little response from other European powers. Encouraged, Hitler began pressing German claims on the Sudetenland, an area of Czechoslovakia with a predominantly ethnic German population; France and Britain conceded this territory to him, against the wishes of the Czechoslovak government, in exchange for a promise of no further territorial demands. However, soon after that, Germany and Italy forced Czechoslovakia to cede additional territory to Hungary and Poland. In March 1939 Germany invaded the remainder of Czechoslovakia and subsequently split it into the German Protectorate of Bohemia and Moravia and the pro-German independent client state, the Slovak Republic.

Alarmed, and with Hitler making further demands on Danzig, France and Britain guaranteed their support for Polish independence; when Italy conquered Albania in April 1939, the same guarantee was extended to Romania and Greece. Shortly after the Franco-British pledge to Poland, Germany and Italy formalized their own alliance with the Pact of Steel. In August 1939 Germany and the Soviet Union signed the Molotov-Ribbentrop Pact, a non-aggression pact. This treaty included a secret protocol placing Western Poland and Lithuania in the German sphere of influence while placing eastern Poland, Finland, Estonia, Latvia and the Romanian province of Bessarabia in the Soviet sphere of influence.

Course of the War

War Breaks out in Europe

On September 1, 1939, Germany and Slovakia — a client state in 1939 — attacked Poland and World War II broke out. France, Britain, and the countries of the Commonwealth declared war on Germany but provided little military support to Poland other than a small French attack into the Saarland. On September 17, 1939, after signing an armistice with Japan, the Soviets launched their own invasion of Poland. By early October, Poland was divided among Germany, the Soviet Union, Lithuania (returned Vilnius capital province) and Slovakia, although Poland never officially surrendered and continued the fight outside its borders. At the same time as the battle in Poland, Japan launched its first attack against Changsha, a strategically important Chinese city, but was repulsed by late September.

Following the invasion of Poland and a German-Soviet treaty governing Lithuania, the Soviet Union forced the Baltic countries to allow it to station Soviet troops in their countries under pacts of "mutual assistance." Finland rejected territorial demands and was invaded by the Soviet Union in November 1939. The resulting conflict ended in March 1940 with Finnish concessions. France and the United Kingdom, treating the Soviet attack on Finland as tantamount to entering the war on the side of the Germans, responded to the Soviet invasion by supporting its expulsion from the League of Nations. In June 1940, the Soviet Armed Forces invaded and occupied the neutral Baltic States.

In Western Europe, British troops deployed to the Continent, but in a phase nicknamed the Phoney War by the British and "Sitzkrieg" by the Germans, neither side launched major operations against the other until April 1940. The Soviet Union and Germany entered a trade pact in February of 1940, pursuant to which the Soviets received German military and industrial equipment in exchange for supplying raw materials to Germany to help circumvent a British blockade. In April, Germany invaded Denmark and Norway to secure shipments of iron ore from Sweden, which the allies would try to disrupt. Denmark immediately capitulated, and despite Allied support, Norway was conquered within two months. British discontent over the Norwegian campaign led to the replacement of Prime Minister Neville Chamberlain by Winston Churchill on May 10, 1940.

Axis Advances

On that same day, Germany invaded France, Belgium, the Netherlands, and Luxemboug. The Netherlands and Belgium were overrun using blitzkrieg tactics in a few days and weeks respectively. The French fortified Maginot Line was circumvented by a flanking movement through the thickly wooded Ardennes region, mistakenly perceived by French planners as an impenetrable natural barrier against armoured vehicles. British troops were forced to evacuate the continent at Dunkirk, abandoning their heavy equipment by the end of the month. On June 10, Italy invaded, declaring war on both France and the United Kingdom; twelve days later France surrendered and was soon divided into German and Italian occupation zones, and an unoccupied rump state under the Vichy Regime. On July 14, the British attacked the French fleet in Algeria to prevent its possible seizure by Germany.

With France neutralised, Germany began an air superiority campaign over Britain (the Battle of Britain) to prepare for an invasion. The campaign failed and by September the invasion plans were cancelled. Using newly captured French ports the German Navy enjoyed success against an over-extended Royal Navy, using U-boats against British shipping in the Atlantic. Italy began operations in the Mediterranean, initiating a siege of Malta in June, conquering British Somaliland in August, and making an incursion into British-held Egypt in September 1940. Japan increased its blockade of China in September by seizing several bases in the northern part of the now-isolated French Indochina.

Throughout this period, the neutral United States took measures to assist China and the Western Allies. In November 1939, the American Neutrality Act was amended to allow 'Cash and carry' purchases by the Allies. In 1940, following the German capture of Paris, the size of the United States Navy was significantly increased and, after the Japanese incursion into Indochina, the United States embargoed iron, steel and mechanical parts against Japan. In September, the United States further agreed to a trade of American destroyers for British bases. Still, a large majority of the American public continued to oppose any direct military intervention into the conflict well into 1941.

At the end of September 1940, the Tripartite Pact united Japan, Italy, and Germany to formalize the Axis Powers. The pact stipulated that any country, with the exception of the Soviet Union, not in the war which attacked any Axis Power would be forced to go to war against all three. During this time, the United States continued to support the United Kingdom and China by introducing the Lend-Lease policy authorizing the provision of war materiel and other items and creating a security zone spanning roughly half of the Atlantic Ocean where the United States Navy protected British convoys. As a result, Germany and the United States found themselves engaged in sustained, if undeclared, naval warfare in the North and Central Atlantic by October 1941, even though the United States remained officially neutral.

The Axis expanded in November 1940 when Hungary, Slovakia, and Romania joined the Tripartite Pact. These countries participated in the subsequent invasion of the USSR, with Romania making the largest contribution to recapture territory ceded to the USSR and pursue its leader Ion Antonescu's desire to combat communism. In October 1940, Italy invaded Greece but within days was repulsed and pushed back into Albania, where a stalemate soon occurred. In December 1940, British Commonwealth forces began counter-offensives against Italian forces in Egypt and Italian East Africa. By early 1941, with Italian forces having been pushed back into Libya by the Commonwealth, Churchill ordered a dispatch of troops from Africa to bolster the Greeks. The Italian Navy also suffered significant defeats, with the Royal Navy putting three Italian battleships out of commission by carrier attack at Taranto, and several more warships neutralised at Cape Matapan.

The Germans soon intervened to assist Italy. Hitler sent German forces to Libya in February, and by the end of March they had launched an offensive against the diminished Commonwealth forces. In under a month, Commonwealth forces were pushed back into Egypt with the exception of the besieged port of Tobruk. The Commonwealth attempted to dislodge Axis forces in May and again in June, but failed on both occasions. In early April following Bulgaria's signing of the Tripartite Pact, the Germans intervened in the Balkans, by invading Greece and Yugoslavia following a coup; here too they made rapid progress, eventually forcing the Allies to evacuate after Germany conquered the Greek island of Crete by the end of May.

The Allies did have some successes during this time. In the Middle East, Commonwealth forces first quashed a coup in Iraq which had been supported by German aircraft from bases within Vichy-controlled Syria, then, with the assistance of the Free French, invaded Syria and Lebanon to prevent further such occurrences. In the Atlantic, the British scored a much-needed public morale boost by sinking the German flagship *Bismarck*. Perhaps most importantly, during the Battle of Britain the Royal Air Force had successfully resisted the Luftwaffe's assault, and on May 11, 1941, Hitler called off the bombing campaign.

In Asia, despite several offensives by both sides, the war between China and Japan was stalemated by 1940. In August of that year, Chinese communists launched an offensive in Central China; in retaliation, Japan instituted harsh measures (the Three Alls Policy) in occupied areas to reduce human and material resources for the communists. Continued antipathy between Chinese communist and nationalist forces culminated in armed clashes in January 1941, effectively ending their cooperation. With the situation in Europe and Asia relatively stable, Germany, Japan, and the Soviet Union made preparations. With the Soviets wary of mounting tensions with Germany and the Japanese planning to take advantage of the European War by seizing resource-rich European possessions in Southeast Asia, the two powers signed the Soviet–Japanese Neutrality Pact in April 1941. By contrast, the Germans were steadily making preparations for an attack on the Soviet Union, amassing forces on the Soviet border.

The War Becomes Global

On June 22, 1941, Germany, along with other European Axis members and Finland, invaded the Soviet Union in Operation Barbarossa. The primary targets of this surprise offensive were the Baltic region, Moscow, and Ukraine, with an ultimate goal of ending the 1941 campaign near the Arkhangelsk-Astrakhan line, connecting the Caspian and White Seas. Hitler's objectives were to eliminate the Soviet Union as a military power, exterminate Communism, generate so-called 'living space' by dispossessing the native population and guarantee access to the strategic resources needed to defeat Germany's remaining rivals. Although before the war the Red Army was preparing for strategic counter-offensives, *Barbarossa* forced the Soviet supreme command to adopt a strategic defence. During the summer, the Axis made significant gains into Soviet territory, inflicting immense losses in personnel and materiel. However, by the middle of August, the German

Army High Command decided to suspend the offensive of a considerably depleted Army Group Centre, and to divert the Second Panzer Group to reinforce troops advancing toward central Ukraine and Leningrad. The Kiev offensive was overwhelmingly successful, resulting in encirclement and elimination of four Soviet armies, and made further advance into Crimea and industrially developed Eastern Ukraine (the First Battle of Kharkov) possible.

The diversion of three quarters of the Axis troops and the majority of their air forces from France and the central Mediterranean to the Eastern Front prompted the United Kingdom to reconsider its grand strategy. In July, the UK and the Soviet Union formed a military alliance against Germany and shortly after jointly invaded Iran to secure the Persian Corridor and Iran's oilfields. In August, the United Kingdom and the United States jointly issued the Atlantic Charter.

By October, when Axis operational objectives in Ukraine and the Baltic region were achieved, with only the sieges of Leningrad and Sevastopol continuing, a major offensive against Moscow had been renewed. After two months of fierce battles, the German army almost reached the outer suburbs of Moscow, where the exhausted troops were forced to suspend their offensive. Despite impressive territorial gains, the Axis campaign had failed to achieve its main objectives: two key cities remained in Soviet hands, the Soviet capability to resist was not broken, and the Soviet Union retained a considerable part of its military potential. The *blitzkrieg* phase of WWII in Europe had ended.

By early December, freshly mobilized reserves allowed the Soviets to achieve numerical parity with Axis troops. This, as well as intelligence data that established a minimal number of Soviet troops in the East sufficient to prevent any attack by the Japanese Kwantung Army, allowed the Soviets to begin a massive counter-offensive that started on December 5 along a 1,000 kilometres (620 mi) front and pushed German troops 100–250 kilometres (62–160 mi) west. Japan had seized military control of southern Indochina the previous year, partly to increase pressure on China by blocking supply routes, but also to better position Japanese forces in the event of a war with the Western powers. Japan, hoping to capitalise on Germany's success in Europe, made several demands, including a steady supply of oil, of the Dutch East

Indies; these attempts, however, broke down in June 1941. The United States, United Kingdom, and other Western governments reacted to the seizure of Indochina with a freeze on Japanese assets, while the United States (which supplied 80 percent of Japan's oil) responded by placing a complete oil embargo. Thus Japan was essentially forced to choose between abandoning its ambitions in Asia and the prosecution of the war against China, or seizing the natural resources it needed by force; the Japanese military did not consider the former an option, and many officers considered the oil embargo an unspoken declaration of war. Japanese Imperial General Headquarters thus planned to rapidly seize European colonies in Asia to create a large defensive perimeter stretching into the Central Pacific; the Japanese would then be free to exploit the resources of Southeast Asia while exhausting the over-stretched Allies by fighting a defensive war. To prevent American intervention while securing the perimeter it was further planned to neutralise the United States Pacific Fleet from the outset. On December 7 (December 8 in Asian time zones), 1941, Japan attacked British and American holdings with near simultaneous offensives against Southeast Asia and the Central Pacific. These included an attack on the American fleet at Pearl Harbour and landings in Thailand and Malaya.

These attacks prompted the United States, United Kingdom, Australia, other Western Allies, and China (already fighting the Second Sino-Japanese War), to formally declare war on Japan. Germany and the other members of the Tripartite Pact responded by declaring war on the United States. In January, the United States, United Kingdom, Soviet Union, China, and twenty-two smaller or exiled governments issued the Declaration by United Nations which affirmed the Atlantic Charter. The Soviet Union did not adhere to the declaration, maintained a neutrality agreement with Japan and exempted itself from the principle of self-determination.

Meanwhile, by the end of April 1942, Japan had almost fully conquered Burma, Malaya, the Dutch East Indies, Singapore, and the key base of Rabaul, inflicting severe losses on Allied troops and taking a large number of prisoners. Despite a stubborn resistance in Corregidor, the Philippines was eventually captured in May 1942, forcing the government of the Philippine

Commonwealth into exile. Japanese forces also achieved naval victories in the South China Sea, Java Sea and Indian Ocean and bombed the Allied naval base at Darwin, Australia. The only real Allied success against Japan was a victory at Changsha in early January 1942. These easy victories over unprepared opponents left Japan severely overconfident, as well as overextended.

Germany retained the initiative as well. Exploiting dubious American naval command decisions, the German navy ravaged Allied shipping off the American Atlantic coast. Despite considerable losses, European Axis members stopped a major Soviet offensive in Central and Southern Russia, keeping most territorial gains they achieved during the previous year. In North Africa, the Germans launched an offensive in January, pushing the British back to positions at the Gazala Line by early February, followed by a temporary lull in combat which Germany used to prepare for their upcoming offensives.

The Tide Turns

In early May 1942, Japan initiated operations to capture Port Moresby by amphibious assault and thus sever communications and supply lines between the United States and Australia. The Allies, however, intercepted and turned back Japanese naval forces, preventing the invasion. Japan's next plan, motivated by the earlier bombing on Tokyo, was to seize Midway Atoll and lure American carriers into battle to be eliminated; as a diversion, Japan would also send forces to occupy the Aleutian Islands. In early June, Japan put its operations into action but the Americans, having broken Japanese naval codes in late May, were fully aware of the plans and force dispositions and used this knowledge to achieve a decisive victory over the Imperial Japanese Navy.

With its capacity for aggressive action greatly diminished as a result of the Midway battle, Japan chose to focus on a belated attempt to capture Port Moresby by an overland campaign in the Territory of Papua. The Americans planned a counter-attack against Japanese positions in the southern Solomon Islands, primarily Guadalcanal, as a first step towards capturing Rabaul, the main Japanese base in Southeast Asia. Both plans started in July, but by mid-September, the battle for Guadalcanal took priority for the Japanese, and troops in New Guinea were ordered to withdraw from the Port Moresby area to the northern part of the island, where they faced Australian and United States troops in the Battle of Buna-Gona. Guadalcanal soon became a focal point for both sides with heavy commitments of troops and ships in the battle for Guadalcanal. By the start of 1943, the Japanese were defeated on the island and withdrew their troops. In Burma, Commonwealth forces mounted two operations. The first, an offensive into the Arakan region in late 1942 went disastrously, forcing a retreat back to India by May 1943. The second was the insertion of irregular forces behind Japanese front-lines in February which, by the end of April, had achieved dubious results.

On Germany's eastern front, the Axis defeated Soviet offensives in the Kerch Peninsula and at Kharkov and then launched their main summer offensive against southern Russia in June 1942, to seize the oil fields of the Caucasus. The Soviets decided to make their stand at Stalingrad which was in the path of the advancing German armies. By mid-November the Germans had nearly taken Stalingrad in bitter street fighting when the Soviets began their second winter counter-offensive, starting with an encirclement of German forces at Stalingrad and an assault on the Rzhev salient near Moscow, though the latter failed disastrously. By early February 1943, the German Army had taken tremendous losses; German troops at Stalingrad had been forced to surrender and the front-line had been pushed back beyond its position before the summer offensive. In mid-February, after the Soviet push had tapered off, the Germans launched another attack on Kharkov, creating a salient in their front line around the Russian city of Kursk.

By November 1941, Commonwealth forces had launched a counter-offensive, Operation Crusader, in North Africa, and reclaimed all the gains the Germans and Italians had made. In the West, concerns the Japanese might utilize bases in Vichy-held Madagascar caused the British to invade the island in early May 1942. This success was offset soon after by an Axis offensive in Libya which pushed the Allies back into Egypt until Axis forces were stopped at El Alamein. On the Continent, raids of Allied commandos on strategic targets, culminating in the disastrous Dieppe Raid, demonstrated the Western allies' inability to launch an invasion of continental Europe without much better preparation, equipment, and operational security. In August 1942, the Allies succeeded in repelling a second attack against El Alamein and, at a high cost, managed to get desperately needed supplies to the besieged Malta. A few months later the Allies commenced an attack of their own in Egypt, dislodging the Axis forces and beginning a drive west across Libya. This attack was followed up shortly after by an Anglo-American invasion of French North Africa, which resulted in the region joining the Allies. Hitler responded to the French colony's defection by ordering the occupation of Vichy France; although Vichy forces did not resist this violation of the armistice, they managed to scuttle their fleet to prevent its capture by German forces. The now pincered Axis forces in Africa withdrew into Tunisia, which was conquered by the Allies by May 1943.

Allies Gain Momentum

Following the Guadalcanal Campaign, the Allies initiated several operations against Japan in the Pacific. In May 1943, American forces were sent to eliminate Japanese forces from the Aleutians, and soon after began major operations to isolate Rabaul by capturing surrounding islands, and to breach the Japanese Central Pacific perimeter at the Gilbert and Marshall Islands. By the end of March 1944, the Allies had completed both of these objectives, and additionally neutralised another major Japanese base in the Caroline Islands. In April, the Allies then launched an operation to retake Western New Guinea.

In the Soviet Union, both the Germans and the Soviets spent the spring and early summer of 1943 making preparations for large offensives in Central Russia. On July 4, 1943, Germany attacked Soviet forces around the Kursk Bulge. Within a week, German forces had exhausted themselves against the Soviets' deeply echeloned and well-constructed defences and, for the first time in the war, Hitler cancelled the operation before it had achieved tactical or operational success. This decision was partially affected by the Western Allies' invasion of Sicily launched on July 9 which, combined with previous Italian failures, resulted in the ousting and arrest of Mussolini later that month. On July 12, 1943, the Soviets launched their own counter-offensives, thereby dispelling any hopes of the German Army for victory or even stalemate in the east. The Soviet victory at Kursk was one of the decisive turning points of the war, giving the Soviet Union the initiative on the Eastern Front. The Germans attempted to stabilise their eastern front along the hastily fortified Panther-Wotan line, however, the Soviets broke through it at Smolensk and by the Lower Dnieper Offensives.

In early September 1943, the Western Allies invaded the Italian mainland, following an Italian armistice with the Allies. Germany responded by disarming Italian forces, seizing military control of Italian areas, and creating a series of defensive lines. German special forces then rescued Mussolini, who then soon established a new client state in German occupied Italy named the Italian Social Republic. The Western Allies fought through several lines until reaching the main German defensive line in mid-November.

German operations in the Atlantic also suffered. By May 1943, as Allied counter-measures became increasingly effective, the resulting sizable German submarine losses forced a temporary halt of the German Atlantic naval campaign. In November 1943, Franklin D. Roosevelt and Winston Churchill met with Chiang Kai-shek in Cairo and then with Joseph Stalin in Tehran. The former conference determined the postwar return of Japanese territory while the latter included agreement that the Western Allies would invade Europe in 1944 and that the Soviet Union would declare war on Japan within three months of Germany's defeat.

In January 1944, the Allies launched a series of attacks in Italy against the line at Monte Cassino and attempted to outflank it with landings at Anzio. By the end of January, a major Soviet offensive expelled German forces from the Leningrad region, ending the longest and most lethal siege in history. The following Soviet offensive was halted on the pre-war Estonian border by the German Army Group North aided by Estonians hoping to re-establish national independence. This delay slowed subsequent Soviet operations in the Baltic Sea region. By late May 1944, the Soviets had liberated Crimea, largely expelled Axis forces from Ukraine and made incursions into Romania, which were repulsed by the Axis troops. The Allied offensives in Italy had succeeded and, at the expense of allowing several German divisions to retreat, on June 4 Rome was captured.

The Allies experienced mixed fortunes in mainland Asia. In March 1944, the Japanese launched the first of two invasions, an operation against British positions in Assam, India, and soon besieged Commonwealth positions at Imphal and Kohima. In May 1944, British forces mounted a counter-offensive that drove Japanese troops back to Burma, and Chinese forces that had invaded Northern Burma in late 1943 besieged Japanese troops in Myitkyina. The second Japanese invasion attempted to destroy China's main fighting forces, secure railways between Japanese-held territory and capture Allied airfields. By June, the Japanese had conquered the province of Henan and begun a renewed attack against Changsha in the Hunan province.

Allies Close In

On June 6, 1944 (known as D-Day), the Western Allies invaded northern France and, after reassigning several Allied divisions from Italy, southern France. These landings were successful, and led to the defeat of the German Army units in France. Paris was liberated by the local resistance assisted by the Free French forces on August 25 and the Western Allies continued to push back German forces in Western Europe during the latter part of the year. An attempt to advance into northern Germany spear-headed by a major airborne operation in Holland was not successful. The Allies also continued their advance in Italy until they ran into the last major German defensive line.

On June 22, the Soviets launched a strategic offensive in Belarus (known as "Operation Bagration") that resulted in the almost complete destruction of the German Army Group Centre. Soon after that, another Soviet strategic offensive forced German troops from Western Ukraine and Eastern Poland. The successful advance of Soviet troops prompted resistance forces in Poland to initiate several uprisings, though the largest of these, in Warsaw, as well as a Slovak Uprising in the south, were not assisted by the Soviets and were put down by German forces. The Red Army's strategic offensive in eastern Romania cut off and destroyed the considerable German troops there and triggered a successful coup d'état in Romania and in Bulgaria, followed by those countries' shift to the Allied side.

In September 1944, Soviet Red Army troops advanced into

Yugoslavia and forced the rapid withdrawal of the German Army Groups E and F in Greece, Albania and Yugoslavia to rescue them from being cut off. By this point, Communist-led partisans under Marshal Josip Broz Tito controlled much of the territory of Yugoslavia and were engaged in delaying efforts against the German forces further south. In northern Serbia, the Red Army, with limited support from Bulgarian forces, assisted the partisans in a joint liberation of the capital city of Belgrade on October 20. A few days later, the Soviets launched a massive assault against German-occupied Hungary that lasted until the fall of Budapest in February 1945. In contrast with impressive Soviet victories in the Balkans, the bitter Finnish resistance to the Soviet offensive in the Karelian Isthmus denied the Soviets occupation of Finland and led to the signing of Soviet-Finnish armistice on relatively mild conditions with subsequent Finland's shift to the Allied side.

By the start of July, Commonwealth forces in Southeast Asia had repelled the Japanese sieges in Assam, pushing the Japanese back to the Chindwin River while the Chinese captured Myitkyina. In China, the Japanese were having greater successes, having finally captured Changsha in mid-June and the city of Hengyang by early August. Soon after, they further invaded the province of Guangxi, winning major engagements against Chinese forces at Guilin and Liuzhou by the end of November and successfully linking up their forces in China and Indochina by the middle of December.

In the Pacific, American forces continued to press back the Japanese perimeter. In mid-June 1944 they began their offensive against the Mariana and Palau islands, scoring a decisive victory against Japanese forces in the Philippine Sea within a few days. These defeats led to the resignation of Japanese Prime Minister Tôjô and provided the United States with air bases to launch intensive heavy bomber attacks on the Japanese home islands. In late October, American forces invaded the Filipino island of Leyte; soon after, Allied naval forces scored another large victory during the Battle of Leyte Gulf, the largest naval battle in history.

Axis Collapse, Allied Victory

On December 16, 1944, Germany attempted its last desperate measure for success on the Western Front by marshalling German reserves to launch a massive counter-offensive in the Ardennes to attempt to split the Western Allies, encircle large portions of Western Allied troops and capture their primary supply port at Antwerp in order to prompt a political settlement. The offensive had been repulsed by January with no strategic objectives fulfilled. In Italy, the Western Allies remained stalemated at the German defensive line. In mid-January 1945, the Soviets attacked in Poland, pushing from the Vistula to the Oder river in Germany, and overran East Prussia. On February 4, U.S., British, and Soviet leaders met in Yalta. They agreed on the occupation of postwar Germany, and when the Soviet Union would join the war against Japan.

In February, the Soviets invaded Silesia and Pomerania, while Western Allied forces entered Western Germany and closed to the Rhine river. In March, the Western Allies crossed the Rhine north and south of the Ruhr, encircling a large number of German troops, while the Soviets advanced to Vienna. In early April the Western Allies finally pushed forward in Italy and swept across Western Germany, while in late April Soviet forces stormed Berlin; the two forces linked up on Elbe river on April 25.

Several changes in leadership occurred during this period. On April 12, U.S. President Roosevelt died and was succeeded by Harry Truman. Benito Mussolini was killed by Italian partisans on April 28. Two days later, Hitler committed suicide, and was succeeded by Grand Admiral Karl Dönitz.

German forces surrendered in Italy on April 29 and in Western Europe on May 7. On the Eastern Front, Germany surrendered to the Soviets on May 8. A German Army Group Centre resisted in Prague until May 11. In the Pacific theatre, American forces accompanied by the forces of the Philippine Commonwealth advanced in the Philippines, clearing Leyte by the end of 1944. They landed on Luzon in January 1945 and seized Manila in March leaving it in ruins; Mindanao was captured later that month. British and Chinese forces defeated the Japanese in northern Burma from October to March, then the British pushed on to Rangoon by May 3. American forces also moved toward Japan, taking Iwo Jima by March, and Okinawa by June. American bombers destroyed Japanese cities, and American submarines cut off Japanese imports.

On July 11, the Allied leaders met in Potsdam, Germany. They confirmed earlier agreements about Germany, and reiterated the demand for unconditional surrender of all Japanese forces by Japan, specifically stating that "the alternative for Japan is prompt and utter destruction". During this conference the United Kingdom held its general election and Clement Attlee replaced Churchill as Prime Minister. When Japan continued to reject the Potsdam terms, the United States then dropped atomic bombs on the Japanese cities of Hiroshima and Nagasaki in early August. Between the two bombs, the Soviets invaded Japanese-held Manchuria, as agreed at Yalta. On August 15, 1945 Japan surrendered, with the surrender documents finally signed aboard the deck of the American battleship USS Missouri on September 2, 1945, ending the war.

Aftermath

In an effort to maintain international peace, the Allies formed the United Nations, which officially came into existence on October 24, 1945, and adopted The Universal Declaration of Human Rights in 1948, as a common standard of achievement for all member nations.

The alliance between the Western Allies and the Soviet Union had begun to deteriorate even before the war was over, and the powers each quickly established their own spheres of influence. In Europe, the continent was essentially divided between Western and Soviet spheres by the so-called Iron Curtain which ran through and partitioned Allied occupied Germany and occupied Austria. The Soviet Union created the Eastern Bloc by directly annexing several countries it occupied as Soviet Socialist Republics that were originally effectively ceded to it by Germany in the Molotov-Ribbentrop Pact, such as Eastern Poland, the three Baltic countries, part of eastern Finland and northeastern Romania. Other states that the Soviets occupied at the end of the war were converted into Soviet Satellite states, such as the People's Republic of Poland, the People's Republic of Hungary, the Czechoslovak Socialist Republic, the People's Republic of Romania, the People's Republic of Albania, and later East Germany from the Soviet zone of German occupation. In Asia, the United States occupied Japan and administrated Japan's former islands in the Western Pacific while the Soviets annexed Sakhalin and the Kuril Islands; the former Japanese governed Korea was divided and occupied between the two powers. Mounting tensions between the United States and the Soviet Union soon evolved into the formation of the American-led NATO and the Soviet-led Warsaw Pact military alliances and the start of the Cold War between them.

Soon after the end of World War II, conflict flared again in many parts of the world. In China, nationalist and communist forces quickly resumed their civil war. Communist forces were eventually victorious and established the People's Republic of China on the mainland while nationalist forces ended up retreating to the reclaimed island of Taiwan. In Greece, civil war broke out between Anglo-American supported royalist forces and communist forces, with the royalist forces victorious. Soon after these conflicts ended, North Korea invaded South Korea, which was backed by the United Nations, while North Korea was backed by the Soviet Union and China. The war resulted in essentially a stalemate and ceasefire, after which North Korean leader Kim Il Sung created a highly centralised and brutal dictatorship, according himself unlimited power and generating a formidable cult of personality.

Following the end of the war, a rapid period of decolonization also took place within the holdings of the various European colonial powers. These primarily occurred due to shifts in ideology, the economic exhaustion from the war and increased demand by indigenous people for self-determination. For the most part, these transitions happened relatively peacefully, though notable exceptions occurred in countries such as Indochina, Madagascar, Indonesia and Algeria. In many regions, divisions, usually for ethnic or religious reasons, occurred following European withdrawal. This was seen prominently in the Mandate of Palestine, leading to the creation of Israel, and in India, resulting in the creation of the Dominion of India and the Dominion of Pakistan.

Economic recovery following the war was varied in differing parts of the world, though in general it was quite positive. In Europe, West Germany recovered quickly and doubled production from its pre-war levels by the 1950s. Italy came out of the war in poor economic condition, but by 1950s, the Italian economy was marked by stability and high growth. The United Kingdom was in a state of economic ruin after the war, and continued to experience relative economic decline for decades to follow. France rebounded quite quickly, and enjoyed rapid economic growth and modernisation.

The Soviet Union also experienced a rapid increase in production in the immediate postwar era. In Asia, Japan experienced incredibly rapid economic growth, and led to Japan becoming one of the most powerful economies in the world by the 1980s. China, following the conclusion of its civil war, was essentially a bankrupt nation. By 1953 economic restoration seemed fairly successful as production had resumed pre-war levels. This growth rate mostly persisted, though it was briefly interrupted by the disastrous Great Leap Forward economic experiment. At the end of the war, the United States produced roughly half of the world's industrial output; by the early 1970s though, this dominance had lessened significantly.

Impact

Casualties and War Crimes

Many of these deaths were a result of genocidal actions committed in Axis-occupied territories and other war crimes committed by German as well as Japanese forces. The most notorious of German atrocities was The Holocaust, the systematic genocide of Jews in territories controlled by Germany and its allies. The Nazis also targeted other groups, including the Roma (targeted in the Porajmos), Slavs, and gay men, exterminating an estimated five million additional people.

The targets of the Axis-aligned Croatian Ustaše regime were mostly Serbs. The best-known Japanese atrocity is the Nanking Massacre, in which several hundred thousand Chinese civilians were raped and murdered. The Japanese military murdered from nearly 3 million to over 10 million civilians, mostly Chinese. Mitsuyoshi Himeta reported 2.7 million casualties occurred during the *Sankô Sakusen*. General Yasuji Okamura implemented the policy in Heipei and Shantung. Limited Axis usage of biological and chemical weapons is also known. The Italians used mustard gas during their conquest of Abyssinia, while the Japanese Imperial Army used a variety of such weapons during their invasion and occupation of China and in early conflicts against the Soviets.

Both the Germans and Japanese tested such weapons against civilians and, in some cases, on prisoners of war.

While many of the Axis's acts were brought to trial in the world's first international tribunals, incidents caused by the Allies were not. Examples of such Allied actions include population transfer in the Soviet Union, the Soviet forced labour camps (Gulag), Japanese American internment in the United States, the Operation Keelhaul, expulsion of Germans after World War II, the Soviet massacre of Polish citizens and the mass-bombing of civilian areas in enemy territory, including Tokyo and most notably at Dresden. Large numbers of famine deaths can also be partially attributed to the war, such as the Bengal famine of 1943 and the Vietnamese famine of 1944–45.

Concentration Camps and Slave Work

The Nazis were responsible for The Holocaust, the killing of approximately six million Jews (overwhelmingly Ashkenazim), as well as two million ethnic Poles and four million others who were deemed "unworthy of life" (including the disabled and mentally ill, Soviet POWs, homosexuals, Freemasons, Jehovah's Witnesses, and the Roma) as part of a programme of deliberate extermination. About 12 million, most of whom were Eastern Europeans, were employed in the German war economy as forced labor in Germany during World War II. In addition to Nazi concentration camps, the Soviet gulags, or labor camps, led to the death of citizens of occupied countries such as Poland, Lithuania, Latvia, and Estonia, as well as German prisoners of war (POWs) and even Soviet citizens who had been or were thought to be supporters of the Nazis. Sixty percent of Soviet POWs of the Germans died during the war. Richard Overy gives the number of 5.7 million Soviet POWs. Of those, 57 percent died or were killed, a total of 3.6 million. Some of the survivors on their return to the USSR were treated as traitors.

Japanese prisoner-of-war camps, many of which were used as labour camps, also had high death rates. The International Military Tribunal for the Far East found the death rate of Western prisoners was 27.1 percent (for American POWs, 37 percent), seven times that of POWs under the Germans and Italians The death rate among Chinese POWs was much larger; a directive ratified on August 5, 1937 by Hirohito declared that the Chinese were no longer protected under international law. While 37,583 prisoners from the UK, 28,500 from the Netherlands and 14,473 from United States were released after the surrender of Japan, the number for the Chinese was only 56. According to a joint study of historians featuring Zhifen Ju, Mark Peattie, Toru Kubo, and Mitsuyoshi Himeta, more than 10 million Chinese were mobilized by the Japanese army and enslaved by the East Asia Development Board for slave labor in Manchukuo and north China. The U.S. Library of Congress estimates that in Java, between 4 and 10 million *romusha* (Japanese: "manual labourers"), were forced to work by the Japanese military. About 270,000 of these Javanese labourers were sent to other Japanese-held areas in South East Asia, and only 52,000 were repatriated to Java.

On February 19, 1942 Roosevelt signed Executive Order 9066, interning thousands of Japanese, Italians, German Americans, and some emigrants from Hawaii who fled after the bombing of Pearl Harbour for the duration of the war. The U.S. and Canadian governments interned 150,000 Japanese-Americans, as well as nearly 11,000 German and Italian residents of the U.S. Allied use of involuntary labor occurred mainly in the east, such as in Poland, but more than a million were also put to work in the west. In Hungary's case, Hungarians were forced to work for the Soviet Union until 1955.

Home Fronts and Production

In Europe, before the outbreak of the war, the Allies had significant advantages in both population and economics. In 1938, the Western Allies (United Kingdom, France, Poland and British Dominions) had a 30 percent larger population and a 30 percent higher gross domestic product than the European Axis (Germany and Italy); if colonies are included, it then gives the Allies more than a 5:1 advantage in population and nearly 2:1 advantage in GDP. In Asia at the same time, China had roughly six times the population of Japan, but only an 89 percent higher GDP; this is reduced to three times the population and only a 38 percent higher GDP if Japanese colonies are included.

Though the Allies' economic and population advantages were largely mitigated during the initial rapid blitzkrieg attacks of

Germany and Japan, they became the decisive factor by 1942, after the United States and Soviet Union joined the Allies, as the war largely settled into one of attrition. While the Allies' ability to out-produce the Axis is often attributed to the Allies having more access to natural resources, other factors, such as Germany and Japan's reluctance to employ women in the labour force, Allied strategic bombing, and Germany's late shift to a war economy contributed significantly. Additionally, neither Germany nor Japan planned to fight a protracted war, and were not equipped to do so. To improve their production, Germany and Japan used millions of slave labourers; Germany used about 12 million people, mostly from Eastern Europe, while Japan pressed more than 18 million people in Far East Asia.

Occupation

In Europe, occupation came under two very different forms. In Western, Northern and Central Europe (France, Norway, Denmark, the Low Countries, and the annexed portions of Czechoslovakia) Germany established economic policies through which it collected roughly 69.5 billion reichmarks by the end of the war; this figure does not include the sizable plunder of industrial products, military equipment, raw materials and other goods. Thus, the income from occupied nations was over 40 percent of the income Germany collected from taxation, a figure which increased to nearly 40 percent of total German income as the war went on. In the east, the much hoped for bounties of lebensraum were never attained as fluctuating front-lines and Soviet scorched earth policies denied resources to the German invaders. Unlike in the west, the Nazi racial policy encouraged excessive brutality against what it considered to be the "inferior people" of Slavic descent; most German advances were thus followed by mass executions. Although resistance groups did form in most occupied territories, they did not significantly hamper German operations in either the east or the west until late 1943.

In Asia, Japan termed nations under its occupation as being part of the Greater East Asia Co-prosperity Sphere, essentially a Japanese hegemony which it claimed was for purposes of liberating colonised peoples. Although Japanese forces were originally welcomed as liberators from European domination in many territories, their excessive brutality turned local public opinions against them within weeks. During Japan's initial conquest it captured 4 million barrels of oil left behind by retreating Allied forces, and by 1943 was able to get production in the Dutch East Indies up to 50 million barrels, 76 percent of its 1940 output rate.

Advances in Technology and Warfare

During the war, aircraft continued their roles of reconnaissance, fighters, bombers and ground-support from World War I, though each area was advanced considerably. Two important additional roles for aircraft were those of the airlift, the capability to quickly move high-priority supplies, equipment and personnel, albeit in limited quantities; and of strategic bombing, the targeted use of bombs against civilian areas in the hopes of hampering enemy industry and morale. Anti-aircraft weaponry also continued to advance, including key defences such as radar and greatly improved anti-aircraft artillery, such as the German 88 mm gun. Jet aircraft saw their first limited operational use during World War II, and though their late introduction and limited numbers meant that they had no real impact during the war itself, the few which saw active service pioneered a mass-shift to their usage following the war.

At sea, while advances were made in almost all aspects of naval warfare, the two primary areas of development were focused around aircraft carriers and submarines. Although at the start of the war aeronautical warfare had relatively little success, actions at Taranto, Pearl Harbour, the South China Sea and the Coral Sea soon established the carrier as the dominant capital ship in place of the battleship. In the Atlantic, escort carriers proved to be a vital part of Allied convoys, increasing the effective protection radius dramatically and helping to seal the Mid-Atlantic gap. Beyond their increased effectiveness, carriers were also more economical than battleships due to the relatively low cost of aircraft and their not requiring to be as heavily armoured. Submarines, which had proved to be an effective weapon during the first World War were anticipated by all sides to be important in the second. The British focused development on anti-submarine weaponry and tactics, such as sonar and convoys, while Germany focused on improving its offensive capability, with designs such as the Type VII submarine and Wolf pack tactics. Gradually, continually improving Allied technologies such as the Leigh light, hedgehog, squid, and homing torpedoes proved victorious.

Land warfare changed drastically from the static front lines predominating in World War I to become much more fluid and mobile. An important change was the concept of combined arms warfare, wherein tight coordination was sought between the various elements of military forces; the tank, which had been used predominantly for infantry support in the First World War, had evolved into the primary weapon of these forces during the second. In the late 1930s, tank design was considerably more advanced in all areas then it had been during World War I, and advances continued throughout the war in increasing speed, armour and firepower. At the start of the war, most armies considered the tank to be the best weapon against itself, and developed special-purpose tanks to that effect. This line of thinking was all but negated by the poor performance of the relatively light early tank armaments against armour, and German doctrine of avoiding tank-versus-tank combat; the latter factor, along with Germany's use of combined arms, were among the key elements of their highly successful blitzkrieg tactics across Poland and France. Many means of destroying tanks, including indirect artillery, anti-tank guns (both towed and self-propelled), mines, short-ranged infantry antitank weapons, and other tanks were utilised. Even with large-scale mechanisation of the various armies, the infantry remained the backbone of all forces, and throughout the war, most infantry equipment was similar to that utilised in World War I. However, the United States became the first country to arm its soldiers with a semi-automatic rifle, in this case the M-1 Garand. Some of the primary advances though, were the widespread incorporation of portable machine guns, a notable example being the German MG42, and various submachine guns which were well suited to close-quarters combat in urban and jungle settings. The assault rifle, a late war development which incorporated many of the best features of the rifle and submachine gun, became the standard postwar infantry weapon for nearly all armed forces. In terms of communications, most of the major belligerents attempted to solve the problems of complexity and security presented by using large codebooks for cryptography with the creation of various ciphering machines, the most well known being the German Enigma machine. SIGINT (*sig*nals *int*elligence) was the countering process of decryption, with the notable examples being the British ULTRA and the Allied breaking of Japanese naval codes. Another important aspect of military intelligence was the use of deception operations, which the Allies successfully used on several occasions to great effect, such as operations Mincemeat and Bodyguard. Other important technological and engineering feats achieved during, or as a result of, the war include the worlds first programmable computers (Z3, Colossus, and ENIAC), guided missiles and modern rockets, the Manhattan Project's development of nuclear weapons, the development of artificial harbours and oil pipelines under the English Channel.

The Post-War World

The end of the Second World War brought many photo opportunities for the victors. The Soviets and the Western Allies had promoted the concept of an antifascist brotherhood during the war, and photos were taken all over the world of the Allies embracing and celebrating their victory. Before the war ended, the three major Allied nations began to discuss the postwar world in a series of conferences with the three leaders. Roosevelt, Churchill, and Stalin met at Yalta in March 1945 and Truman, Atlee and Stalin met in Potsdam in July 1945. Roosevelt had first used the term "United Nations" when 26 Nations signed the Declaration of the United Nations on January 1, 1942. From April to October 1945, 51 nations met in San Francisco and created the United Nations. The Headquarters were set up in New York after the Charter was ratified by a majority of the member nations. The major Allies (China, Soviet Union, France, Great Britain, and the United States) held seats on the Security Council, each country held veto power over any decision the United Nations made.

The reality was that huge cracks were appearing in the Allied unity. With no more enemies to fight, the suspicions held at bay until victory was obvious became public and bitter. Churchill later wrote that he already suspected the Soviets were replacing the Axis as the aggressors before the European war ended. America, enjoying a brief monopoly on the atom bomb, conducted tests in the Bikini Atoll on July 25, 1946. The world was impressed by the casual destruction of so many warships as much as it was by the bomb itself. The Berlin Airlift heightened the Cold War tension in 1948. In 1949 the Western Powers came together to form the North Atlantic Treaty Organization (NATO). When the Soviets and soon the French, British, and Chinese acquired the bomb, huge arsenals were quickly built. The ability to annihilate the planet many times over evolved into the concept of Mutual Assured Destruction (MAD) which meant that neither side would start a war if they were guaranteed to be destroyed.

In the Pacific, the seeds for more conflict were being sown all over Asia. Soviet Forces occupied Northern Korea on August 12, 1945 and the United States landed in September 18. Within two years, the Koreas were at war, along with the Western powers and the Soviets.

The United Nations supported the West after the Soviets walked out of the Security Council. Only after Stalin died could the North Koreans sign an armistice in July 1953. Two million Koreans and 53,000 Americans died. In French Indochina, the American-armed French fought to hold onto their prewar colonial empire. Vietminh leader Ho Chi Minh, who had agitated for Vietnamese independence since the Versailles Conference of 1919, wrote the Indochinese declaration of independence from Japanese occupation based on the American Declaration of Independence. But Truman felt he had to support the French. Sporadic fighting culminated in the defeat of the French at Dien Bien Phu in 1954.

America wholly occupied the Japanese Home Islands, in a government that was secretly completely controlled by MacArthur. The only Soviet-occupied islands were part of the Kuriles, occupied in August 1945. The Soviets refused to relinquish control.

MacArthur reinvented the Japanese government. With an eye to running for President against Truman, whom he disliked, MacArthur wrote in sweeping changes into the new constitution, including women's suffrage, representative democracy, and establishment of political parties, including the Communist Party. One of the most controversial articles prevented the use of Japanese forces overseas. The 1940's and 1950's were hard times, with the black market providing most of the consumer goods for the Japanese, and the United States supplying most of the food.

The Americans ended their occupation of the Home Islands in 1952. Okinawa and Iwo Jima were continually occupied until the 1970's, with massive military operations denying the Soviets a warm-water port for their Navy. At the end of the occupation, it was proposed that a giant statue of MacArthur would be erected in Tokyo Bay. That was never accomplished, but he had left his mark on the Japanese people. MacArthur was recalled in 1952 after advocating the use of atomic weapons in Korea and war with China. The Japanese attitude towards the war was varied and intense. Relatives of those killed all over the Pacific still travel to recover bones from sunken ships or battlefields, and ritually burn them in ceremonial fires. The massive destruction of Japan had instilled a fervent opposition to the use of Japanese forces overseas. The announcement of the creation of a new "Self-Defence Force" was met with student riots throughout the 1960's. A fringe group, called the Red Army, participated in several terrorist attacks in the 1960's and 1970's.

America took up the anti-Communist bastion in Vietnam, fighting with their old enemy Ho Chi Minh. In fighting that lasted from 1962 to 1975, millions of Vietnamese and 59,000 Americans were killed. The war left Vietnam as the fourth largest military power, and severely tested American ideals and morale. The 1980's saw resurgence in anti-Japanese sentiment in the United States, as public opinion and the media converged to anoint Japan as an economic enemy. The Japanese gained dominance in several industries, including the electronics industry. The Japanese made several purchases of American companies and stock, leading to widespread fears in the United States that Japan had an industrial lead.

Japanese Emperor Hirohito was the last wartime leader to die in 1989. He was mourned amid a reexamination of his complacency in wartime actions in Nanjing, Manila, and the start of the war. The war passed into history as thousands of veterans died during the 1990's. As the twentieth century dawned, the scope of the violence and the millions who died were reexamined in film and television.

With the millennium, thousands of people entered a new century with the hope that such a war would never be fought again.

6

Origin and Evolution of the Cold War

Cold War

The Cold War (1945–1991) was the continuing state of political conflict, military tension, and economic competition existing after World War II (1939–1945), primarily between the USSR and its satellite states, and the powers of the Western world, including the United States. Although the primary participants' military forces never officially clashed directly, they expressed the conflict through military coalitions, strategic conventional force deployments, a nuclear arms race, espionage, proxy wars, propaganda, and technological competition, such as the Space Race. Despite being allies against the Axis powers and having the most powerful forces, the USSR and the US disagreed about the configuration of the postwar world while occupying most of Europe. The Soviet Union created the Eastern Bloc with the eastern European countries it occupied, annexing some as Soviet Socialist Republics and maintaining others as satellite states, some of which were later consolidated as the Warsaw Pact (1955–1991). The US and some western European countries established containment of communism as a defensive policy, establishing alliances such as NATO to that end.

Several such countries also coordinated the rebuilding of western Europe, especially western Germany, which the USSR opposed. Elsewhere, in Latin America and Southeast Asia, the USSR fostered communist revolutions, opposed by several western countries and their regional allies; some they attempted to roll back, with mixed results. Some countries aligned with NATO and the Warsaw Pact, yet nonaligned country blocs also emerged.

The Cold War featured periods of relative calm and of international high tension – the Berlin Blockade (1948–1949), the Korean War (1950–1953), the Berlin Crisis of 1961, the Vietnam War (1959–1975), the Cuban Missile Crisis (1962), the Soviet war in Afghanistan (1979–1989), and the Able Archer 83 NATO exercises in November 1983. Both sides sought détente to relieve political tensions and deter direct military attack, which would likely guarantee their mutual assured destruction with nuclear weapons.

In the 1980s, the United States increased diplomatic, military, and economic pressures against the USSR, which had already suffered severe economic stagnation. Thereafter, Soviet President Mikhail Gorbachev introduced the liberalizing reforms of *perestroika* ("reconstruction", "reorganization", 1987) and *glasnost* ("openness", ca. 1985). The Cold War ended after the Soviet Union collapsed in 1991, leaving the United States as the dominant military power, and Russia possessing most of the Soviet Union's nuclear arsenal. The Cold War and its events have had a significant impact on the world today, and it is commonly referred to in popular culture such as fiction.

Origins of the Term

The first use of the term *Cold War* describing the post–World War II geopolitical tensions between the USSR and its Western European Allies is attributed to Bernard Baruch, a US financier and presidential advisor. In South Carolina, on April 16, 1947, he delivered a speech (by journalist Herbert Bayard Swope) saying, "Let us not be deceived: we are today in the midst of a cold war." Newspaper reporter-columnist Walter Lippmann gave the term wide currency, with the book *Cold War* (1947).

Previously, during the war, George Orwell used the term *Cold War* in the essay "You and the Atomic Bomb" published October 19, 1945, in the British newspaper *Tribune*. Contemplating a world living in the shadow of the threat of nuclear war, he warned of a "peace that is no peace", which he called a permanent "cold war", Orwell directly referred to that war as the ideological confrontation between the Soviet Union and the Western powers.

Moreover, in *The Observer* of March 10, 1946, Orwell wrote that "... [a]fter the Moscow conference last December, Russia began to make a 'cold war' on Britain and the British Empire."

Background

There is disagreement among historians regarding the starting point of the Cold War. While most historians trace its origins to the period immediately following World War II, others argue that it began towards the end of World War I, although tensions between the Russian Empire, other European countries and the United States date back to the middle of the 19th century.

As a result of the 1917 Bolshevik Revolution in Russia (followed by its withdrawal from World War I), Soviet Russia found itself isolated in international diplomacy. Leader Vladimir Lenin stated that the Soviet Union was surrounded by a "hostile capitalist encirclement", and he viewed diplomacy as a weapon to keep Soviet enemies divided, beginning with the establishment of the Soviet Comintern, which called for revolutionary upheavals abroad.

Subsequent leader Joseph Stalin, who viewed the Soviet Union as a "socialist island", stated that the Soviet Union must see that "the present capitalist encirclement is replaced by a socialist encirclement." As early as 1925, Stalin stated that he viewed international politics as a bipolar world in which the Soviet Union would attract countries gravitating to socialism and capitalist countries would attract states gravitating toward capitalism, while the world was in a period of "temporary stabilization of capitalism" preceding its eventual collapse.

Several events fueled suspicion and distrust between the western powers and the Soviet Union: the Bolsheviks' challenge to capitalism; the 1926 Soviet funding of a British general workers strike causing Britain to break relations with the Soviet Union; Stalin's 1927 declaration that peaceful coexistence with "the capitalist countries... is receding into the past"; conspiratorial allegations in the Shakhty show trial of a planned French and British-led coup d'etat; the Great Purge involving a series of campaigns of political repression and persecution in which over half a million Soviets were executed; the Moscow show trials including allegations of British, French, Japanese and German espionage; the controversial death of 6-8 million people in the Ukrainian Soviet Socialist Republic in the 1932-3 Ukrainian famine; western support of the White Army in the Russian Civil War; the US refusal to recognize the Soviet Union until 1933; and the Soviet entry into the Treaty of Rapallo. This outcome rendered Soviet–American relations a matter of major long-term concern for leaders in both countries.

Origins of the Cold War

The Origins of the Cold War are widely regarded to lie most directly within the relations between the Soviet Union and its World War II allies the United States, Britain and France in the years 1945–1947. Those events led to the Cold War that endured for just under half a century. Events preceding the Second World War, and even the Russian Revolution of 1917, underlay pre-World War II tensions between the Soviet Union, western European countries and the United States. A series of events during and after World War II exacerbated tensions, including the Soviet-German pact during the first two years of the war leading to subsequent invasions, the perceived delay of an amphibious invasion of German-occupied western Europe, the western allies' support of the Atlantic Charter, disagreement in wartime conferences over the fate of Eastern Europe, the Soviets' creation of an Eastern Bloc of Soviet Socialist Republics and Soviet satellite states, western allies scrapping the Morgenthau Plan to support the rebuilding of German industry and the Marshall Plan.

Tsarist Russia and the West

Differences between the political and economic systems of Russia and the West predated the Russian Revolution of 1917. From the neo-Marxist World Systems perspective, Russia differed from the West as a result of its late integration into the capitalist world economy in the 19th century. Struggling to catch up with the industrialized West as of the late 19th century, Russia upon the revolution in 1917 was essentially a semi-peripheral or peripheral state whose internal balance of forces, tipped by the domination of the Russian industrial sector by foreign capital, had been such that it suffered a decline in its relative diplomatic power internationally. From this perspective, the Russian Revolution represented a break with a form of dependent industrial development and a radical withdrawal from the capitalist world economy.

Other scholars have argued that Russia and the West developed fundamentally different political cultures shaped by Eastern Orthodoxy and rule of the tsar. Others have linked the Cold War to the legacy of different heritages of empire-building between the Russians and Americans. From this view, the United States, like the British Empire, was fundamentally a maritime power based on trade and commerce, and Russia was a bureaucratic and land-based power that expanded from the centre in a process of territorial accretion.

Imperial rivalry between the British and tsarist Russia preceded the tensions between the Soviets and the West following the Russian Revolution. Throughout the 19th century, improving Russia's maritime access was a perennial aim of the tsars' foreign policy. Despite Russia's vast size, most of its thousands of miles of seacoast was frozen over most of the year, or access to the high seas was through straits controlled by other powers, particularly in the Baltic and Black Seas. The British, however, had been determined since the Crimean War in the 1850s to slow Russian expansion at the expense of Ottoman Turkey, the "sick man of Europe." With the completion of the Suez Canal in 1869, the prospect of Russia seizing a portion of the Ottoman seacoast on the Mediterranean, potentially threatening the strategic waterway, was of great concern to the British. British policymakers were also apprehensive about the close proximity of the Tsar's territorially expanding empire in Central Asia to India, triggering a series of conflicts between the two powers in Afghanistan, dubbed The Great Game.

The British long exaggerated the strength of the relatively backward sprawling Russian empire, which according to the Wisconsin school was more concerned with the security of its frontiers than conquering Western spheres of influence. British fears over Russian expansion, however, subsided following Russia's stunning defeat in the Russo-Japanese War in 1905.

Historians associated with the Wisconsin school see parallels between 19th century Western rivalry with Russia and the Cold War tensions of the post-World War II period. From this view,

Western policymakers misinterpreted postwar Soviet policy in Europe as expansionism, rather than a policy, like the territorial growth of imperial Russia, motivated by securing vulnerable Russian frontiers.

Russian Revolution

In World War I, the US, Britain, and Russia had been allies for a few months from April 1917 until the Bolsheviks seized power in Russia in November. In 1918, the Bolsheviks negotiated a separate peace with the Central Powers at Brest-Litovsk, This separate peace contributed to American mistrust of the Soviets, since it left the Western Allies to fight the Central Powers alone.

As a result of the 1917 Bolshevik Revolution in Russia followed by its withdrawal from World War I, Soviet Russia found itself isolated in international diplomacy. Leader Vladimir Lenin stated that the Soviet Union was surrounded by a "hostile capitalist encirclement" and he viewed diplomacy as a weapon to keep Soviet enemies divided, beginning with the establishment of the Soviet Comintern, which called for revolutionary upheavals abroad. Tensions between Russia (including its allies) and the West turned intensely ideological. The landing of U.S. troops in Russia in 1918, which became involved in assisting the anti-Bolshevik Whites in the Russian Civil War helped solidify lasting suspicions among Soviet leadership of the capitalist world. This was the first event which made Russian-American relations a matter of major, long-term concern to the leaders in each country.

Interwar Diplomacy (1918-1939)

After winning the civil war, the Bolsheviks proclaimed a worldwide challenge to capitalism. Subsequent Soviet leader Joseph Stalin, who viewed the Soviet Union as a "socialist island", stated that the Soviet Union must see that "the present capitalist encirclement is replaced by a socialist encirclement."

As early as 1925, Stalin stated that he viewed international politics as a bipolar world in which the Soviet Union would attract countries gravitating to socialism and capitalist countries would attract states gravitating toward capitalism while the world was in a period of "temporary stabilization of capitalism" preceding its eventual collapse. Several events fueled suspicion and distrust between the western powers and the Soviet Union: the Bolsheviks' challenge to capitalism; the 1926 Soviet funding of a British general workers strike causing Britain to break relations with the Soviet Union; Stalin's 1927 declaration that peaceful coexistence with "the capitalist countries... is receding into the past"; conspiratorial allegations in the Shakhty show trial of a planned French and British-led coup d'etat; the Great Purge involving a series of campaigns of political repression and persecution in which over half a million Soviets were executed; the Moscow show trials including allegations of British, French, Japanese and German espionage; the controversial death of 6-8 million people in the Ukrainian Soviet Socialist Republic in the 1932-3 Ukrainian famine; western support of the White Army in the Russian Civil War; the US refusal to recognize the Soviet Union until 1933; and the Soviet entry into the Treaty of Rapallo. This outcome rendered Russian–American relations a matter of major long-term concern for leaders in both countries.

Differences existed in the political and economic systems of western democracies and the Soviet Union—capitalism versus socialism, economic autarky versus free trade, state planning versus private enterprise—became simplified and refined in national ideologies to represent two ways of life. Following the postwar Red Scare, many in the U.S. saw the Soviet system as a threat. The atheistic nature of Soviet communism also concerned many Americans. The American ideals of free determination and President Woodrow Wilson's Fourteen Points conflicted with many of the USSR's policies. Up until the mid-1930s, both British and U.S. policymakers commonly assumed the communist Soviet Union to be a much greater threat than disarmed and democratic Germany and focused most of their intelligence efforts against Moscow. However it has also been stated that in the period between the two wars, the U.S. had little interest in the Soviet Union or its intentions. America, after minimal contribution to World War I and the Russian Civil War, began to favour an isolationist stance when concerned with global politics (something which contributed to its late involvement in the Second World War). An example of this can be seen from its absence in the League of Nations, an international political forum, much like the United Nations; President Woodrow Wilson was one of the main advocates for the

League of Nations; the United States Congress, however, voted against joining. America was enjoying unprecedented economic growth throughout the 1910s and early 20s. However, the world soon plunged into the Great Depression and the U.S. was therefore even less inclined to make contributions to the international community while it suffered from serious financial and social problems at home.

The Soviets further resented Western appeasement of Adolf Hitler after the signing of the Munich Pact in 1938.

Molotov-Ribbentrop Pact and the start of World War II (1939-1941)

Suspicions intensified when, during the summer of 1939, after conducting negotiations with both a British-French group and Germany regarding potential military and political agreements, the Soviet Union and Germany signed a Commercial Agreement providing for the trade of certain German military and civilian equipment in exchange for Soviet raw materials and the Molotov-Ribbentrop Pact, commonly named after the foreign secretaries of the two countries (Molotov-Ribbentrop), which included a secret agreement to split Poland and Eastern Europe between the two states.

One week after the Molotov-Ribbentrop Pact's signing, the partition of Poland commenced with the German invasion of western Poland. Relations between the Soviet Union and the West further deteriorated when, two weeks after the German invasion, the Soviet Union invaded eastern Poland while coordinating with German forces. The Soviet Union then invaded Finland, which was also ceded to it under the Molotov-Ribbentrop Pact's secret protocol, resulting in stiff losses and the entry of an interim peace treaty granting it parts of eastern Finland. In June, the Soviets issued an ultimatum demanding Bessarabia, Bukovina and the Hertza region from Romania, after which Romania caved to Soviet demands for occupation. That month, the Soviets also invaded the Baltic countries of Lithuania, Estonia and Latvia

From August 1939 to June 1941 (when Germany broke the Pact and invaded the Soviet Union), relations between the West and the Soviets deteriorated further when the Soviet Union and Germany engaged in an extensive economic relationship by which the Soviet Union sent Germany vital oil, rubber, manganese and other material in exchange for German weapons, manufacturing machinery and technology. In late 1940, the Soviets also engaged in talks with Germany regarding potential membership in the Axis, culminating in the countries trading written proposals, though no agreement for Soviet Axis entry was ever reached.

Wartime Alliance (1941-1945)

On June 22, 1941, Germany broke the Molotov-Ribbentrop Pact with Operation Barbarossa, the invasion of the Soviet Union through the territories that the two countries had previously divided. The Soviets and the Western Allies were forced to cooperate, despite their past tensions. The U.S. shipped vast quantities of Lend Lease material to the Soviets. Britain and the Soviets signed a formal alliance, but the U.S. did not join until after the Attack on Pearl Harbour on December 7, 1941.

During the war, both sides disagreed on military tactics, especially the question of the opening of a second front against Germany in Western Europe. As early as July 1941, Stalin had asked Britain to invade northern France, but that country was in no position to carry out such a request. Stalin had asked the Western Allies to open a second front since the early months of the war—which finally occurred on D-Day, June 6, 1944.

The Soviets believed at the time, and charged throughout the Cold War, that the British and Americans intentionally delayed the opening of a second front against Germany in order to intervene only at the last minute so as to influence the peace settlement and dominate Europe. Historians such as John Lewis Gaddis dispute this claim, citing other military and strategic calculations for the timing of the Normandy invasion. In the meantime, the Russians suffered heavy casualties, with as many as twenty million dead. Nevertheless, Soviet perceptions (or misconceptions) of the West and *vice versa* left a strong undercurrent of tension and hostility between the Allied powers.

Both sides, moreover, held very dissimilar ideas regarding the establishment and maintenance of postwar security. The Americans tended to understand security in situational terms, assuming that, if US-style governments and markets were established as widely as possible, countries could resolve their differences peacefully, through international organizations. The key to the US vision of security was a postwar world shaped according to the principles laid out in the 1941 Atlantic Charter — in other words, a liberal international system based on free trade and open markets. This vision would require a rebuilt capitalist Europe, with a healthy Germany at its centre, to serve once more as a hub in global affairs.

This would also require US economic and political leadership of the postwar world. Europe needed the USA's assistance if it was to rebuild its domestic production and finance its international trade. The USA was the only world power not economically devastated by the fighting. By the end of the war, it was producing around fifty percent of the world's industrial goods.

Soviet leaders, however, tended to understand security in terms of space. This reasoning was conditioned by Russia's historical experiences, given the frequency with which the country had been invaded over the last 150 years.

The Second World War experience was particularly dramatic for the Russians: the Soviet Union suffered unprecedented devastation as a result of the Nazi onslaught, and over 20 million Soviet citizens died during the war; tens of thousands of Soviet cities, towns, and villages were levelled; and 30,100 Soviet factories were destroyed.

In order to prevent a similar assault in the future, Stalin was determined to use the Red Army to gain control of Poland, to dominate the Balkans and to destroy utterly Germany's capacity to engage in another war. The problem was that Stalin's strategy risked confrontation with the equally powerful United States, who viewed Stalin's actions as a flagrant violation of the Yalta agreement.

Even before the war came to an end, it seemed highly likely that cooperation between the Western powers and the USSR would give way to intense rivalry or conflict. This was due primarily to the starkly contrasting economic ideologies of the two superpowers, now quite easily the strongest in the world. Whereas the USA was a liberal, multiparty democracy with an advanced capitalist economy, based on free enterprise and profit-making, the USSR was a one-party Communist dictatorship with a state-controlled economy where private wealth and initiative was all but outlawed.

Postwar Relations

Wartime Conferences

Several postwar disagreements between western and Soviet leaders were related to their differing interpretations of wartime and immediate postwar conferences. The Tehran Conference in late 1943 was the first Allied conference in which Stalin was present. At the conference the Soviets expressed frustration that the Western Allies had not yet opened a second front against Germany in Western Europe. In Tehran, the Allies also considered the political status of Iran. At the time, the British had occupied southern Iran, while the Soviets had occupied an area of northern Iran bordering the Soviet republic of Azerbaijan. Nevertheless, at the end of the war, tensions emerged over the timing of the pull out of both sides from the oil-rich region.

At the February 1945 Yalta Conference, the Allies attempted to define the framework for a postwar settlement in Europe. The Allies could not reach firm agreements on the crucial questions: the occupation of Germany, postwar reparations from Germany, and loans. No final consensus was reached on Germany, other than to agree to a Soviet request for reparations totaling $10 billion "as a basis for negotiations." Debates over the composition of Poland's postwar government were also acrimonious.

Following the Allied victory in May, the Soviets effectively occupied Eastern Europe, while the US had much of Western Europe. In occupied Germany, the US and the Soviet Union established zones of occupation and a loose framework for four-power control with the ailing French and British.

At the Potsdam Conference starting in late July 1945, the Allies met to decide how to administer the defeated Nazi Germany, which had agreed to unconditional surrender nine weeks earlier on May 7 and May 8, 1945, VE day. Serious differences emerged over the future development of Germany and Eastern Europe. At Potsdam, the US was represented by a new president, Harry S. Truman, who on April 12 succeeded to the office upon Roosevelt's death. Truman was unaware of Roosevelt's plans for postwar engagement with the Soviet Union, and more generally uninformed about foreign policy and military matters. The new president, therefore, was initially reliant on a set of advisers (including

Ambassador to the Soviet Union Averell Harriman, Secretary of War Henry L. Stimson and Truman's own choice for secretary of state, James F. Byrnes). This group tended to take a harder line towards Moscow than Roosevelt had done. Administration officials favouring cooperation with the Soviet Union and the incorporation of socialist economies into a world trade system were marginalized. The UK was represented by a new prime minister, Clement Attlee, who had replaced Churchill after the Labour Party's defeat of the Conservatives in the 1945 general election.

One week after the Potsdam Conference ended, the atomic bombings of Hiroshima and Nagasaki added to Soviet distrust of the United States, when shortly after the attacks, Stalin protested to U.S. officials when Truman offered the Soviets little real influence in occupied Japan.

The immediate end of Lend-Lease from America to the USSR after the surrender of Germany also upset some politicians in Moscow, who believed this showed the U.S. had no intentions to support the USSR any more than they had to.

Challenges of Post-war Demilitarization

The formal accords at the Yalta Conference, attended by U.S President Franklin Roosevelt, British Prime Minister Winston Churchill, and Soviet leader Joseph Stalin, was key in shaping Europe's balance of power in the early postwar period.

However, toward the end of the war, the prospects of an Anglo-American front against the Soviet Union seemed slim from Stalin's standpoint. At the end of the war, Stalin assumed that the capitalist camp would resume its internal rivalry over colonies and trade, giving opportunity for renewed expansion at a later date, rather than pose a threat to the USSR. Stalin expected the United States to bow to domestic popular pressure for postwar demilitarization. Soviet economic advisors such as Eugen Varga predicted that the U.S. would cut military expenditures, and therefore suffer a crisis of overproduction, culminating in another great depression. Based on Varga's analysis, Stalin assumed that the Americans would offer the Soviets aid in postwar reconstruction, needing to find any outlet for massive capital investments in order to sustain the wartime industrial production that had brought the U.S. out of the Great Depression. However, to the surprise of Soviet leaders, the U.S. did not suffer a severe postwar crisis of overproduction. As Stalin had not anticipated, capital investments in industry were sustained by maintaining roughly the same levels of government spending.

In the United States, a conversion to the prewar economy nevertheless proved difficult. Though the United States military was cut to a small fraction of its wartime size, America's military-industrial complex that was created during the Second World War was not eliminated. Pressures to "get back to normal" were intense. Congress wanted a return to low, balanced budgets, and families clamored to see the soldiers sent back home. The Truman administration worried first about a postwar slump, then about the inflationary consequences of pent-up consumer demand. The G.I. Bill, adopted in 1944, was one answer: subsidizing veterans to complete their education rather than flood the job market and probably boost the unemployment figures. In the end, the postwar U.S. government strongly resembled the wartime government, with the military establishment—along with military-security industries—heavily funded. The postwar capitalist slump predicted by Stalin was averted by domestic government management, combined with the U.S. success in promoting international trade and monetary relations.

Conflicting Visions of Post-war Reconstruction

There were fundamental contrasts between the visions of the United States and the Soviet Union, between the ideals of capitalism and communism. Those contrasts had been simplified and refined in national ideologies to represent two ways of life, each vindicated in 1945 by previous disasters. Conflicting models of autarky versus exports, of state planning against private enterprise, were to vie for the allegiance of the developing and developed world in the postwar years. U.S. leaders, following the principles of the Atlantic Charter, hoped to shape the postwar world by opening up the world's markets to trade and markets. Administration analysts eventually reached the conclusion that rebuilding a capitalist Western Europe that could again serve as a hub in world affairs was essential to sustaining U.S. prosperity.

World War II resulted in enormous destruction of infrastructure and populations throughout Eurasia with almost no country left unscathed. The only major industrial power in the world to emerge intact—and even greatly strengthened from an economic perspective—was the United States. As the world's greatest industrial power, and as one of the few countries physically unscathed by the war, the United States stood to gain enormously from opening the entire world to unfettered trade. The United States would have a global market for its exports, and it would have unrestricted access to vital raw materials. Determined to avoid another economic catastrophe like that of the 1930s, U.S. leaders saw the creation of the postwar order as a way to ensure continuing U.S. prosperity.

Such a Europe required a healthy Germany at its centre. The postwar U.S. was an economic powerhouse that produced 50% of the world's industrial goods and an unrivaled military power with a monopoly of the new atom bomb. It also required new international agencies: the World Bank and International Monetary Fund, which were created to ensure an open, capitalist, international economy. The Soviet Union opted not to take part.

The American vision of the postwar world conflicted with the goals of Soviet leaders, who, for their part, were also motivated to shape postwar Europe. The Soviet Union had, since 1924, placed higher priority on its own security and internal development than on Leon Trotsky's vision of world revolution. Accordingly, Stalin had been willing before the war to engage non-communist governments that recognized Soviet dominance of its sphere of influenced and offered assurances of non-aggression.

Creation of the Eastern Bloc

After the war, Stalin sought to secure the Soviet Union's western border by installing communist-dominated regimes under Soviet influence in bordering countries. During and in the years immediately after the war, the Soviet Union annexed several countries as Soviet Socialist Republics within the Union of Soviet Socialist Republics. Many of these were originally countries effectively ceded to it by Nazi Germany in the Molotov-Ribbentrop Pact, before Germany invaded the Soviet Union. These later annexed territories include Eastern Poland (incorporated into two different SSRs), Latvia (became Latvia SSR), Estonia (became Estonian SSR), Lithuania (became Lithuania SSR), part of eastern

Finland (Karelo-Finnish SSR and annexed into the Russian SFSR) and northern Romania (became the Moldavian SSR).

Other states were converted into Soviet Satellite states, such as East Germany, the People's Republic of Poland, the People's Republic of Hungary, the Czechoslovak Socialist Republic, the People's Republic of Romania and the People's Republic of Albania, which aligned itself in the 1960s away from the Soviet Union and towards the People's Republic of China.

The defining characteristic of the Stalinist communism implemented in Eastern Bloc states was the unique symbiosis of the state with society and the economy, resulting in politics and economics losing their distinctive features as autonomous and distinguishable spheres. Initially, Stalin directed systems that rejected Western institutional characteristics of market economies, democratic governance (dubbed "bourgeois democracy" in Soviet parlance) and the rule of law subduing discretional intervention by the state. They were economically communist and depended upon the Soviet Union for significant amounts of materials. While in the first five years following World War II, massive emigration from these states to the West occurred, restrictions implemented thereafter stopped most East-West migration, except that under limited bilateral and other agreements.

Cold War Evolution and Interpretations

Interpreting the history of the Cold War has been a notoriously controversial pursuit. New evidence, unearthed in recent years from archives on both sides of the Atlantic and the Pacific, has not resolved old debates, but it has added immensely to our collective knowledge. Much remains to be learned and understood about the history of the global power struggle, the impact of which on the latter half of the twentieth century can scarcely be exaggerated. As it recedes into history, the passions of presentism (interpreting history on the basis of contemporary prejudices) have receded as well. These developments open up new possibilities for stimulating discussion of the evolution and interpretations of the Cold War.

Five key interpretive themes can be employed to explain the evolution of the Cold War and to interpret the history of the conflict: ideology, national expansionism, economic hegemony, militarization, and patriotic culture. These forces help explain the origins, evolution, and end of the Cold War. Despite the primary focus on Soviet-American relations, no one questions that the Cold War became a *global* phenomenon enveloping the fates of scores of nations, some modern and industrial, others premodern and developing. Nations such as Great Britain and China played key roles in the evolution of the Cold War, but so did smaller states as diverse as Angola, Cuba, Egypt, Greece, India, Israel, Japan, Korea, South Africa, Vietnam, and many more. As this list suggests, the Cold War encompasses a vast and complex history, overshadowing the latter half of the twentieth century.

Ideological Divide

Ideology is a central element in coming to grips with the Cold War. In this respect, the Cold War actually began in 1917, with the triumph of the Bolshevik communist revolutionaries in Russia. The Bolsheviks, led by Vladimir Ilich Lenin, a committed Marxist revolutionary, denounced capitalism as an exploitative and moribund social system. Lenin's contribution to Marxism was his theory that imperialism was the last gasp of capitalism. The Bolsheviks believed that the bloodletting then under way in World War I reflected the penultimate crisis of modern capitalism. Lenin and other communists sought to build socialism in Russia while doing what they could to facilitate expansion of Marxism-Leninism abroad. The West greeted the Bolshevik Revolution with implacable hostility, including an ill-fated Allied intervention against the Bolsheviks in the Russian civil war, which the Marxists eventually won. The Western worldview was capably represented in the rhetoric of President Woodrow Wilson, who had called for U.S. intervention in World War I to make the world "safe for democracy." Wilson spoke not just for constitutional government but also for free-trade capitalism as well. Bolshevism, with its emphasis on state economic planning, was anathema to the deep-seated faith in free enterprise, a cornerstone of American ideology. Moreover, Wilson, like millions of Americans deeply religious, found Marxist atheism, which had condemned religion as the "opiate of the masses," profoundly offensive.

Hence, an ideological gulf between the Soviet Union and the United States, between communism and capitalism, emerged from

World War I and divided East and West throughout the interwar period. Beginning in 1929 the Soviet Union came under the iron authority of Joseph Stalin, a pitiless autocrat responsible for the deaths of millions of his own countrymen in purges, forced agricultural collectivization, and breakneck industrialization. Washington declined to accord formal diplomatic recognition of the Soviet Union until 1933. Among other consequences, East-West hostility ensured that efforts to forge an antifascist alliance against Nazi Germany during the late 1930s would come to grief. When the Western powers rejected Soviet overtures for an alliance against the Nazis, Stalin negotiated his own pact with Adolf Hitler in 1939, paving the way for World War II. After sacking much of Europe, Hitler turned on the Soviets, long his primary target, in an invasion of Russia launched on 22 June 1941. The West quickly embraced the Soviet cause as its own in a mutual conflict against Nazi aggression.

Clearly the wartime Grand Alliance, forged by the Nazi bid to dominate Europe, was little more than a marriage of convenience. Indeed, nothing less than Hitler's bid to dominate Europe could have brought Stalin and the Soviet Union into alliance with Great Britain and the United States. Winston Churchill's memorable comment that he would ally with "the devil himself" against the Nazi regime was no mere quip; Churchill was explaining just how extraordinary the prime minister himself considered the unlikely alliance between East and West. Equally cosmopolitan, but markedly less anti-Soviet than Churchill, President Franklin D. Roosevelt saw the war as an opportunity not only to defeat Nazi aggression but to create a framework through Soviet-American cooperation for something like the world order Wilson had envisioned all too prematurely during the previous European war.

Roosevelt came to understand, however, in the weeks before his death on 12 April 1945, that his vision might not stand up to the hard realities embodied in a renascent Stalinist Russia. Once seemingly on the brink of destruction, the Soviet Union had turned the battle at Stalingrad in the winter of 1942–1943 and never looked back. Despite the unparalleled destruction of the Soviet state, including some 27 million dead in the war, the Red Army found itself ensconced in the heart of Europe, all with the blessing of its wartime allies. The onetime pariah state now stood poised to exert unprecedented influence on the postwar world.

National Expansion

World War II redrew the map of the world, creating vast power vacuums from the defeat of Nazi Germany in Europe and imperial Japan in Asia. Given his own ruthlessness and the lens of Marxist historicism, Stalin could only interpret the Soviet victory as an opportunity both to ensure his nation's security and to promote the inevitable expansion of the communist system. None of the new archival evidence that began emerging in the 1990s has contradicted Stalin's explanation to a group of comrades in 1945 that to the victors would go the spoils; that is, whichever power occupied a liberated European country could be expected to impose his own social system on that state. Stalin heard his allies' pleas for him to pay lip service to a postwar democratic order, best embodied in the Declaration of Liberated Europe issued at the Yalta Conference in February 1945, but at the end of the day this was "algebra," as far as the Soviet dictator was concerned, and he averred a preference for simple math.

Presiding over a vast global empire—though one verging on dissolution rather than expansion—Winston Churchill understood simple math as well. He and Stalin had engaged in just such an exercise in coming to the so-called percentages agreement during a tête-à-tête in Moscow in 1944. Running down the nations of East-Central Europe one by one, the two Allied leaders came to agreement as to which powers would call the shots in the states then being liberated from the Nazis. In effect, Churchill went a long way toward acquiescing in the very division of Europe that he later bitterly decried in his 5 March 1946 "Iron Curtain" address in Fulton, Missouri. Churchill hoped to temper Soviet ambitions, but when it came to the fates of neighbouring states such as Poland and Romania, Stalin understood only one language—domination.

U.S.–Soviet relations, vastly improved during the war under Roosevelt, began to deteriorate. Within less than a year after the end of the European war, Cold War declarations emanated from both capitals. In a February 1946 address, Stalin offered up a plateful of Marxist verities, including the warning that conflict between communism and Western imperialism was inevitable and would continue. George F. Kennan, America's foremost Soviet expert, dispatched the "long telegram" from Moscow that same month warning of an unstable, xenophobic, and expansionist regime. The policy Kennan urged in response— "containment" of Russia's "expansive tendencies"—soon became the watchword of American foreign policy. Churchill's address in Fulton, delivered in Truman's presence in his home state, followed on the heels of Kennan's landmark 8,000-word telegram. Stalin responded to Churchill's speech by labeling Britain's wartime leader a "convinced reactionary" and accusing the Western powers of planning a new cordon sanitaire against the Soviet Union.

Rising Cold War tensions focused next on the Near East. Only a showdown in the new United Nations prompted Stalin's grudging withdrawal from neighbouring Iran, where the Red Army had remained past an agreed-upon March 1946 deadline. By the spring of 1947, the threat of a leftist triumph in Greece, fear of Soviet influence in Turkey, and the decline of British power in the Mediterranean region combined to give rise to the Truman Doctrine. In a speech that has long been interpreted as an American declaration of cold war, Truman averred in April 1947 that the world had become divided between "alternative ways of life" and that "it must be the policy of the United States to support free peoples who are resisting attempted subjugation by armed minorities or by outside pressures." Despite its own history of often bellicose national expansion (such as the Mexican War or annexation of the Philippines), the United States would not accommodate itself to postwar Soviet expansion. Washington dominated postwar Japan and western Europe, both of which were reoriented along Western lines, and established a system of military bases across the world. The United States built and controlled the Panama Canal and backed British and French control of the Suez Canal, yet it rejected Soviet efforts to extend influence over the Black Sea straits. In addition to resenting these double standards, Stalin and his comrades feared America's ability to wield its unprecedented economic clout.

American Financial Hegemony

In addition to the ideological divide and issues of national expansion, U.S. economic hegemony fueled the Cold War. The

Soviets—who had suffered far more devastation, both human and material, in World War II than the United States (or any other country)—sought loans, grants, and reparations to rebuild. Washington had contributed immeasurably to the Soviet war effort through lend-lease and other forms of aid. The United States also promised a postwar loan but delayed the matter and then linked economic assistance with political issues, notably the fates of postwar governments in East-Central Europe. No loan was ever made.

In striking contrast to the devastation of Russia's economy, World War II had been phenomenally good for American business. Government-fueled war production ended the Great Depression and brought full employment and rapid economic growth to the United States. Unscathed by war and prosperous at home, the United States emerged as the unquestioned economic powerhouse of the postwar world. The dollar dwarfed all other currencies and New York displaced London as the world's financial centre. At the 1944 Bretton Woods (New Hampshire) Conference, the United States established the World Bank and the International Monetary Fund, agencies that would issue loans and assistance to anchor postwar economic recovery. Such assistance came with strings attached. In order to be eligible, countries would have to meet certain criteria compatible with free-market capitalism. After attending the conference, the Soviet Union never joined the Washington-based and U.S.-dominated international financial agencies.

If there was any hope of heading off the Cold War, it ended with the Marshall Plan. The European Recovery Program, launched by the U.S. Army general turned secretary of state George C. Marshall, laid the foundation for decades of American and western European economic and political integration. The program of loans, assistance, and psychological recovery from the destitution of war succeeded brilliantly in effecting the economic and political recovery of western Europe, especially in France and Italy, where communist parties backed by Moscow had been poised to bid for power. The Marshall Plan exemplified "empire by invitation," an interpretive framework that emphasized that American economic assistance and political influence were welcomed by the western European governments and the majority of public opinion. U.S.

propaganda and covert operations, especially in Italy, played a significant role in the process, however. Nevertheless, there is little doubt that western Europeans welcomed American power and influence far more than Eastern Europeans welcomed Soviet power. This single reality carries a great deal of explanatory power as to both the origins and the eventual end of the Cold War.

By the late 1940s, the Marshall Plan had begun to achieve its aims of fostering western European economic recovery and political confidence building. It gave rise to a postwar order in which the United States emerged as the unquestioned world leader. It advanced an American campaign of global financial hegemony. As successful as the Marshall Plan was in advancing Western political and economic integration, the economic recovery program also cemented the division of Europe. Although the Soviets had attended the initial discussions in Paris, Stalin and his foreign minister, V. I. Molotov, understood all too clearly that they would be left, by design, on the outside looking in. With American economic clout dwarfing that of the devastated Soviet Union, Stalin and Molotov understood that the Marshall Plan posed a grave threat to the budding "people's democracies" of East-Central Europe. After Molotov strode out of the Paris discussions, Stalin ordered out the Czech delegation as well. Within months the Kremlin orchestrated a coup, brutally ousting Czech liberals in tactics that revived vivid memories of Hitler. "Moral Godfearing peoples," Truman declared, "must save the world from Atheism and totalitarianism."

The Division of Germany

There was, of course, no precise moment when the Cold War can be said to have begun, yet there is no question that it was in place by 1948, the same year in which the term itself was popularized. The breakdown of Allied cooperation in Germany brought the division of the postwar world into the capital of the vanquished former common enemy. American, British, and French forces colluded in floating a new German currency without notifying the Soviets. The Kremlin and its German comrades cut off road, rail, and canal links to Berlin in an effort to force the Western powers out of the former Reich capital, which reposed in the heart of Soviet-occupied eastern Germany. The subsequent

American airlift broke the back of the Kremlin blockade, which Stalin abandoned after eleven months in May 1949. The emergence of two rival German states, and years of bitter propaganda and covert operations, followed in the wake of the Berlin blockade and airlift.

The United States and its west European allies accepted the division of Germany under a strategy of "dual containment." The larger, more productive western Germany—soon to become the Federal Republic of Germany—would anchor the postwar European economy under U.S. occupation and supervision. This approach would not only fuel recovery but would reassure France and other past victims of aggression that Germany was now contained within the Western alliance. The Soviets incorporated into their sphere the smaller eastern rump Germany—which became the German Democratic Republic—and which the West subjected to unremitting psychological warfare in the form of radio propaganda, covert operations, and various forms of subversion. In any case, the division of Germany cemented, in both real and symbolic terms, the division of Europe.

Militarization

One of the most significant outcomes of World War II was the enormous momentum of militarization. Four years of global conflict—indeed, two world wars in a single generation—had left a powerful imprint. Neither the Soviet Union nor the United States ever fully demobilized. Troops from both nations remained encamped in the heart of Europe, while U.S. air and naval bases spread throughout the world. Although the Soviet Red Army was the world's largest ground force, the United States possessed a formidable two-ocean navy and the most powerful air force the world had ever seen. As the Soviet economy and society struggled to rebuild from the ruins of war, U.S. economic might laid the foundation for the emergence of an awesome military power.

Sole possession of the atomic bomb offered both real and symbolic evidence of U.S. military superiority. Some historians have argued that the United States dropped the two bombs on Japan as much to make an impression on the Soviets as to end the Pacific war. "Atomic diplomacy" did not work, however, as Stalin adopted a nonchalant stance toward the bomb and refused to adjust Soviet political aims in deference to the U.S. monopoly. While Washington had shared atomic information with Great Britain during the war, the Soviets were kept in the dark—or so Americans thought. In actuality, Soviet spies had penetrated the atomic research program and stolen the secrets of the atom. Talks on international control of atomic weapons quickly foundered and became another casualty of the Cold War.

Both sides cultivated their military prowess and vowed to defend their territory and spheres of influence. While the Soviets trumpeted the heroic defence of the motherland against the Nazis, the Americans reorganized their defence establishment, now housed in the sprawling new Pentagon building. Under the National Security Act (1947), Washington created a new Department of Defence and departments of Air Force and Marines to join the Army and the Navy, all four branches coordinated by a new phalanx of generals, the Joint Chiefs of Staff. The legislation also created the National Security Council to advise the president on global foreign policy and the Central Intelligence Agency to gather information and carry out covert operations.

The West took the lead in dividing Europe into hostile military alliances. In 1949, acting under a UN provision for collective security arrangements, the West promulgated the North Atlantic Treaty Organization (NATO), a military alliance aimed squarely at the Soviet Union. The actual threat of a Soviet military attack on western Europe was remote, yet memories of Nazi blitzkrieg and Pearl Harbour remained vivid. More to the point, however, NATO furthered the course of Western economic and political integration and created a market for perpetuating the profitable wartime collusion between science, government, and the defence industry. The successful Soviet atomic test in 1949 fueled the nuclear arms race, as both powers pushed ahead with development of hydrogen, or thermonuclear, weapons. From this point forward, the two superpowers each cultivated the power to destroy one another in an all-out war.

The Cold War in Asia

Tumultuous developments in Asia ensured that the Cold War would become global. U.S. policy appeared well in hand in the early postwar years, as the occupation of Japan provided an unprecedented opportunity to further Washington's economic and political agenda in Asia. Establishing Japan as the focal point of an economic program across the "great crescent" of Asia, Washington sought to ensure an anticommunist order friendly to the supremacy of the dollar and U.S. ideology. The Japanese proved largely compliant, but the triumph of the communists in the Chinese civil war promptly shattered the American quest for a noncommunist Asian postwar order.

The rise to power of the Chinese Communist Party in October 1949 was a stunning blow to Americans, who had long waxed sentimental about the prospects of expanding Western influence in "the Orient." Roosevelt had given rise to false hopes during the war by floating the ill-fated concept that China would serve as one of the "four policemen" of the postwar world. In reality, the democratic China was a chimera. And while Stalin had repeatedly shown himself willing to sell out the Chinese communists during the war, now that they had come to power, he entered into an alliance with Mao Zedong's regime in 1950. Inexperienced in foreign affairs, and plagued by demagogues and opportunists in Congress, millions of Americans believed the leaders who told them that only domestic subversion could account for the dastardly turn of affairs in East Asia. Still adjusting to the burdens of world power, Americans became resentful when events did not unfold as they expected.

Korea and NSC 68

With capitalist and communist regimes ensconced in Japan and China, respectively, Korean communists led by Kim Il Sung sought to "liberate" their peninsula through armed aggression. Archival evidence found in the 1990s revealed that Kim practically pleaded with Stalin, on numerous occasions, before gaining the Kremlin autocrat's assent to an attack against southern forces backed by the American-educated Syngman Rhee. The outbreak of war in Korea in June 1950 stunned the Truman administration and an American public already reeling from a series of Cold War setbacks. Unaware and unwilling to consider that Kim, and not Stalin, had fomented the war in Korea, the Truman administration decided immediately to respond with force to what it was sure was a deliberate *Soviet* provocation. Within months, U.S. and UN forces reversed the battle, prompting a massive Chinese intervention that turned the Korean War into a bloody three-year stalemate. Korea would remain a divided nation for at least the rest of the century, yet another casualty of the Cold War.

The outbreak of war in Korea, punctuated by the approval of the historic U.S. foreign policy document National Security Council Document 68 (NSC 68) marked the end of the first phase of the Cold War. The apocalyptic policy paper envisioned a fight to the finish with Soviet-sponsored world communism. The document, approved by Truman, literally envisioned spending whatever was necessary in the name of national security. During the course of the Korean War, defence spending more than tripled, ensuring the predominance of military Keynesianism for the remainder of the century. Military Keynesianism encompassed stimulation of the economy through federal investment and expenditure on defence.

Among other significant repercussions of the Korean bloodletting was the establishment of U.S. military bases in Asia; lasting involvement in the dispute between Taiwan and mainland China; assignment of U.S. troops to Europe on a permanent basis; and West German rearmament. Approval of NSC 68 culminated the first phase of the Cold War. The Korean War cemented militarization and the adoption of worst case scenarios of "enemy" behaviour on both sides. Sometimes referred to as the "forgotten war," insofar as it was sandwiched between World War II and the Vietnam War, the Korean War was one of most significant conflicts in modern world history.

Patriotic Culture in the United States

Cold War anxiety reached new heights, or depths, during the Korean War and had a profound effect on American society. Conservatism outpaced reform. The process began early in World War II, when Roosevelt himself announced that "Dr. New Deal" had been replaced by "Dr. Win the War." The reform era was over, replaced by the inevitable conservative reaction of war, mirroring the World War I experience. War and Cold War provided an opportunity that conservative elites, alarmed by the specter of creeping socialism in the New Deal, would not let pass. The profitable matrix revolving around science, business, government, and defence cemented military Keynesianism over government spending on domestic concerns. While federal dollars fueled Cold War militarization, spending on social programs, deemed socialistic by many conservatives, would be contained at home. An inveterate New Dealer, Henry Wallace, launched a last-gasp campaign against the new order but was thoroughly repudiated in the 1948 election. Truman's stunning upset victory over Thomas Dewey underscored that containment, anticommunism, and militarization would illuminate the path to electoral triumph.

Hysteria over domestic communism brought repression and exercised a lasting chilling effect on left-wing sentiment. Beginning with the "Hollywood Ten" in 1946, former communists and left-wing sympathizers were harassed, purged, and put on notice. In 1950 the Alger Hiss case, in which a former high-level State Department diplomat was convicted of perjury for lying about being a communist agent, put liberals and former New Dealers on the defensive while giving rise to a new breed of politician, best embodied by Richard Nixon, for whom the Cold War provided the core of their identity. Federal Bureau of Investigation director J. Edgar Hoover—accountable to no one and since World War I obsessed with destroying radicalism—launched a campaign against thousands of Americans who had harbored left-wing sentiments. Despite the extraordinarily crude and reckless tactics of Joseph McCarthy, the junior senator from Wisconsin conducted a four-year campaign against thousands of alleged subversives. The victims of the postwar hysteria were not only the tens of thousands of men and women harassed by McCarthy and the FBI, but the basic constitutional rights of freedom of thought and association as well.

The Failed Quest for "liberation"

While U.S. national security elites still hoped to force the Soviet Union to allow political independence throughout Eastern Europe, the State Department grasped the possibilities inherent in the independent communist course being pursued in Yugoslavia since the open breach in 1948 between Stalin and Josip Broz Tito. Both Truman and his successor, Dwight D. Eisenhower, sought to promote "Titoism" in Eastern Europe, but the confrontational quest for "liberation" of the "captive nations" undermined this effort. Right-wing critics insisted that containment was a fatalistic and unmanly (even "pantywaist," to some critics) policy, which supposedly acquiesced in Soviet hegemony over Eastern Europe. In reality, Kennan's conceptualization of containment, embraced as U.S. Cold War policy, had always encompassed liberation, or rollback, of communist power in Eastern Europe.

Eisenhower intensified a campaign of "psychological warfare" that had begun under Truman in an effort to destabilize Soviet hegemony. A variety of strategies, focused especially on radio propaganda, did indeed help shake the foundations of Communist Party authority in Eastern Europe. When necessary, however, as in East Germany in 1953 and Hungary in 1956, the Soviet Union simply resorted to direct military intervention to maintain its hard sphere of influence over East-Central Europe. Nothing the United States and its NATO allies could have done, short of initiating World War III, would have altered this fundamental geopolitical reality flowing from the World War II settlement and the postwar ideological clash.

A more subtle Western approach might have enhanced the possibility of the post-Stalinist leadership loosening the bonds of authority over the East-Central European Communist Party regimes. However, by confronting the Soviet Union with both NATO and aggressive psychological warfare, Washington gave the Kremlin no opportunity to allow for liberalization, or Titoism, in the region. It was all too clear to Soviet leaders that if the "satellites" were allowed to go their own way they would end up ultimately—as in fact occurred decades later after the end of the Cold War—being transferred directly into the hostile NATO orbit. The Kremlin had no choice, short of capitulation to the West, but to protect its sphere at all costs. With psychological warfare having failed to deliver the ultimate prize of liberation, the Eisenhower administration was compelled to adopt an evolutionary approach emphasizing toned-down radio propaganda, exchanges of film, trade fairs, exhibitions, and people-to-people contacts.

Following the death of Stalin in 1953, Nikita S. Khrushchev eventually emerged as the new Kremlin leader. In 1956, Khrushchev stunned communists throughout the world by denouncing Stalin for his many "crimes" against the people. A dedicated Marxist-Leninist known for his thundering denunciations of the West, Khrushchev also took concrete steps, including meaningful cuts in Soviet defenses, toward achieving "peaceful coexistence" with the West. Khrushchev's brash style, however, combined with deeply ingrained American Cold War anxieties, continued to plague any progress toward a genuine détente. A hysterical American reaction to the Soviet launch of *Sputnik*, the first Earth satellite, in 1957 complicated Eisenhower's hopes for a breakthrough in the Cold War. The president's own decision to authorize a campaign of aerial spying over Soviet airspace doomed the Eisenhower-Khrushchev "thaw" in the Cold War. Hopes for achieving what would later be called détente came crashing down with Gary Powers's U-2 spy plane in May 1960. Eisenhower limped out of office decrying the "unwarranted influence" of the military-industrial complex, a phenomenon that, ironically, had gained substantial momentum on his own watch.

Kennedy and Crises

The essential forces that fueled the Cold War— ideology, geopolitics, economics, militarization, and patriotic culture— persisted throughout the conflict. The Cold War manifested itself in waves, or cycles, of varying intensity. After the brief thaw of the mid-1950s, another intense wave of conflict emerged during the presidency of John F. Kennedy. Bitter confrontation over the anomalous western enclave in Berlin, deep inside East Germany, ended with construction of the Berlin Wall in August 1961. The wall brought a pernicious settlement to the German problem, but the concrete and barbed wire divide gave substance to Churchill's metaphor of an Iron Curtain. Despite scores of bold and often successful escapes by East Germans, the wall was an effective physical barrier, though ultimately a devastating propaganda liability and harbinger of the West's eventual triumph in the Cold War.

The 1962 Cuban missile crisis marked the apogee of Cold War confrontation, including a palpable threat of nuclear annihilation. Already livid over the loss of Cuba to communism under Fidel Castro, Americans were angered even further by Khrushchev's decision to place mediumrange nuclear warheads ninety miles off U.S. shores. From the Cuban and Soviet perspective— a perspective rarely considered under a monolithic U.S. patriotic culture—the action might have been seen as an understandable response to blatant American efforts to topple Castro, which had failed once in the Bay of Pigs invasion in April 1961 but would continue in no fewer than eight assassination plots against the Cuban leader. Moreover, as Khrushchev pointed out, nuclear missiles in Cuba would confront the United States with an analogous situation to that faced by the Soviet Union, which had nuclear weapons targeting its cities and defence sites from a variety of hostile NATO states.

Kennedy ultimately rejected the most hawkish advice he received—unilateral bombing of Cuba—but the president opted for a national television address rather than private diplomacy to demand that Khrushchev dismantle the missile sites. Kennedy then confronted the Soviets with a naval blockade, an act of war that the administration tried to soften by employing the euphemism of a "quarantine." Khrushchev backed down, but only after Kennedy renounced intervention in Cuba and pledged privately to dismantle U.S. missile sites in Turkey.

The last months of Kennedy's abortive presidency marked a turning point in the history of the Cold War. Following the crises in Berlin and Cuba, a sobered Kennedy and Khrushchev began to usher in a new thaw by establishing a "hotline" for instant communication and signing the 1963 Limited Test Ban Treaty, terminating aboveground nuclear test blasts. Cultural exchange picked up throughout the 1960s as well. Cold War rivalry continued on a global scale, but after 1963 the shadow of Armageddon began to recede, particularly as the Soviets achieved a rough parity in the nuclear arms race by the end of the decade.

The Third World

While both sides accepted the status quo in Europe and embraced mutual deterrence through MAD (mutually assured destruction), the Cold War continued to rage in the so-called Third World of developing nations. From 1946 to 1960, thirty-seven new nations emerged from under a history of colonial domination to gain independent status. Both the United States and the Soviet Union, backed by their respective allies, competed intensively for influence over the new nations of Africa, Asia, Latin America, and the Middle East. Strategists in both camps believed that ultimate victory or defeat in the Cold War depended on the outcome of Third World conflicts. Moreover, many of these areas harbored vital natural resources, such as oil in the Middle East, upon which the developed world had become dependent. With American and allied automobiles, industry, and consumerism dependent on ready access to vast supplies of crude oil, maintaining access to foreign energy sources emerged as a key element of U.S. foreign policy.

Both the United States and the Soviet Union abhorred neutralism, that is, they demanded that their allies and Third World nations side with them against their Cold War rival. Both powers equated neutralism with appeasement and sought to punish not just states that sided against them but those that attempted to remain equivocal. Both the United States and the Soviet Union worked tirelessly in Asia, Africa, Latin America, and the Middle East to convince Third World leaders that their ideology was on the right side of history and held out the best hope for those nations to grapple with their pressing social problems, including poverty, disease, and rampant population growth. The Soviets had less money and a weaker economy than their Western rivals, but they did have the advantage of arguing that communist ideology offered liberation from the legacy of colonialism.

Adopting a much harsher line toward the West than Khrushchev, China's leader, Mao Zedong, called on Third World revolutionaries to launch "wars of national liberation" against the capitalist world.

The message had resonance since the overwhelming majority of Third World states had been under the control of foreign powers, including Belgium, Britain, France, Germany, Holland, and the United States, for much of the previous century.

Washington sought desperately to counteract the Soviet message and to contain revolutionary movements in the Third World. U.S. leaders went to great lengths to stave off defeat in even the most obscure and strategically insignificant corners of the globe out of fear of a bandwagon or domino effect. They insisted that a communist victory anywhere would encourage other revolutionaries and thus precipitate the much-feared red avalanche.

While the United States was most sensitive to revolutionary movements in neighbouring Latin America, Cold War intervention was a global phenomenon.

For years Washington coveted as a strategic partner South Africa, at the time a racist white minority regime that attempted to isolate and contain black radical movements in southern Africa. In North Africa and the Middle East, Washington backed Egypt and Israel against more radical regimes, some of which, such as Syria, became close Soviet allies.

The United States and the Soviet Union supported different sides in the Middle East Arab-Israeli conflict. The United States backed the Zionist state, a policy supported by most American Jews—the largest population in the world in any one country—but also by a majority of overall public opinion. While Washington became Israel's chief diplomatic benefactor and weapons supplier, the Soviet Union embraced the cause of Arab nationalism and Palestinian statehood. When wars erupted in 1956, 1967, and 1973, however, Washington and Moscow ultimately found the common language to work together to prevent the conflicts from escalating into longer wars.

While the Soviets and Chinese appealed to the Third World on the basis of Lenin's theory of imperialism, Washington offered its democratic ideology as well as its advanced economy to woo Third World nations. Through its supervision of the World Bank and the International Monetary Fund, the United States offered aid and loans on the condition that the recipients join the capitalist camp in the Cold War struggle.

The United States confronted serious obstacles, however, in its efforts to win over the Third World. First of all, most of the Third World consisted of populations of people of color. The leaders and peoples of those nations condemned America's history of slavery, racism, and support for imperialism based on a racial hierarchy. Many scholars believe, in fact, that the Cold War played a significant role in the slow emergence of federal government support for the civil rights movement, which culminated in the United States in the mid-1960s. U.S. leaders recognized that they could not hope to appeal successfully to the Third World while sanctioning segregation, denial of voting rights, and other forms of racial discrimination in the United States itself.

Cia Covert Operations

When economic, ideological, and cultural appeals failed, the United States, like the Soviet Union, employed spies and covert operations in an effort to achieve its aims in the developing world. Both employed a variety of tactics, including bribes, intimidation, propaganda, and violence. As a Communist Party dictatorship, the Soviets were less accountable to their public than the Americans were to theirs.

Anxious to avoid public scrutiny, the Central Intelligence Agency and other covert branches of the national security state conducted their operations in secret. U.S. covert operations included extralegal coups against revolutionary regimes in Africa, Asia, Latin America, and the Middle East.

In 1953, for example, a CIA operation, approved directly by Eisenhower, led to the overthrow of the elected leader of Iran, Mohammad Mosaddeq. The Iranian leader had moved to assert national control over his nation's oil supplies, an action that menaced the interest of U.S. and British oil conglomerates and smacked of socialism. The coup succeeded, as the CIA paved the way for Shah Reza Pahlavi to assume power and keep Iran open to the West. The foreign policy of intervention proved shortsighted a quarter-century later, however, as Iranian fundamentalists overthrew the shah, condemned the United States as the "Great Satan" in world affairs, and held fifty-three American hostages for more than a year.

In 1954 another CIA coup overthrew Jacobo Arbenz Guzmán, the legitimate ruler of the Central American nation of Guatemala. Arbenz had engaged in land redistribution, threatening the interest of the United Fruit Company, a U.S. corporation. Moreover, Washington was determined to curb such socialist-style behaviour out of fear that it would inspire similar actions by other nations of the region. The coup replaced Arbenz with a more compliant leader but ultimately led to more than a quarter-century of factionalism, poverty, and state terror in Guatemala. In part it was the success of the Guatemalan coup that led the Eisenhower and

Kennedy administrations to confidently approve plans for a takeover in Cuba, an initiative that failed spectacularly at the Bay of Pigs. Castro's fully prepared forces destroyed the U.S.-backed Cuban exile guerillas shortly after their landing at Cochinos Bay.

Lack of air support and widespread publicity on the eve of a putatively "covert" operation doomed the invasion and left a humiliated Kennedy administration even more determined to contain communism. An even more disastrous intervention subsequently unfolded in Asia.

The Vietnam War

While securing Japan as the centerpiece of the "great crescent" strategy, Washington successfully fended off a leftist insurgency in the Philippines after granting independence to the archipelago in 1946. U.S. economic and strategic influence (weapons sales, for example) helped contain radical movements in the new nations of Indonesia and Malaysia. Taiwan depended heavily on the United States to maintain its defensive posture and separation from mainland China.

In 1954, just a year after the Korean armistice, a new Cold War crisis arose in Indochina (Cambodia, Laos, and Vietnam) as France suffered a humiliating defeat following an eight-year campaign to reassert imperial authority.

The Viet Minh, a nationalist group led by a communist, Ho Chi Minh, won the battle of Dien Bien Phu, forcing France to capitulate. Determined to prevent Vietnam from falling to communism, the United States helped sabotage an international agreement that elections would be held in 1956 to unify the Southeast Asian nation. The problem with the elections, as the Eisenhower administration well understood, was that Ho Chi Minh would have won them. Washington threw its support behind Ngo Dinh Diem, who proclaimed the existence of a separate Republic of Vietnam (South Vietnam) in opposition to Ho's regime in the northern half of the country. The United States thus began a commitment that would eventually cost billions of dollars and more than 58,000 American lives while bringing unparalleled death and destruction to Indochina.

Despite occupying the country with more than half a million ground troops and pummeling the region with the most intensive bombing campaign in world history, Washington could neither subdue the Vietnamese opposition nor create a viable government in Saigon. By the time President Richard M. Nixon pulled out in January 1973, the United States itself had become deeply divided over the war. Saigon fell to the communists two years later. The much-feared domino effect never transpired in Southeast Asia. Laos and Cambodia did "go communist," but well before the end of the Indochina war, the Soviet Union and China had become enemies.

In 1979, Communist Party governments of the region were at war with one another, as China briefly invaded Vietnam, a Soviet ally, for its attack on the blood-thirsty regime of the Khmer Rouge in Cambodia, a Chineseally.

The consensus interpretation is that the Vietnam War was a tragic foreign policy blunder. Some diehard elements of the patriotic culture insisted that Washington could have won the war with a divergent strategy, but this argument ignores the decisive political aspects of the struggle as well as the very real possibility that an unlimited assault on North Vietnam in the mid-1960s would have brought China into the war, much as events had transpired in Korea. The nation as a whole struggled for decades to recover from a foreign policy debacle that, however tragic, had flowed logically from U.S. Cold War ideology and perceptions.

Detente

Despite the aggressive U.S. militarism in Southeast Asia, and a brutal Soviet invasion of Czechoslovakia in 1968, a new thaw in East-West relations emerged in the 1960s and 1970s. Détente (relaxation of tensions) emerged as part of the cyclical pattern of Cold War history in which periods of relative calm followed periods of bitter great-power conflict. Kennedy and Khrushchev started the process in the wake of the missile crisis, but both were removed from the scene with Kennedy's assassination in Dallas and Khrushchev's ouster in a 1964 Kremlin power shift. The new, hard-line regime of Leonid Brezhnev aggressively pursued Soviet aims, including sending the Red Army into Czechoslovakia to repress the "Prague Spring." Although the Czechs had not rejected the Warsaw Pact alliance with the Soviet Union, the Brezhnev Doctrine proclaimed that none of the East European states would be allowed to vacate the communist camp.

Preoccupied with his foreign policy debacle in Vietnam, Lyndon Johnson made little progress toward détente, but his successor, Nixon, was keenly interested in improved East-West relations. Nixon's support for détente was ironic, since he had made his reputation in politics as a fervent anticommunist, yet he would achieve a breakthrough in the Cold War. The impetus for détente, however, actually came from European leaders Charles de Gaulle, president of France, and Willy Brandt, the West German chancellor.

Bitterly opposed to the U.S. war in the former French colony of Indochina, De Gaulle excoriated U.S. foreign policy, withdrew France from NATO's integrated military command, and met with Brezhnev in Moscow in 1966. Brandt, a former mayor of West Berlin, pursued a diplomacy of *Ostpolitik* (Eastern policy), improving relations with neighbouring East Germany.

Nixon and Henry A. Kissinger, a refugee from Nazi Germany and a former Harvard professor turned national security adviser, pursued détente in part to prevent the Europeans from undermining Washington's leadership. Nixon and Kissinger also hoped to use improved relations to gain the assistance of Moscow and Beijing in bringing an end to the Vietnam War without the United States suffering a humiliating defeat.

Nixon and Kissinger exploited the Sino-Soviet rift with a "triangular diplomacy" that sought to play off the great communist powers against one another to the betterment of U.S. national interests. After Kissinger travelled secretly to Beijing for talks in 1969, the momentum toward rapprochement (reconciliation) was irreversible. During a dramatic state visit in 1971, Nixon clinked cocktail glasses with Mao Zedong in Beijing and posed for photographers atop the Great Wall of China. The next year the two powers issued the Shanghai Communique, a joint statement that China and the United States would strive to improve their relations and to contain "hegemony," a euphemism for the Soviet Union.

The dramatic "Nixinger" summit diplomacy with the onetime archenemy "Red" China wowed the American public and created anxiety in Moscow. The Kremlin warned the Americans against playing the "China card" but also received Nixon in Moscow in 1972 despite the American mining of Haiphong Harbour in North Vietnam, where Soviet supply ships regularly anchored. The high point of the U.S.–Soviet détente was the signing of the 1972 Strategic Arms Limitation Agreement, known as SALT I.

The treaty established ceilings on offensive missiles and sharply limited destabilizing defensive weapons systems, but it was more important as a political vehicle for improved relations than for its actual achievements in limiting the weapons of mass destruction. Nixon and Kissinger failed completely in their quest to go through China and the Soviets to prevail upon North Vietnam to accept an independent South Vietnam, which instead fell in April 1975.

The momentum of détente began to wane in the mid-1970s. Nixon, its chief architect, met his political demise in the Watergate scandal. With the Soviet Union maintaining its hegemony over Eastern Europe, sponsoring revolutionary movements in the Third World, and denying human rights to many of its own citizens, American critics began to equate détente with appeasement.

In the southwest African nation of Angola, the two superpowers backed competing forces in a raging civil war. Cuban troops, viewed as Soviet "proxies," fought in behalf of leftist rebels in Angola while the United States and China supported the opposition. A Cold War battle also emerged in Ethiopia and throughout the horn of Africa. Soviet and Cuban influence was confined mainly to those two countries, as U.S. trade and diplomacy proved advantageous in several other key African states.

Critics of détente advocated "linkage"— linking trade, arms control, and improved relations with Soviet behaviour in world affairs and in the regime's human rights policies. The Soviets bitterly resented this approach and any effort to influence their internal affairs. They had left themselves vulnerable to such criticism, however, not only by denying freedom of intellectual and religious expression in Russia but by violating pledges to respect human rights embodied in the 1975 Helsinki Accords. Under this agreement, the United States, Soviet Union, and governments throughout Europe recognized current borders as permanent, thus in effect renouncing the old U.S. Cold War depiction of Eastern Europe as a set of "captive nations."

Jimmy Carter, elected president in 1976, advocated arms control but made human rights the centerpiece of his diplomacy and criticized the Soviets for their violations. U.S. relations with China continued to improve, however, a process that culminated in 1979 with formal recognition of Beijing at the expense of the longtime U.S. on Taiwan.

The Japanese, too, expressed dismay at not being consulted about the dramatic shift in U.S. East Asian policy. Détente deteriorated under Carter, who adopted conflicting policies that reflected the conflicting advice he received from Secretary of State Cyrus Vance, an advocate of détente, and national security adviser Zbigniew Brzezinski, a Polish emigré who adopted a harder line toward the Soviets. Carter himself allowed the SALT process to break down. Although a SALT II treaty was negotiated, Carter never took it before the U.S. Senate, where it faced rejection.

Two climactic events in 1979 destroyed détente and ensured Carter's defeat in the 1980 presidential election. First, in November a militant fundamentalist regime in Iran took over the U.S. embassy in Tehran, holding fifty-three Americans hostage. Carter began painstaking negotiations aimed at securing their release, which would not come for more than year.

Meanwhile, the United States appeared helpless as Iranian radicals burned the U.S. flag and shouted "Death to Carter" in daily rituals outside the embassy. In December the Soviet Union launched an invasion of neighbouring Afghanistan, where the pro-Soviet government in Kabul had come under siege. The Soviet assault seemed to confirm critics' charges that détente had been a form of appeasement. Carter declared that Brezhnev had lied to him and instituted a variety of sanctions, including a U.S. boycott of the 1980 Olympic games in Moscow.

Reagan's Cold War

Yet another cycle of Cold War confrontation followed in the wake of the collapse of détente and the foreign policy disasters in Iran and Afghanistan. Like the previous similar waves, this one featured hostile rhetoric, military escalation, little or no diplomacy, and fear of a superpower conflict. What distinguished the new cycle of conflict was the dynamic personality of President Ronald W. Reagan, an inveterate cold warrior who labelled the Soviet Union an "evil empire." A former Hollywood actor and two-term California governor, Reagan declared that the country had grown weak but soon would once again "stand tall" in world affairs. The new president embarked on an enormous campaign of militarization reminiscent of similar spurts following NSC 68 (1950) and in the wake of the "missile gap" controversy in the late 1950s and early 1960s.

U.S.–Soviet relations deteriorated sharply in Reagan's first term. Diplomacy virtually ceased. In March 1983 Reagan stunned the Soviets, and threatened to destabilize the nuclear arms race, by announcing his support for a space-based defensive shield. The president glibly declared that nuclear weapons could be rendered "impotent and obsolete" by developing a perfect defence against incoming ballistic missiles.

The program, known as the Strategic Defence Initiative (SDI), was both costly and a violation of the 1972 treaty limiting defensive systems. The Kremlin feared, however, that the initiative would force the Soviets, already suffering from a badly flagging economy, into a costly new arena of superpower competition. The Kremlin bitterly criticized SDI, launched an offensive missile buildup of its own, and accused the United States of enhancing the threat of another world war.

On 1 September 1983, U.S.–Soviet relations reached their nadir when a Soviet pilot carried out an order to shoot down Korean Airlines Flight 007 en route from Anchorage, Alaska, to Seoul, Korea. The passenger jumbo jet had deviated from its course and flown hundreds of miles into Soviet territory. The Soviet pilot could not distinguish the Boeing aircraft from U.S. reconnaissance jets, which routinely played "chicken" with Soviet forces along their vast border. The Reagan administration claimed that the Kremlin had deliberately destroyed the civilian airliner, which had gone off course as a result of a computer programming error. The Soviets, after remaining silent for days, insisted, apparently truthfully, that they had not recognized the plane as a civilian airliner. The Kremlin charged that the civilian jet clearly had been on a U.S.– and South Korean–backed intelligence mission.

While Reagan unnerved the Soviets, most of the American public supported his policies. Even foreign policy disasters did not undermine the president's appeal. In one such incident in 1983, Reagan dispatched U.S. forces to Lebanon on an uncertain mission to combat "terrorism" and contain Syrian "aggression." The action brought little more than the deaths of 241 U.S. marines from a radical suicide assault on their position.

Reagan also overthrew a leftist government in Grenada by direct invasion and conducted a series of raids against the Libyan dictator Muammar Qaddafi. The most intense arena of the revived Cold War, however, was Central America.

In Nicaragua, the Sandinista rebels, named for a martyred reform leader from the 1930s, came to power in 1979 and launched a socialist government. In neighbouring El Salvador, leftist rebels battled a murderous U.S.-backed military regime. Although Carter had initiated the move to contain the perceived threat, it was Reagan who embarked on an all-out campaign to destroy the left in America's "backyard." While employing every possible means to isolate and economically weaken Castro's Cuba, Reagan sharply increased aid to the Salvadoran military, which allied with "death squads" responsible for executing not only leftist leaders but liberal critics of the government, students, citizens, Catholic priests, and even American churchwomen. The CIA authorized funding for the contras, rebels whose aim was to overthrow the government in Managua. Funded, armed, and trained on U.S. bases in Florida as well as in Honduras, the contras began to fight their way through the Nicaraguan jungles.

Although the United Nations, the Organization of American States, and the World Court condemned the United States for actions such as the illegal mining of Nicaragua's harbors in 1982,

Reagan ignored the world community. Reagan's campaign against the left led to the Iran-Contra scandal, which tarnished his presidency.

The president either authorized illegal actions or failed to exercise supervision over his subordinates—he was not sure himself which had been the case. What became clear was that the administration had secretly sold arms to Iran—officially a terrorist nation with which Washington had refused to conduct diplomacy—as part of a scheme to gain the release of hostages being held in Lebanon as well as to circumvent congressional restrictions on funding for the contra rebels in Nicaragua.

While Reagan remained a popular president, the damage done by the Iran-Contra scandal as well as changes in the Soviet Union prompted him to reconsider his hard-line Cold War policies. Throughout the 1980s, antinuclear protesters in the United States and Europe, as well as liberal and moderate critics, also brought pressure to bear on the White House to pursue an arms-control agreement and a renewal of East-West diplomacy. Some of the president's advisers, including his wife, Nancy, urged him to leave a legacy of peace rather than one simply of zealotry and confrontation.

The Gorbachev Phenomenon

A dynamic new Soviet leader, Mikhail S. Gorbachev, prompted Reagan's turn to moderation. Following the death of Brezhnev in 1982, two more Soviet leaders assumed the helm but died within a short period. Born in 1931, well after the Bolshevik Revolution, Gorbachev represented a new generation of Communist Party leadership in Moscow. Assuming power in 1985, Gorbachev sought to revitalize Soviet society through a series of dramatic reforms. He called the program *perestroika,* or restructuring, a concept that included sweeping economic and social reforms. The Soviet government authorized joint ventures with foreign companies, allowing some free enterprise to emerge in the socialist economy, and lifted restrictions on free speech and intellectual expression. Gorbachev called that reform *glasnost,* or openness.

Decrying the Cold War as dangerous and wasteful, Gorbachev unilaterally reduced Soviet investment in the great-power struggle.

Declaring that intervention in Afghanistan had been a mistake, he pulled out Soviet troops in 1989. Gorbachev implemented sharp cuts in Soviet defence spending, including the withdrawal of tens of thousands of Red Army troops occupying Eastern Europe. Reagan and his advisers reacted with skepticism to Gorbachev's initiatives in world affairs, but the sweeping changes promoted by the charismatic new Russian leader soon became impossible to ignore.

Gorbachev pressed Reagan to join him in bold new diplomatic ventures, and the U.S. president nearly responded at the Reykjavik summit in Iceland in 1986. There the two world leaders flirted with the "zero option"—an agreement to eliminate all nuclear weapons by the year 2000. This breathtaking proposal collapsed, however, over Reagan's refusal to sacrifice research and development of his Strategic Defence Initiative. Despite the summit breakdown, Reagan and Gorbachev had formed a bond, one that led the next year to a successful nuclear arms summit in Washington, D.C. Under the INF Treaty, both sides agreed to dismantle all intermediate range nuclear forces throughout the world. The Soviets agreed to on-site verification of their missile installations, a concession that would not have been possible in the pre-Gorbachev era.

By the time Reagan left office in 1989, the warlike atmosphere he had fostered in the early 1980s was but a distant memory. Both the U.S. and Soviet presidents were calling for an end to the Cold War, but no one envisioned just how sudden, dramatic, and complete that end would be. *Perestroika* and *glasnost* could not help but reverberate beyond Russia's borders.

The sweeping economic reforms and loosening of restrictions on freedom of speech, the press, and artistic and intellectual life unleashed powerful forces that proved impossible to contain. Before they had run their course, the Communist Party regimes would topple throughout Europe and the Soviet Union and the Cold War would come to an end. Skeptics assumed Gorbachev would inevitably respond in the fashion of the Chinese Communist Party, which conducted a bloody crackdown on student demonstrators in June 1989 at Beijing's mammoth Tiananmen Square. The United States condemned the repression at Tiananmen but maintained trade, diplomatic, and cultural ties with the People's Republic of China. U.S. national security elites concluded that continuing dialogue with China was too important to make an issue of the regime's repressive action. Rejecting the Chinese model, Gorbachev concluded that the costs—militarily and politically, and in world opinion—were too high to forcefully maintain Soviet hegemony over Eastern Europe. The Soviet leader stunned Western national security experts by renouncing the Brezhnev Doctrine, which held that the Kremlin would use force to maintain communist regimes.

The End of the Cold War

Once Soviet intervention had been renounced, the people of Eastern Europe took matters into their own hands. Poland had assumed the lead, well before Gorbachev's time, under Lech Walesa and the Solidarity trade-union movement. Similar pro-democracy reform movements emerged in Czechoslovakia and throughout Eastern Europe.

The movement climaxed in 1989 with the sudden dissolution of the Soviet empire. A leader of Solidarity became prime minister of Poland, where a year later the first free elections in sixty-eight years were held to turn out the communists. Soviet troops departed from Hungary, where a new government unearthed the remains of the martyred reform leader Imre Nagy, executed by the Soviets after the 1956 rebellion, in order to give him a burial ceremony with full honors. The poet and playwright Vaclav Havel led the "velvet revolution" in Czechoslovakia. In November 1989 security forces bludgeoned hundreds of protesters in Wenceslas Square in Prague, but even more massive crowds returned on successive days, shouting for an end to communism. The regime came tumbling down.

The most dramatic change came in Berlin, the heart of the nation that had been divided by the Cold War. After the East German authorities announced under pressure that citizens would no longer be prevented from traveling to the western sector of the city, the Berlin Wall, the ultimate symbol of the Cold War, literally crumbled in the hands of crowds of jubilant, hammer-wielding Germans. German reunification soon followed. Contending parties agreed on free elections in Albania and Bulgaria, but the regime of Nicolae Ceausescu in Romania grimly clung to power. In December, after his security police fired into crowds murdering hundreds of protesters, the Romanian army joined forces with the street protesters to topple the regime. Ceausescu and his wife were summarily executed by firing squad on Christmas Day 1989.

Meanwhile, in the Soviet Union itself, the three Baltic states of Estonia, Latvia, and Lithuania, forcibly annexed by Stalin in the 1939 pact with Hitler, demanded independence. All across the vast Eurasian empire, ethnic republics such as Azerbaijan, Belarus, Georgia, Moldavia, Tajikistan, Ukraine, and Uzbekistan rejected the essence of Soviet political life: the central authority of the Kremlin. Gorbachev repeatedly ruled out military intervention against the breakaway republics, but violence erupted in regions throughout the Soviet Union. Finally, in August 1991, on the eve of Gorbachev's planned signing of a new union treaty that would have created a formal confederation, hard-liners effected a coup, placing Gorbachev under house arrest in the Crimea. Protests, led by renegade Russian Communist Party leader Boris Yeltsin, overwhelmed the plotters of the coup after three days of tense standoff.

The collapse of the coup left a changed world in its wake. Gorbachev attempted to return to power after the coup, but in fact— because he was the leader of the discredited Communist Party—he had no real authority left. The Soviet reformer had won the Nobel Peace Prize but had lost the real prize: state power. Yeltsin assumed the Russian presidency under a new democratic system. Russia, and most of the fifteen other republics, rejected the Soviet system, though individual communists could remain engaged in parliamentary politics. The infamous KGB security police assumed a new name and no longer hounded intellectual critics of communism but otherwise remained active. Western Europe and the United States embraced the newly independent East European regimes, even encouraging several to join NATO over the opposition of Yeltsin and many residents of the former Soviet Union.

The United States confronted a world in which the nation's preeminent adversary for almost a half century had suddenly ceased to exist. President George H. W. Bush, who had succeeded Reagan in 1989, reacted cautiously to the dramatic change before declaring the triumph of the United States in the Cold War. The Cold War had been costly and dangerous but had provided a pernicious kind of stability in world affairs. With regional conflicts raging in the former Yugoslavia, Africa, parts of Asia, and in ethnic enclaves of Russia, many wondered if the post–Cold War world might bring even greater instability and uncertainty to world affairs.

Interpreting the Cold War

From the outset of the Cold War, the two adversaries blamed one another for the conflict. For a long time, historians, echoing the patriotic culture of their nations, followed in train. In the Soviet Union, historical interpretation adhered to the rigid Communist Party line, which held the "imperialist" United States responsible for the Cold War. The Americans had tried to strangle the Soviet Union during its infancy and had sought ever since, with the brief interlude of World War II (known there as the Great Patriotic War) to contain Russia by surrounding it with hostile states. The United States and its allies had menaced the Soviet Union with the atomic bomb and had tried to isolate and destroy the "motherland" with their economic power and trade restrictions. The Soviet Union depicted itself as a defensive outpost of progressive reform in a world dominated by ruthless but ultimately doomed capitalist imperialists.

Until a wave of revisionism emerged in the 1960s, historians in the United States interpreted the evolution of the Cold War in orthodox terms: that it was a struggle to contain an expansionist and "totalitarian" Soviet regime. The totalitarian model linked Nazi Germany and the Soviet Union as two ruthless military powers that forced their will upon neighbouring states and employed terror at home against their own people. Like the Soviets, Americans insisted that their actions in the Cold War had been primarily defensive, as the term "containment" suggested. The essential argument, reflected in the language of NSC 68, was that the United States represented the "free world" in a struggle against atheist totalitarianism.

Revisionists of various shades began to emerge in the United States in the late 1950s, reaching their apogee in the wake of the disastrous U.S. intervention in Indochina. Revisionists challenged the patriotic culture with their will-ingness to consider the Soviet point of view. Some argued that economic necessity, specifically the need for foreign markets, determined the direction of U.S. Cold War diplomacy. Revisionists emphasized that the United States, not just the Soviet Union, had been an expansionist power throughout its history. They also underscored the willingness of U.S. national security elites to ally themselves with a host of dictators across the globe, as long as those rulers embraced anticommunism and left their nations open to U.S. economic penetration.

Orthodox interpretations returned with a vengeance with the end of the Cold War and the collapse of the Soviet Union. The triumphalist argument held that the Cold War policies of the United States and its allies had been necessary to contain communism and that they had proven spectacularly successful. Despite the violence of the era, some viewed the Cold War as a "long peace," because, in fact, the superpowers had not gone to war. One scholar went so far as to assert that the end of the Cold War marked the "end of history" insofar as democratic politics and capitalism soon would be embraced by everyone.

Others rejected the triumphalist interpretation of the history of the Cold War as well as the notion that the long struggle had been worth the effort. They argued that the Cold War had been extremely expensive, diverting resources to the respective militaries and away from economic and social development. Moreover, the superpowers typically carried out military conflicts on Third World battlefields, leaving many of those nations divided and wracked by poverty and degradation.

The East-West struggle might have come to an end, but the great divide in wealth and quality of life between North and South had never been greater. Moreover, market reforms failed to revive the Russian economy. Indeed, "shock therapy" brought a sharply lower standard of living for most of the population, which had lost the guaranteed employment and safety net once provided under the Soviet system. In 1999, Yeltsin stepped down for Vladimir Putin, a little known former KGB officer, who became the new Russian president.

Interpretations of the Cold War will continue to evolve as scholars gain access to more evidence and as world events continue to unfold and illuminate fresh perspectives on the past. New archival evidence, made available by the collapse of the former Communist Party regimes, has revealed fascinating insight into Cold War conflicts such as the Korean War and the Cuban missile crisis. Scholars now argue that Third World countries, rather than being mere pawns in the Cold War, often shaped the agenda for their superpower allies. Others argue that the real significance of the Cold War was its impact on science, technology, and culture, including popular culture and consumerism.

By century's end, the Cold War may have been over but many legacies remained. Russian-American and Sino-American relations continued to be strained. Ethnic and regional conflicts simmered across the globe. The threat posed by nuclear, chemical, and biological weapons remained real, whether they might be wielded by terrorists or by so-called outlaw regimes. At the same time, information technology, rapid population growth, and environmental threats such as global warming began to establish an agenda for the new millennium. The efforts of the people of the world and their leaders to meet these challenges would determine the character of the post–Cold War world.

7

Non-Aligned Movement

Non-Aligned Movement

The Non-Aligned Movement (NAM) is an international organisation of states considering themselves not formally aligned with or against any major power bloc. The movement is largely the brainchild of India's first Prime Minister Jawaharlal Nehru, former president of Egypt Gamal Abdul Nasser and Yugoslav president Josip Broz Tito. It was founded in April 1955; as of 2006, it has 118 members. The purpose of the organisation as stated in the *Havana Declaration of 1979* is to ensure "the national independence, sovereignty, territorial integrity and security of nonaligned countries" in their "struggle against imperialism, colonialism, neo-colonialism, racism, and all forms of foreign aggression, occupation, domination, interference or hegemony as well as against great power and bloc politics." They represent nearly two-thirds of the United Nations's members and comprise 55% of the world population, particularly countries considered to be developing or part of the third world.

Members have, at various times, included: Yugoslavia, India, Ghana, Pakistan, Algeria, Bangladesh, Libya, Sri Lanka, Egypt, Indonesia, Cuba, Colombia, Venezuela, post-1994 South Africa, Iran, Malaysia, and, for a time, the People's Republic of China. Brazil has never been a formal member of the movement, but shares many of the aims of NAM and frequently sends observers to the Non-Aligned Movement's summits. While the organisation was intended to be as close an alliance as NATO or the Warsaw Pact, it has little cohesion and many of its members were actually quite closely aligned with one or another of the great powers.

Additionally, some members were involved in serious conflicts with other members (e.g. India and Pakistan, Iran and Iraq). The movement fractured from its own internal contradictions when the Soviet Union invaded Afghanistan in 1979. While the Soviet allies supported the invasion, other members (particularly Islamic nations) of the movement did not.

Because the Non-Aligned Movement was formed as an attempt to thwart the Cold War, it has struggled to find relevance since the Cold War ended. After the breakup of Yugoslavia, a founding member, its membership was suspended in 1992 at the regular Ministerial Meeting of the Movement, held in New York during the regular yearly session of the General Assembly of the United Nations. At the Summit of the Movement in Jakarta, Indonesia (September 1, 1992-September 6, 1992) Yugoslavia was suspended or expelled from the Movement The successor states of the SFR Yugoslavia have expressed little interest in membership, though some have observer status. In 2004, Malta and Cyprus ceased to be members and joined the European Union. Belarus remains the sole member of the Movement in Europe. Turkmenistan, Belarus and Dominican Republic are the most recent entrants. The application of Bosnia-Herzegovina and Costa Rica were rejected in 1995 and 1998.

Origins

Independent countries, who chose not to join any of the Cold War blocs, were also known as non aligned nations.

The term "nonalignment" itself was coined by Indian Prime Minister Nehru during his speech in 1954 in Colombo, Sri Lanka. In this speech, Nehru described the five pillars to be used as a guide for Sino-Indian relations, which were first put forth by Chinese Premier Zhou Enlai. Called Panchsheel (five restraints), these principles would later serve as the basis of the Non-Aligned Movement. The five principles were:

- Mutual respect for each other's territorial integrity and sovereignty
- Mutual non-aggression
- Mutual non-interference in domestic affairs
- Equality and mutual benefit

- Peaceful co-existence.

A significant milestone in the development of the Nonaligned movement was the 1955 Bandung Conference, a conference of Asian and African states hosted by Indonesian president Sukarno. The attending nations declared their desire not to become involved in the Cold War and adopted a "declaration on promotion of world peace and cooperation", which included Nehru's five principles. Six years after Bandung, an initiative of Yugoslav president Tito led to the first official Non-Aligned Movement Summit, which was held in September 1961 in Belgrade.

At the Lusaka Conference in September 1970, the member nations added as aims of the movement the peaceful resolution of disputes and the abstention from the big power military alliances and pacts. Another added aim was opposition to stationing of military bases in foreign countries. The founding fathers of the Nonaligned movement were: Nehru of India, Sukarno of Indonesia and Josip Broz Tito of Yugoslavia, Gamal Abdul Nasser of Egypt and Kwame Nkrumah of Ghana. Their actions were known as 'The Initiative of Five'.

Organisational Structure and Membership

Requirements of the NAM with the key beliefs of the United Nations. The latest requirements are now that the candidate country has displayed practices in accordance with:

- Respect for fundamental human rights and for the purposes and principles of the Charter of the United Nations.
- Respect for the sovereignty and territorial integrity of all nations.
- Recognition of the equality of all races and of the equality of all nations, large and small.
- Abstention from intervention or interference in the internal affairs of another country.
- Respect for the right of each nation to defend itself singly or collectively, in conformity with the Charter of the United Nations.
- Refraining from acts or threats of aggression or the use of force against the territorial integrity or political independence of any country.

- Settlement of all international disputes by peaceful means, in conformity with the Charter of the United Nations.
- Promotion of mutual interests and cooperation.
- Respect for justice and international obligations.

Policies and Ideology

Secretaries General of the NAM had included such diversified figures as Suharto, an authoritarian anti-communist, and Nelson Mandela, a democratic socialist and famous anti-apartheid activist. Consisting of many governments with vastly different ideologies, the NAM is unified by its commitment in world peace and security. At the seventh summit held in New Delhi in March 1983, the movement described itself as the "history's biggest peace movement". The movement places equal emphasis on disarmament. NAM's commitment to peace pre-dates its formal institutionalisation in 1961. The Brioni meeting between heads of governments of India, Egypt and Yugoslavia in 1956 recognised that there exists a vital link between struggle for peace and endeavours for disarmament.

The Nonaligned movement believes in policies and practices of cooperation, especially those that are multilateral and provide mutual benefit to all those involved. Many of the members of the NAM are also members of the United Nations and both organisations have a stated policy of peaceful cooperation, yet successes that the NAM has had in multilateral agreements tends to be ignored by the larger, western and developed nation dominated UN. African concerns about apartheid were linked with Arab-Asian concerns about Palestine and success of multilateral cooperation in these areas has been a stamp of moderate success for the NAM. The NAM has played a major role in various ideological conflicts throughout its existence, including extreme opposition to apartheid regimes and support of liberation movements in various locations including Zimbabwe and South Africa. The support of these sorts of movements stems from a belief that every state has the right to base policies and practices with national interests in mind and not as a result of relations to a particular power bloc. The Nonaligned movement has become a voice of support for issues facing developing nations and is still contains ideals that are legitimate within this context.

Contemporary Relevance

Since the end of the Cold War and the formal end of colonialism, the Nonaligned movement has been forced to redefine itself and reinvent its purpose in the current world system. A major question has been whether many of its foundational ideologies, principally national independence, territorial integrity, and the struggle against colonialism and imperialism, can be applied to contemporary issues. The movement has emphasised its principles of multilateralism, equality, and mutual non-aggression in attempting to become a stronger voice for the global South, and an instrument that can be utilised to promote the needs of member nations at the international level and strengthen their political leverage when negotiating with developed nations. In its efforts to advance Southern interests, the movement has stressed the importance of cooperation and unity amongst member states, but as in the past, cohesion remains a problem since the size of the organisation and the divergence of agendas and allegiances present the ongoing potential for fragmentation. While agreement on basic principles has been smooth, taking definitive action vis-à-vis particular international issues has been rare, with the movement preferring to assert its criticism or support rather than pass hard-line resolutions. The movement continues to see a role for itself, as in its view, the world's poorest nations remain exploited and marginalised, no longer by opposing superpowers, but rather in a uni-polar world, and it is Western hegemony and neo-colonialism that that the movement has really re-aligned itself against. It opposes foreign occupation, interference in internal affairs, and aggressive unilateral measures, but it has also shifted to focus on the socio-economic challenges facing member states, especially the inequalities manifested by globalization and the implications of neo-liberal policies. The nonaligned movement has identified economic underdevelopment, poverty, and social injustices as growing threats to peace and security.

Current Activities and Positions

Criticism of US Policy

In recent years the US has become a target of the organisation. The US invasion of Iraq and the War on Terrorism, its attempts to stifle Iran and North Korea's nuclear plans, and its other actions have been denounced as human rights violations and attempts to run roughshod over the sovereignty of smaller nations. The movement's leaders have also criticised the American control over the United Nations and other international structures. While the organisation has rejected terrorism, it condemns the association of terrorism with a particular religion, nationality, or ethnicity, and recognises the rights of those struggling against colonialism and foreign occupation.

Self-determination of Puerto Rico

Since 1961, the group have supported the discussion of the case of Puerto Rico's self-determination before the United Nations. A resolution on the matter will be proposed on the XV Summit by the Hostosian National Independence Movement.

Anti-Zionism

NAM's Havana Declaration of 1979 adopted anti-Zionism as part of the movement's agenda. The movement has denounced Israel's occupation of the West Bank and Gaza Strip. It has called upon Israel to halt its settlement activities, open up border crossings, and cease the use of force and violence against civilians. The UN has also been asked to pressure Israel and to do more to prevent human rights abuses.

Sustainable Development

The movement is publicly committed to the tenets of sustainable development and the attainment of the Millennium Development Goals, but it believes that the international community has not created conditions conducive to development and has infringed upon the right to sovereign development by each member state. Issues such as globalization, the debt burden, unfair trade practices, the decline in foreign aid, donor conditionalities, and the lack of democracy in international financial decision-making are cited as factors inhibiting development.

Reforms of the UN

The Non-Aligned Movement has been quite outspoken in its criticism of current UN structures and power dynamics, mostly in how the organisation has been utilised by powerful states in ways that violate the movement's principles. It has made a number of recommendations that would strengthen the representation and power of 'nonaligned' states. The proposed reforms are also aimed at improving the transparency and democracy of UN decision-making. The UN Security Council is the element considered the most distorted, undemocratic, and in need of reshaping.

South-south Cooperation

Lately the Non-Aligned Movement has collaborated with other organisations of the developing world, primarily the Group of 77, forming a number of joint committees and releasing statements and document representing the shared interests of both groups. This dialogue and cooperation can be taken as an effort to increase the global awareness about the organisation and bolster its political clout.

Cultural Diversity and Human Rights

The movement accepts the universality of human rights and social justice, but fiercely resists cultural homogenisation. In line with its views on sovereignty, the organisation appeals for the protection of cultural diversity, and the tolerance of the religious, sociocultural, and historical particularities that define human rights in a specific region. Working groups, task forces, committees

- High-Level Working Group for the Restructuring of the United Nations
- Working Group on Human Rights
- Working Group on Peace-Keeping Operations
- Working Group on Disarmament
- Task Force on Somalia
- Non-Aligned Security Caucus
- Standing Ministerial Committee for Economic Cooperation
- Joint Coordinating Committee (chaired by Chairman of G-77 and Chairman of NAM).

India and the Non-Aligned Movement

India played an important role in the multilateral movements of colonies and newly independent countries that developed into the Non-Aligned Movement.

Origin of Nonalignment Movement

Nonalignment had its origins in India's colonial experience and the nonviolent Indian independence struggle led by the Congress, which left India determined to be the master of its fate in an international system dominated politically by Cold War alliances and economically by Western capitalism and Soviet communism.

The principles of nonalignment, as articulated by Nehru and his successors, were preservation of India's freedom of action internationally through refusal to align India with any bloc or alliance, particularly those led by the United States or the Soviet Union; nonviolence and international cooperation as a means of settling international disputes. Nonalignment was a consistent feature of Indian foreign policy by the late 1940s and enjoyed strong, almost unquestioning support among the Indian elite.

The term "Non-Alignment" itself was coined by Indian Prime Minister Jawaharlal Nehru during his speech in 1954 in Colombo, Sri Lanka. In this speech, Nehru described the five pillars to be used as a guide for Sio-Indian relations, which were first put forth by Chinese Premier Zhou Enlai. Called Panchsheel (five restraints), these principles would later serve as the basis of the Non-Aligned Movement. The five principles were:

1. Mutual respect for each other's territorial integrity and sovereignty
2. Mutual non-aggression
3. Mutual non-interference in domestic affairs
4. Equality and mutual benefit
5. Peaceful co-existence.

Jawaharlal Nehru's concept of nonalignment brought India considerable international prestige among newly independent states that shared India's concerns about the military confrontation between the superpowers and the influence of the former colonial powers. New Delhi used nonalignment to establish a significant role for itself as a leader of the Third World in such multilateral organizations as the United Nations (UN) and the Nonaligned Movement. The signing of the Treaty of Peace, Friendship, and Cooperation between India and the Soviet Union in 1971 and

India's involvement in the internal affairs of its smaller neighbours in the 1970s and 1980s tarnished New Delhi's image as a nonaligned nation and led some observers to note that in practice, nonalignment applied only to India's relations with countries outside South Asia.

Early Developments

The movement had its origins in the 1947 Asian Relations Meeting in New Delhi and the 1955 Asian-African Conference in Bandung, Indonesia. India also participated in the 1961 Belgrade Conference that officially established the Nonaligned Movement, but Jawaharlal Nehru's declining prestige limited his influence.

In the 1960s and 1970s, New Delhi concentrated on internal problems and bilateral relations, yet retained membership in an increasingly factionalized and radicalized movement. During the contentious 1979 Havana summit, India worked with moderate nations to reject Cuban president Fidel Castro's proposition that "socialism" (that is, the Soviet Union) was the "natural ally" of nonalignment.

In 1980s

Under Indira Gandhi in the early 1980s, India attempted to reassert its prominent role in the Nonaligned Movement by focusing on the relationship between disarmament and economic development.

By appealing to the economic grievances of developing countries, Indira Gandhi and her successors exercised a moderating influence on the Nonaligned Movement, diverting it from some of the Cold War issues that marred the controversial 1979 Havana meeting. Although hosting the 1983 summit boosted Indian prestige within the movement, its close relations with the Soviet Union and its pro-Soviet positions on Afghanistan and Cambodia limited its influence.

The end of the Cold War left the Nonaligned Movement without its original raison d'être, and its membership became deeply divided over international disputes, strategy, and organization. During the 1992 Jakarta summit, India took a middle position between countries favouring confrontation with developed nations on international economic issues, such as Malaysia, and those that favoured a more cooperative approach, such as Indonesia. Although New Delhi played a minor role compared with Kuala Lumpur and Jakarta on most issues facing the summit, India formulated the Nonaligned Movement position opposing developed countries' linkage of foreign aid to human rights criteria.

Consequences

The early 1990s demise of the bipolar world system, which had existed since the end of World War II, shook the underpinnings of India's foreign policy. The Cold War system of alliances had been rendered meaningless by the collapse of the East European communist states, the dissolution of the Warsaw Treaty Organization (Warsaw Pact), and the demise of the Soviet Union.

In the early 1990s, most colonies had become independent, and apartheid in South Africa was being dismantled, diminishing the value of anticolonialism and making it impossible for antiracism to serve as a rallying point for international political action (India and South Africa restored full diplomatic relations in 1993 after a thirty nine year lapse).

The Panchsheel (Panch Shila), peaceful resolution of international disputes, and international cooperation to spur economic development which was being enhanced by domestic economic reforms were broad objectives in a changing world. Thus, the 1990s saw India redefining nonalignment and the view of India's place in the world.

India also is a founding member of the Group of fifteen, a group of developing nations established at the ninth Nonaligned Movement summit in Belgrade in 1989 to facilitate dialogue with the industrialized countries.

India played host to the fourth Group of Fifteen summit in March 1994. At the summit, Prime Minister Narsimha Rao and other leaders expressed concern over new trade barriers being raised by the industrialized countries despite the conclusion of a new world trade agreement.

Relevance of being 'Nonaligned' and Irrelevance of NAM

Historian Ramachandra Guha has described Jawaharlal Nehru's policy of nonalignment as an attempt to place India "beyond and above the rivalries of Great Powers." While critics would describe nonalignment as utopian and counterproductive, cynics and realists would argue that despite professions of high moral principles, what Nehru was trying to do was to adopt a posture that led to India being wooed by both superpowers — the US and the Soviet Union.

The hard reality is that in 1947 India was economically and militarily weak and needed assistance from both the superpowers. American and British hostility, particularly on Jammu and Kashmir, led to India depending on a Soviet veto in the Security Council.

In return, India was forced to endorse the Soviet invasions of Hungary and Czechoslovakia. But Indian diplomacy was skilfully conducted to ensure continuing Western economic assistance and particularly food aid, at time when our food production could not meet growing demand and our foreign exchange reserves were woefully inadequate.

India today is very different from the India of the Cold War days. We are now recognised as an emerging economic power, no longer dependant on the charity of others for our economic progress. In these circumstances, does it make any sense to cling to old shibboleths and slogans such as "nonaligned solidarity" in a vastly transformed world order?

High Praise for India

Addressing the US-India Business Summit in Washington on June 27, the US Secretary of State, Ms Condoleezza Rice, voiced high praise for India's democratic institutions and the "rise" of India as an emerging economic power.

She observed: "I am happy that India and the US are accomplishing a great deal together these days, but I would say that we are only scratching the surface of what we can do. We, in America, look on the rise of India as an opportunity, a chance to work with a friendly democracy." She added: "India and the

US can work together bilaterally, but multilaterally as well, together with other free countries like Japan, as well, together with other free countries like Australia and (South) Korea and our allies in Europe, working with large multiethnic and multi-religious democracies like Brazil, Indonesia and South Africa."

India is already cooperating and interacting with states extensively within Asia and beyond, through regional groupings such as SAARC and BIMSTEC, multilateral ties with ASEAN and as a participant in the East Asia Summit. It has moved to complement its trilateral dialogue with Russia and China with a new association embracing Australia, Japan and the US.

It is a full-fledged dialogue partner of the European Union and a special invitee to the G-8 summits, joining a select group of emerging economic powers to interact with the most powerful economies.

Moreover, groupings such as the India-South Africa-Brazil partnership are becoming increasingly important in dealing with global economic issues and fostering cooperation between like-minded countries spanning three continents. This association positions India to seek cooperative arrangements with regional groupings such as the Southern African Customs Union (SACU) and the Mercosur in South America.

Ms Rice triggered a controversy in her July 27 speech by asserting that "nonalignment" had lost its meaning after the end of the Cold War and the disintegration of the Soviet Union. She had evidently been irked by the shrill anti-American rhetoric that emerged at the recent Non-Aligned Movemnet Summit in Havana.

This summit is now remembered in India only for the curious assertion, (described by a respected columnist to me as the "Havana Hallucinations,") of the Prime Minister, Dr. Manmohan Singh, that Pakistan, like India, is also a "victim of terrorism".

If Ms Rice failed to draw a distinction between being "nonaligned" and being a member of the "Non-Aligned Movement" (NAM), the External Affairs Minister, Mr Pranab Mukherjee, whose diplomatic skills have been an asset to the conduct of our foreign policy, curiously responded by speaking about NAM rather than "nonalignment". He recalled that the

NAM had played an important role in the process of decolonisation (that ended four decades ago) and the end of apartheid in South Africa (16 years ago). Mr Mukherjee said little about NAM's contemporary relevance, beyond a reference to its importance in promoting "South-South Cooperation".

NAM has little relevance today. Only 52 Heads of Government out of the 118 NAM members bothered to participate in the Havana Summit. Many of the NAM members are economic basket cases, dependant on the West for survival. They invariably bend to Western pressure in multilateral forums such as the World Trade Organisation. Over 50 NAM members figure high in the index of failed states.

The only noteworthy features of the Havana Summit were a return to ritualistic condemnations of Israel and noises of support for Iran's nuclear programme. Interestingly, the nonaligned UN Security Council members which supported Iran's nuclear programme in Havana had no qualms supporting resolutions in the Security Council that imposed sanctions on Teheran for continuing with nuclear enrichment, confirming that 'nonaligned solidarity' rhetoric is farcical.

Similarly, a number of Arab countries which voice strong condemnation of Israel in NAM meetings have no qualms about clandestine ties with Israel on sensitive security issues.

At the 1979 NAM Summit in Havana, radical Arab states sought to have Egypt expelled from the Movement for signing a separate peace agreement with Israel — a move that was rejected. Peace in West Asia is, however, promoted today primarily by the "Quartet" comprising the US, the EU, Russia and the UN, with the peace process based on hard realities and not bombastic NAM rhetoric. And Egypt is no longer threatened by its Arab partners with expulsion from multilateral forums for its links with Israel.

Creditable Foreign Policy

While membership of the NAM does little to promote our national interests in the contemporary world, those who have conducted foreign policy in the post Cold War years deserve credit for the skill with which they have guided an economically resurgent India into partnerships with ASEAN and East Asia, while pressing ahead with plans for economic integration in the neighbourhood through groupings such as SAARC and BIMSTEC.

But India still faces major challenges on issues of terrorism and its quest for energy security in a volatile neighbourhood to its west, at a time when global demand for energy resources is rapidly expanding. A resurgent China appears bent on "containing" India with its nuclear and missile transfers to Pakistan and its quest for naval facilities across the sea lanes of the Indian Ocean. While it would be inadvisable to deal with these challenges through military alliances with distant powers, India has to fashion relationships with powers across the entire Asia-Pacific Region, which promote a stable balance of power in this region.

Non-alignment in the post-Cold War era is still relevant and really means the freedom to choose a wide range of partners to cooperate with on different issues, to protect our national interests. Thus, while being nonaligned gives us the flexibility to choose our partners and partnerships, the Non-Aligned Movement is a forum of little relevance in today's world.

Egypt and the Non-Aligned Movement (NAM)

Egypt is one of the most important founding countries of the Non-Aligned Movement, and has a key role in establishing the movement and realizing its development along with supporting its survival and continuation given Egypt's regional and international status.

Around two-thirds of the United Nations countries are members of the NAM which represents the most important forum for coordinating stances of the developing countries regarding the various political, economic, and social issues on the agenda of the world order.

Egypt had its own contribution in transforming the ideas associated with the NAM to a tangible reality when the movement was first established. Egypt also hosted the second NAM summit in 1964.

And once again Egypt is back to host the events of the 15th summit of the Nam leaders in Sharm el-Sheikh during the period from 11-16 July. It is expected that the summit will be a quantum leap in the march of the Non-Aligned Movement in the 21st century as was the case at Cairo Summit in 1964.

Egyptian vision on the Non-Aligned Movement

Egypt believes that the Non-Aligned Movement represents the most important and broader framework for coordinating stances of the developing countries regarding the various political, economic, and social issues on the agenda of the United Nations along with supporting collective action in the face of unilateral policies, which constitute a challenge facing the third world countries, the majority of them are members of the movement.

Egypt is very much interested in the movement and the need to preserve it for its regional and international influence One of the pillars on which the Egyptian stance on the NAM is based is that the movement had emerged under a bipolar world order. The difference in these circumstances requires developing mechanisms in a way that enable the NAM to contribute-through constructive and realistic stands that are approved by all its members-to international developments.

Egypt has played a key role not only in founding the NAM at the first summit in the Yugoslav capital Belgrade in 1961, but its role started even before the birth of the movement, when Egypt played a leading role in developing the idea of its establishment, and then converted this idea into a significant entity on the ground since the very beginning at the 1955 Bandung Conference.

Egypt believes that the international arena today is witnessing the collapse of the principles on which the Non-Aligned Movement was established. This is an alarming situation, particularly with respect to non-interference in the internal affairs of States, respect of their sovereignty, stability and independence of their decision, and the inadequacy of the national sovereignty and territorial integrity to prevent interference in the internal affairs of States.

More and above internal affairs became a pretext for imposing hegemony on others. All these are massive challenges that require maintaining the movement with rebuilding and promoting its capabilities.

NAM documents and its march assert the role of Egypt in promoting the movement.

This leading Egyptian role in establishing and building the Non-Aligned Movement, in addition to its cultural and political weight, constitutes the basis on which Egypt depends for supporting the movement in the future, through intensifying joint efforts with many countries seeking to support the movement for the development of objectives and mechanisms, and to make them more efficient in dealing with major political, economic and cultural changes in the global arena, especially after the movement shifted from a 25-nation at the first constituent summit to a large entity currently comprising 118 members from Africa, Asia, Europe, and Latin America.

Egypt demonstrates through its active participation of the NAM summits-since founding the movement – its continued interaction and leading role, not only at the regional level, but also at the global one to promote issues of the developing countries to get their fair share at the political and development level in the international arena.

Egypt is acting out of its belief in the importance of the collective action through the support of the United Nations, and its organizations and organs, especially the General Assembly and the rehabilitation and restructuring of the UN Security Council in order to make its resolutions binding to the member states.

Egypt hosted the second NAM summit in 1964 amid a flurry of moves of national independence at the global level, that summit was a quantum leap in the history of the Non-Aligned Movement since its emergence as it moved the movement from the general political framework to the level of fine details and handling issues in depth. Egypt will host during the period from July 11 to 16 the 15th Summit of Heads of State of the Movement to be held in Sharm el-Sheikh with the participation of delegations of more than 140 countries, including 118 members of the movement, which would double Egyptian efforts exerted to support the presence of the movement in the international arena, particularly that Egypt is holding one of the three seats for the leadership of the movement since the Havana Summit in 2006.

By virtue of its membership in the movement's troika Egypt will remain the movement chairman until 2012.. Egypt also undertakes the role of coordinator in two of the six working groups of the movement, namely: the working group on reform of the UN Security Council, and the working group on legal affairs. Choosing Egypt to lead the NAM reflects the Movement 's confidence in the Egyptian diplomacy and respect enjoyed by Egypt at the international level.

Egypt, in its capacity as the chairman of the movement in the coming period, has its own strategic vision on the future of the Movement, and its role on the international arena including more ideas about the movement's action regarding several political and security issues including disarmament, arms control, along with economic issues such as the global financial crisis, and its repercussions on developing countries, and the social, cultural, and legal files, including the issues of human rights and humanitarian assistance, and the dialogue of civilizations.

The most important elements of this vision include the following:

1. Developing and improving the work methods of the movement through a comprehensive review of its role and structure of work so that they would conform with the requirements of our time and even the future in a bid to defend its interests and assume a leading role in the United Nations and world order.
2. Giving high priority to cooperation in the areas which would raise the rates of development in the movement countries and strengthen cooperation among the developing countries and seek to narrow the gap of their stances and achieve their common interests.
3. Consolidating ranks of developing countries in general and the movement in particular, and to strengthen cohesion and solidarity, and to seek once again to negotiate as a one bloc.
4. Undertaking a collective effort by the NAM members at the United Nations with a view to adopting a resolution by the General Assembly banning the use of veto in cases

of genocide, crimes against humanity, with empowering the General Assembly – in case of the failure of the UNSC in carrying out its responsibilities – to undertake the responsibility the Council had been entrusted to undertake and intervene to maintain international peace and security according to the article 24 of the Charter of the Organization.

5. Maintaining coordination among the Non-Aligned Movement and bodies defending the interests of the South, and speaking on behalf of South countries at all international forums, in order to avoid duplication of work.
6. Drafting an international media message that is aimed at identifying the role of the Non-Aligned Movement, and the needs of its members and promoting dialogue and understanding among different civilizations and cultures.
7. Boosting media integration among the members of the Movement, and narrowing the qualitative gap between the North and South, and to support the developing countries through the transfer of technology and knowledge to reach a new international information order based on respect of the freedom of expression, freedom of information, the right of the media men to undertake their job under the respect of the specific values of each society.

8

Detente and the End of Cold War

Détente

Détente is a French term, meaning a relaxing or easing; the term has been used in international politics since the early 1970s. Generally, it may be applied to any international situation where previously hostile nations not involved in an open war de-escalate tensions through diplomacy and confidence-building measures. However, it is primarily used in reference to the general reduction in the tension between the Soviet Union and the United States and a thawing of the Cold War, occurring from the late 1960s until the start of the 1980s.

Causes

The NATO powers and the Warsaw Pact both had pressing reasons to seek relaxation in tensions. Leonid Brezhnev and the rest of the Soviet leadership felt that the economic burden of the nuclear arms race was unsustainable. The American economy was also in financial trouble as the Vietnam War drained government finances at the same time as Lyndon Johnson (and to a lesser extent, Richard Nixon) sought to expand the government welfare state. In West Germany, the Ostpolitik of Willy Brandt was decreasing tensions; the Soviets hoped that with Détente, more trade with Western Europe would be possible. Soviet thinkers also felt that a less aggressive policy could potentially detach the Western Europeans from their American WRC.

Worsening relations with the People's Republic of China, leading to the Sino-Soviet Split, had caused great concern in the Soviet Union. The leadership feared the potential of a Sino-

American alliance against them and believed it necessary to improve relations with the United States. Improved relations with China had already thawed the general American view of communism. Rough parity had been achieved in stockpiling nuclear weapons with a clear capability of mutually assured destruction (MAD). There was also the realization that the "relative gains" theory as to the predictable consequences of war might no longer be appropriate. A "sensible middle ground" was the goal.

Brezhnev and Nixon each hoped improved relations would boost their domestic popularity and secure their power. Several anti-nuclear movements supported détente. The Cuban missile crisis showed how dangerous the relations between the USSR and the USA were becoming. Kennedy and Khruchshev wished to reduce the risk of a nuclear war, as they were aware that the nuclear arsenals on each side granted mutually assured destruction.

Summits and Treaties

The most obvious manifestation of Détente was the series of summits held between the leaders of the two superpowers and the treaties that resulted from these meetings. Earlier in the 1960s, before Détente, the Partial Test Ban Treaty had been signed in 1963. Later in the decade, the Nuclear Non-Proliferation Treaty and Outer Space Treaty were two of the first building blocks of Détente. However, these early treaties did little to curb the superpowers' abilities, and served primarily to limit the nuclear ambitions of third parties that could endanger both superpowers.

The most important treaties were not developed until the advent of the Nixon Administration, which came into office in 1969. The Political Consultative Committee of the Warsaw Pact sent an offer to the West, urging to hold a summit on "security and cooperation in Europe".

The West agreed and talks began towards actual limits in the nuclear capabilities of the two superpowers. This ultimately led to the signing of the SALT I treaty in 1972. This treaty limited each power's nuclear arsenals, though it was quickly rendered out-of-date as a result of the development of MIRVs. In the same year that SALT I was signed, the Biological Weapons Convention and the Anti-Ballistic Missile Treaty were also concluded. Talks on SALT II also began in 1972.

In 1975, the Conference on Security and Cooperation in Europe met and produced the Helsinki Accords, a wide ranging series of agreements on economic, political, and human rights issues. The CSCE was initiated by the USSR, involving thirty-five states throughout Europe. Amongst other issues, one of the most prevalent and discussed after the conference was that of human rights violations in the Soviet Union. The Soviet Constitution directly violated the Declaration of Human Rights from the United Nations, and this issue became a prominent point of separation between the United States and the Soviet Union. The Carter administration had been supporting human rights groups inside the Soviet Union, and Brezhnev accused the administration of interference in other countries' internal affairs. This prompted intense discussion of whether or not other nations may interfere if basic human rights are being violated, such as freedom of speech and religion. The basic disagreement in the philosophies of a democracy and a single-party state did not allow for reconciliation of this issue. Furthermore, the Soviets proceeded to defend their internal policies on human rights by attacking American support of countries like South Africa and Chile which were known to violate many of the same human rights issues.

In July of the same year, the Apollo-Soyuz Test Project became the first international space mission, wherein three American astronauts and two Russian cosmonauts docked their spacecraft and conducted joint experiments. This mission had been preceded by five years of political negotiation and technical cooperation, including exchanges of US and Russian engineers between the two countries' space centres.

Trade relations between the two blocs increased substantially during the era of détente. Most significant were the vast shipments of grain that were sent from the West to the Soviet Union each year, which helped make up for the failure of kolkhoz, Soviet collectivized agriculture.

At the same time, the Jackson-Vanik amendment, signed into law by Gerald Ford on January 3, 1975, after a unanimous vote by both houses of the United States Congress, was designed to leverage trade relations between the U.S. and the USSR, making the United States dependent upon improvements of human rights within the Soviet Union, in particular allowing refusniks to emigrate; it added to the Most Favoured Nation status a clause that provided that no countries resisting emigration could be awarded this status. This provided Jackson with a method of adding some ideological content to détente, linking geopolitics to human rights.

Continued Conflicts

As direct relations thawed, increased tensions continued between the superpowers through their surrogates, especially in the Third World. Conflicts in South Asia, and the Middle East in 1973, saw the Soviet and U.S. backing their respective surrogates with war materiel and diplomatic posturing. In Latin America the United States continued to block any leftward electoral shifts in the region by supporting right wing military coups. During much of the early Détente period, the Vietnam War continued to rage. Neither side trusted the other fully and the potential for nuclear war remained constant. Each side continued to aim thousands of nuclear warheads atop intercontinental ballistic missiles (ICBMs) at each other's cities, maintain submarines with long range nuclear weapon capability (Submarine-launched ballistic missiles or SLBMs) in the world's oceans, keep hundreds of nuclear-armed aircraft on constant alert, and guard contentious borders in Korea and Europe with large ground forces. Espionage efforts remained a high priority as defectors, reconnaissance satellites, and signal intercepts measured intentions and attempted to gain strategic advantage..

End of Détente

The main problem with détente is that there was no clear definition of how friendly and cooperative these two nations were to become. Some historians and politicians have argued that this lack of clarity in the détente relationship was mainly to blame for the collapse of American-Soviet relations at the end of the 1970s. The Soviet invasion of Afghanistan that was to shore up a struggling allied regime led to harsh criticisms in the west and a boycott of the 1980 Summer Olympics, which were to be held in Moscow. American President Jimmy Carter boosted the U.S. defence budget and began financially aiding the President of Pakistan General Muhammad Zia-ul-Haq heavily, who would in turn subsidize the anti-Soviet Mujahideen fighters in the region. The 1980 American presidential election saw Ronald Reagan elected on a platform opposed to the concessions of Détente. Negotiations on SALT II were abandoned.

Detente and the End of the Cold War

During the late 1950s and early 60s both European alliance systems began to weaken somewhat; in the Western bloc, France began to explore closer relations with Eastern Europe and the possibility of withdrawing its forces from NATO. In the Soviet bloc, Romania took the lead in departing from Soviet policy.

U.S. involvement in the Vietnam War in Southeast Asia led to additional conflict with some of its European allies and diverted its attention from the cold war in Europe. All these factors combined to loosen the rigid pattern of international relationships and resulted in a period of detente.

In the 1980s, U.S. President Ronald Reagan revived cold-war policies and rhetoric, referring to the Soviet Union as the "evil empire" and escalating the nuclear arms race; some have argued this stance was responsible for the eventual collapse of Soviet Communism while others attribute it to the inherent weakness of the Soviet state.

From 1989 to 1991 the cold war came to an end with the opening of the Berlin Wall, the collapse of Communist party dictatorship in Eastern Europe, the reunification of Germany, and the disintegration of the Soviet Union.

The End of the Cold War, 1961-1991

Massachusetts Democratic senator John F. Kennedy won the 1960 presidential election partly by assailing the torpor many contemporary observers believed had overcome the Eisenhower administration. The Cold War held dangers as perilous as any conflict in which shots were fired, and Kennedy raised the horrifying specter that the United States might lose: "I think that there is a danger that history will make a judgment that these were the days when the tide began to run out for the United States," Kennedy stated. "These were the times the Communist tide began to pour in" (1). Over the next thirty years, many high officials voiced variations on this theme of dread and threat. Some leading Americans inside and outside of government expressed doubts about the magnitude of the threat posed by communism and the Soviets, while an even greater number considered the cost of the Cold War born by the United States to be too high.

The result was the breakdown of a broad American consensus over the wisdom of a policy of confrontation with the Soviet Union. In the end, of course, the tide ran out on Soviet-style communism.

Surveying the last three decades of the Cold War from the brief period of time that has elapsed since it ended, the following questions stand out.

In ascending order of complexity and controversy, they are: What policies did the participants follow? How and why did these policies alter over time? What effects did the policies of the U.S. and the Soviet Union have on altering the behaviour of their adversary? What effects did the last thirty years of the Cold War have on the political cultures of the United States and the Soviet Union? Did U.S. policies hasten or prolong the end of the Cold War? What did the Cold War cost—financially, economically, culturally and politically? Was the cost worth it?

Answering all of these questions depends on interpretations of the evidence, and the answers given to the last four of them invariably reflect the political and moral values of the interpreter. The last three questions stand at or near the centre of contemporary political discussion.

From the Kennedy administration to the presidency of George Bush, the Cold War alternated between periods of tension—characterized by apocalyptic warnings and anxiety about a devastating nuclear war—and times of detente in which people in both the United States and the Soviet Union believed that the rivalry between the superpowers could be peacefully managed. Under the former scenario, the fate of civilization hung in the balance.

Under the latter, superpower competition might be endless, but each side would refrain from pushing its adversary past the brink of war. Yet throughout these thirty years, neither leaders nor most members of the articulate public anticipated that the end of the Cold War would come the way it did: in relative peace and with the disintegration of the social system of one of the rivals.

The pattern began during the Kennedy administration. The first two years, 1961-1962, saw some of the most hostile confrontations of the Cold War between the United States and its allies and the Soviet Union and its partners.

Kennedy and his principal advisers saw the Cold War as a global competition, and they moved assertively across a broad front. Kennedy authorized the Central Intelligence Agency to proceed with its ill-fated invasion of Cuba in April, and he asked Congress for increases in the budget for both conventional and nuclear forces.

After the failure of the Cuban invasion at the Bay of Pigs, Kennedy approved a CIA plan for a campaign of covert operations against Fidel Castro. He also oversaw an expansion of the activities of American military personnel advising the Army of the Republic of Vietnam. The president and Soviet Communist Party General Secretary Nikita Khrushchev held an unsatisfactory meeting in Vienna in June 1961.

A crisis soon followed over access to Berlin. War loomed as Kennedy told the American public that "we cannot and will not permit the Communists to drive us out of Berlin.... The fulfillment of our pledge to that city is essential to the morale and security of Western Germany, to the unity of Western Europe, and to the faith of the entire free world." A military showdown over the fate of Berlin was averted only after the Soviets surprised the Americans by approving plans of the Communist government of the German Democratic Republic (East Germany) to construct an ugly concrete and barbed wire wall preventing its citizens from fleeing to the West (2).

During the Cuban Missile Crisis of October 1962, the United States and the Soviet Union came closer to nuclear war than at any other time during the Cold War era. The Soviet Union installed intermediate-range ballistic missiles in Cuba in response to frantic pleas from Castro to protect him personally and his government from the CIA's covert operations.

Kennedy characterized the installation of the missiles as "a deliberately provocative and unjustified change in the status quo which cannot be accepted by this country if our courage and our commitments are ever to be trusted again by either friend or foe." The Soviets, confronted by overwhelming military force, agreed to withdraw their missiles (3).

Yet the real prospect of nuclear war with the Soviet Union presented by the Cuban Missile Crisis also moved the Kennedy administration toward a policy of detente with the Soviets. In the wake of the crisis, the two governments opened a telegraphic "hotline," directly connecting the Kremlin with the White House, to be used to defuse tensions in future crises. In June 1963, Kennedy encouraged Americans to "reexamine our attitude toward the Soviet Union" (4). In August of that year, the superpowers signed a treaty banning the testing of nuclear weapons in the atmosphere, under the oceans or in outer space. They promised progress on a treaty banning all nuclear testing and future agreements limiting the growth in the number of nuclear armed missiles possessed by both sides.

Similar alterations between confrontation and detente persisted over the next twenty-five years. Changes in leadership in both the United States and the Soviet Union and the growing U.S. involvement in Vietnam stalled further movement toward detente from November 1963 to the end of 1968. Two years after the missile crises, the Politburo of the Communist Party replaced the humiliated Khrushchev with the dual leadership of Leonid Brezhnev as General Secretary of the Party and Alexei Kosygin as Prime Minister of the Soviet Union.

The new Soviet leadership resolved never to be intimidated again by the United States, and they embarked on a military construction program aimed at gaining parity with the other superpower.

The new American administration of Lyndon B. Johnson became mired in Vietnam, and high officials had little time or intellectual energy to spare on other policy problems. Many U.S. officials believed that the Soviet Union was waging a proxy war against the non-communist world, using North Vietnam as a surrogate. For their part, Soviet leaders expressed similar suspicions that the United States had no real interest in improving relations as long as it fought in Vietnam.

Detente had not died, however. As the sixties progressed, developments in the technology of nuclear weapons and long-range ballistic missiles made both the United States and the Soviet Union feel less secure.

Johnson and Soviet Prime Minister Kosygin met in Glassboro, New Jersey in June 1967, and they promised to negotiate a treaty limiting the growth of ballistic missiles. Johnson anticipated visiting the Soviet Union to sign such a treaty in the fall of 1968, but the Soviet invasion of Czechoslovakia in August of that year once more inhibited movement toward lowering superpower tensions. Johnson called it "a sad commentary on the Communist mind that a sign of liberty in Czechoslovakia is deemed a fundamental threat to the security of the Soviet system".

Despite the invasion of Czechoslovakia, and the continuing conflict in Southeast Asia, detente became a major objective of U.S. policy from 1969 to 1976. Disarray within the Democratic party over foreign affairs helped Richard Nixon win the presidency in 1968.

Democrats split over the war in Vietnam which began to appear to many Americans as peripheral to containment. When Nixon took office he and Henry Kissinger, his national security adviser, sought to "manage" relations with the Soviet Union. Their threefold objectives were to assure a peaceful transition in Soviet status from a regional to a global power; to diminish the American public's obsession with the war in Vietnam; and, as a consequence of the first two, to restore domestic consensus over the value of containment as a unifying foreign policy principle.

Nixon addressed the U.S.-Soviet arms race at his first press conference. He called for a change in U.S. nuclear capability from "superiority" over the Soviet Union, which might foster an arms race, to a "sufficiency" of military strength. Working secretly through a so-called backchannel, Kissinger and Soviet Foreign Minister Andrei Gromyko spent the next three years negotiating agreements on arms control, political relations and trade. Eager to gain favour with voters in the 1972 presidential election year for his foreign affairs acumen, Nixon cautioned Kissinger to delay the announcements of progress on detente until the president met personally with Brezhnev. Otherwise, Nixon feared, "there will be no real news value" to a summit conference.

Nixon met Brezhnev at a highly publicized summit conference to sign agreements on arms control, trade and the future political relations between the two superpowers in May 1972. Other meetings between Nixon and Brezhnev followed in the summers of 1973 and 1974. These regular summits appeared to validate Nixon's and Kissinger's claim that the United States and the Soviet Union had agreed to limit the areas of disagreement between the two countries.

Unfortunately for the hopes of its sponsors, the detente of the 1970s rested on fragile foundations. Critics on both the right and the left of the political spectrum criticized Nixon's and Kissinger's approach. Conservatives argued that the United States yielded too much to the Soviet military in arms control negotiations. Liberals, concerned about the promotion of human rights, stressed that Nixon and Kissinger had done nothing to improve the lot of ordinary Soviet citizens.

Detente also provoked criticism among the Soviet military leadership and ardent communists. They cautioned against the "underestimation of the military danger from imperialism". As a result, the improvement in relations between the United States and the Soviet Union began to unravel in the last year of Nixon's presidency. The two powers disagreed sharply over the October 1973 Middle East War. The growing Watergate scandal distracted Nixon in 1974, and the United States and the Soviet Union did not conclude a full-scale Strategic Arms Limitation Treaty by the end of that year as they had promised.

Detente slipped further during the twenty-nine month presidency of Gerald R. Ford. Domestic American politics thwarted the achievement of an arms control treaty before the election of 1976. Detente as well as Kissinger's and Nixon's approach to world politics became increasingly unpopular. Part of the public feared Soviet ambitions, while another segment of opinion believed that the debacle of involvement in Vietnam had raised the cost of the Cold War out of reach. When former California Governor Ronald Reagan challenged Ford for the Republican presidential nomination, he assailed Ford and his predecessor for underestimating the danger posed by Soviet military power. "Despite concessions granted by our government to the Soviet Union while pursuing detente," Reagan argued, "the Soviets' belligerent attitude toward us and our allies has not changed". Ford became so alarmed by Reagan's criticism that the president ordered all of his subordinates to stop referring to detente.

Democrat Jimmy Carter, the eventual winner of the 1976 presidential election, on the other hand, attacked recent U.S. foreign policy for secrecy, inattention to morality, and a fixation on superpower relations. Carter's criticism of Republican foreign policy during the campaign of 1976 lacked tight focus, and this diffusion bedeviled the foreign policy of his administration.

Carter supported some elements of detente, notably the effort to reduce military tensions between the superpowers. Early in his term he indicated that the Cold War might even be irrelevant beside other more important foreign policy issues, since "we are now free of that inordinate fear of communism that led us to embrace any dictator in that fear." At the same time, Carter's emphasis on the expansion of human rights abroad led him to excoriate Soviet repression at home. These apparently mixed messages confused Soviet leaders who thought that the new U.S. president either lacked foreign policy sophistication or wanted to trap them.

Nevertheless, the United States and the Soviet Union made fitful progress toward arms control from 1977 until the middle of 1979. In June of that year, the two powers signed a treaty setting limits on each sides' ballistic missiles and long-range bombers. Yet six months after the treaty was signed, Carter withdrew it from consideration by the Senate. He did so because Cold War tensions resumed in the latter part of 1979. Americans became fearful of a reassertion of Soviet power in Africa, the Western Hemisphere, and the Middle East. American anxieties increased further after Iranian militants occupied the U.S. Embassy in Teheran, seizing over fifty diplomats and marine guards as hostages in November. Finally, by the end of December, the Soviet Union occupied

Afghanistan, a move which Carter characterized as "the greatest threat to peace since the Second World War".

Ronald Reagan capitalized on public fear of Soviet assertiveness and won the presidency from Jimmy Carter in 1980. Throughout most of his administration, it appeared that the pattern of confrontation and detente of the previous twenty years was to recur. Instead of another turn of an endlessly repeating cycle, however, the 1980s became the final days of the Cold War.

The Reagan administration began by formally declaring detente dead and embarking on the largest peacetime military buildup in U.S. history. In the eight years—from 1981 to 1988—the United States increased spending on the military from about $117 billion per year to approximately $290 billion per year.

"We do not know how much time we have left," Secretary of Defence Caspar Weinberger regularly warned Congress as he argued for approval of the additional appropriations. Reagan employed some of the harshest anti-Soviet rhetoric used by an American official since the early 1960s.

He asserted that Soviet leaders "reserve unto themselves the right to commit any crime, to lie, to cheat." He also reversed John Kennedy's warning of 1960 when he proclaimed in a speech to the British parliament in 1982 that "the Soviet Union runs against the tide of human history". Reagan's strident anticommunism alarmed some Americans and Europeans who feared that war might erupt between the superpowers. During the years 1982 to 1984, some of the largest antiwar demonstrations of the entire Cold War period occurred in cities across Europe and the United States.

Even as he identified in his speech to the British parliament "a great revolutionary crisis" within the Soviet system, Reagan did not predict its imminent collapse. The selection of Mikhail Gorbachev as the new General Secretary of the Communist party of the Soviet Union in March 1985 set in motion the death of Soviet-style communism and the end of the Cold War. Gorbachev quickly recognized that his nation's backward economy could not bear the burden of an arms race with the richer, more technologically advanced United States. Gorbachev and Reagan moved slowly and uneasily toward detente with summit meetings in 1985 in Geneva and Reykjavik. Thereafter, the pace of accommodation quickened markedly.

The two sides concluded an Intermediate Nuclear Forces Treaty in December 1987, eliminating a whole class of ballistic missiles stationed in Europe. Reagan and Gorbachev received hero's welcomes on visits to each other's capitals. "They've changed," the U.S. president replied when a reporter asked if he still considered the Soviet Union the "evil empire" he had called it in 1982.

Americans, Europeans and Soviets realized that the Cold War ended before the Soviet Union ceased to exist. Revolutions swept across Eastern Europe in 1989, and the Berlin Wall came down in November of that year. George Bush, the new American president, who came of age politically during the Cold War, adjusted slowly to its end. He formed a close friendship with Gorbachev by 1990 and backed him in 1991, even to the point of refraining from verbally supporting democrats within the Soviet Union. The U.S. did, however, help Russian president Boris Yeltsin resist a communist coup d'etat in August 1991. Gorbachev resigned on 25 December 1991, and the Soviet Union finally died on 31 December.

Now that the Cold War has ended, the historical postmortems have just begun. The ocean of original documents from U.S. government archives has now been augmented by rivers flowing from previously closed Soviet and Eastern European depositories. This mass of information provides analysts with a basis from which to form answers to the questions raised at the beginning of this essay about the costs and benefits of the Cold War to the societies engaged in it. Those who praise the conduct of American foreign policy believe that the collapse of the Soviet Union validates the actions of U.S. officials and makes the costs of the Cold War worthwhile.

Yet this celebration of the intelligence, judgment and competence of the practitioners of recent U.S. foreign policy is not the final word. Some critics of American diplomacy claimed that the Cold War might have ended sooner, at less cost to all participants had the United States pursued more creative and less confrontational policies. The end of conflict with the Soviet Union coincided with a time of profound domestic anxiety inside the United States. As Americans confronted a disorderly world and a fractious society, some observers argued that the Cold War delayed badly needed domestic reforms and damaged the U.S. economy. Several political candidates during the 1992 presidential campaign noted the excessive cost of the Cold War when they proclaimed: "The Cold War is over. Japan won." Bill Clinton, the victorious candidate in 1992, implied that America's apparent victory in the Cold War had strained the country's resources when he declared the day after his election that he would "focus like a laser on the economy. Foreign policy in large measure will come into play as it affects the economy".

Earlier postwar periods experienced similar fears of the future leading to reevaluations of the recent past. Whatever synthesis develops over the virtues of the policy of containment, the competence of officials, or the wisdom of the general public, the Cold War remains one of the premier forces in defining the contours of the history of the second half of the twentieth century.

9

United Nations

Introduction

The United Nations Organization (UNO) or simply United Nations (UN) is an international organization whose stated aims are facilitating cooperation in international law, international security, economic development, social progress, human rights, and the achieving of world peace. The UN was founded in 1945 after World War II to replace the League of Nations, to stop wars between countries, and to provide a platform for dialogue. It contains multiple subsidiary organizations to carry out its missions.

There are currently 192 member states, including nearly every sovereign state in the world. From its offices around the world, the UN and its specialized agencies decide on substantive and administrative issues in regular meetings held throughout the year. The organization is divided into administrative bodies, primarily: the General Assembly (the main deliberative assembly); the Security Council (for deciding certain resolutions for peace and security); the Economic and Social Council (for assisting in promoting international economic and social cooperation and development); the Secretariat (for providing studies, information, and facilities needed by the UN); the International Court of Justice (the primary judicial organ). Additional bodies deal with the governance of all other UN System agencies, such as the World Health Organization (WHO), the World Food Programme (WFP) and United Nations Children's Fund (UNICEF). The UN's most visible public figure is the Secretary-General, currently Ban Ki-moon of South Korea, who attained the post in 2007. The organization is financed from assessed and voluntary contributions from its member states, and has six official languages: Arabic, Chinese, English, French, Russian and Spanish.

History

Following in the wake of the failed League of Nations (1919–1946), which the United States never joined, the United Nations was established in 1945 to maintain international peace and promote cooperation in solving international economic, social and humanitarian problems. The earliest concrete plan for a new world organization was begun under the aegis of the U.S. State Department in 1939.

Franklin D. Roosevelt first coined the term 'United Nations' as a term to describe the Allied countries. The term was first officially used on January 1, 1942 when 26 governments signed the Atlantic Charter, pledging to continue the war effort. On 25 April 1945, the UN Conference on International Organization began in San Francisco, attended by 50 governments and a number of non-governmental organizations involved in drafting the Charter of the United Nations.

The UN officially came into existence on 24 October 1945 upon ratification of the Charter by the five permanent members of the Security Council—France, the Republic of China, the Soviet Union, the United Kingdom and the United States—and by a majority of the other 46 signatories. The first meetings of the General Assembly, with 51 nations represented, and the Security Council, took place in Westminster Central Hall in London in January 1946.

Since its creation, there has been controversy and criticism of the UN organization. In the United States, an early opponent of the UN was the John Birch Society, which began a "get US out of the UN" campaign in 1959, charging that the UN's aim was to establish a "One World Government." After the Second World War, the French Committee of National Liberation was late to be recognized by the US as the government of France, and so the country was initially excluded from the conferences that aimed at creating the new organization. Charles de Gaulle criticized the UN, famously calling it *le machin* ("the thingie"), and was not convinced that a global security alliance would help maintaining world peace, preferring direct defence treaties between countries.

Organization

The United Nations system is based on five principal organs (formerly six – the Trusteeship Council suspended operations in 1994); the General Assembly, the Security Council, the Economic and Social Council (ECOSOC), the Secretariat, and the International Court of Justice.

Four of the five principal organs are located at the main United Nations headquarters located on international territory in New York City. The International Court of Justice is located in The Hague, while other major agencies are based in the UN offices at Geneva, Vienna, and Nairobi. Other UN institutions are located throughout the world.

The six official languages of the United Nations, used in intergovernmental meetings and documents, are Arabic, Chinese, English, French, Russian, and Spanish, while the Secretariat uses two working languages, English and French. Five of the official languages were chosen when the UN was founded; Arabic was added later in 1973. The United Nations Editorial Manual states that the standard for English language documents is British usage and Oxford spelling (en-gb-oed), and the Chinese writing standard is Simplified Chinese. This replaced Traditional Chinese in 1971 when the UN representation of China was changed from the Republic of China to People's Republic of China.

General Assembly

The General Assembly is the main deliberative assembly of the United Nations. Composed of all United Nations member states, the assembly meets in regular yearly sessions under a president elected from among the member states. Over a two-week period at the start of each session, all members have the opportunity to address the assembly. Traditionally, the Secretary-General makes the first statement, followed by the president of the assembly. The first session was convened on 10 January 1946 in the Westminster Central Hall in London and included representatives of 51 nations.

When the General Assembly votes on important questions, a two-thirds majority of those present and voting is required. Examples of important questions include: recommendations on peace and security; election of members to organs; admission, suspension, and expulsion of members; and, budgetary matters. All other questions are decided by majority vote. Each member country has one vote. Apart from approval of budgetary matters, resolutions are not binding on the members. The Assembly may make recommendations on any matters within the scope of the UN, except matters of peace and security that are under Security Council consideration.

Conceivably, the one state, one vote power structure could enable states comprising just eight percent of the world population to pass a resolution by a two-thirds vote. However, as no more than recommendations, it is difficult to imagine a situation in which a recommendation by member states constituting just eight percent of the world's population, would be adhered to by the remaining ninety-two percent of the population, should they object.

Security Council

The Security Council is charged with maintaining peace and security among countries. While other organs of the United Nations can only make 'recommendations' to member governments, the Security Council has the power to make binding decisions that member governments have agreed to carry out, under the terms of Charter Article 25. The decisions of the Council are known as United Nations Security Council resolutions.

The Security Council is made up of 15 member states, consisting of 5 permanent members – China, France, Russia, the United Kingdom and the United States – and 10 non-permanent members, currently Austria, Burkina Faso, Costa Rica, Croatia, Japan, Libya, Mexico, Turkey, Uganda, and Vietnam. The five permanent members hold veto power over substantive but not procedural resolutions allowing a permanent member to block adoption but not to block the debate of a resolution unacceptable to it. The ten temporary seats are held for two-year terms with member states voted in by the General Assembly on a regional basis. The presidency of the Security Council is rotated alphabetically each month, and is held by Burkina Faso for the month of December 2009.

Secretariat

The United Nations Secretariat is headed by the Secretary-

General, assisted by a staff of international civil servants worldwide. It provides studies, information, and facilities needed by United Nations bodies for their meetings. It also carries out tasks as directed by the UN Security Council, the UN General Assembly, the UN Economic and Social Council, and other UN bodies. The United Nations Charter provides that the staff be chosen by application of the "highest standards of efficiency, competence, and integrity," with due regard for the importance of recruiting on a wide geographical basis.

The Charter provides that the staff shall not seek or receive instructions from any authority other than the UN. Each UN member country is enjoined to respect the international character of the Secretariat and not seek to influence its staff. The Secretary-General alone is responsible for staff selection.

The Secretary-General's duties include helping resolve international disputes, administering peacekeeping operations, organizing international conferences, gathering information on the implementation of Security Council decisions, and consulting with member governments regarding various initiatives. Key Secretariat offices in this area include the Office of the Coordinator of Humanitarian Affairs and the Department of Peacekeeping Operations. The Secretary-General may bring to the attention of the Security Council any matter that, in his or her opinion, may threaten international peace and security.

Secretary-General

The Secretariat is headed by the Secretary-General, who acts as the *de facto* spokesman and leader of the UN. The current Secretary-General is Ban Ki-moon, who took over from Kofi Annan in 2007 and will be eligible for reappointment when his first term expires in 2011.

Envisioned by Franklin D. Roosevelt as a "world moderator", the position is defined in the UN Charter as the organization's "chief administrative officer", but the Charter also states that the Secretary-General can bring to the Security Council's attention "any matter which in his opinion may threaten the maintenance of international peace and security", giving the position greater scope for action on the world stage. The position has evolved into a dual role of an administrator of the UN organization, and a diplomat and mediator addressing disputes between member states and finding consensus to global issues.

The Secretary-General is appointed by the General Assembly, after being recommended by the Security Council. The selection can be vetoed by any member of the Security Council, and the General Assembly can theoretically override the Security Council's recommendation if a majority vote is not achieved, although this has not happened so far.

There are no specific criteria for the post, but over the years it has become accepted that the post shall be held for one or two terms of five years, that the post shall be appointed on the basis of geographical rotation, and that the Secretary-General shall not originate from one of the five permanent Security Council member states.

International Court of Justice

The International Court of Justice (ICJ), located in The Hague, Netherlands, is the primary judicial organ of the United Nations. Established in 1945 by the United Nations Charter, the Court began work in 1946 as the successor to the Permanent Court of International Justice. The Statute of the International Court of Justice, similar to that of its predecessor, is the main constitutional document constituting and regulating the Court.

It is based in the Peace Palace in The Hague, Netherlands, sharing the building with the Hague Academy of International Law, a private centre for the study of international law. Several of the Court's current judges are either alumni or former faculty members of the Academy. Its purpose is to adjudicate disputes among states. The court has heard cases related to war crimes, illegal state interference and ethnic cleansing, among others, and continues to hear cases.

A related court, the International Criminal Court (ICC), began operating in 2002 through international discussions initiated by the General Assembly. It is the first permanent international court charged with trying those who commit the most serious crimes under international law, including war crimes and genocide. The ICC is functionally independent of the UN in terms of personnel and financing, but some meetings of the ICC governing body, the Assembly of States Parties to the Rome Statute, are held at the UN.

There is a "relationship agreement" between the ICC and the UN that governs how the two institutions regard each other legally.

Economic and Social Council

The Economic and Social Council (ECOSOC) assists the General Assembly in promoting international economic and social cooperation and development. ECOSOC has 54 members, all of which are elected by the General Assembly for a three-year term. The president is elected for a one-year term and chosen amongst the small or middle powers represented on ECOSOC. ECOSOC meets once a year in July for a four-week session. Since 1998, it has held another meeting each April with finance ministers heading key committees of the World Bank and the International Monetary Fund (IMF). Viewed separate from the specialized bodies it coordinates, ECOSOC's functions include information gathering, advising member nations, and making recommendations. In addition, ECOSOC is well-positioned to provide policy coherence and coordinate the overlapping functions of the UN's subsidiary bodies and it is in these roles that it is most active.

Specialized institutions

There are many UN organizations and agencies that function to work on particular issues. Some of the most well-known agencies are the International Atomic Energy Agency, the Food and Agriculture Organization, UNESCO (United Nations Educational, Scientific and Cultural Organization), the World Bank and the World Health Organization.

It is through these agencies that the UN performs most of its humanitarian work. Examples include mass vaccination programmes (through the WHO), the avoidance of famine and malnutrition (through the work of the WFP) and the protection of vulnerable and displaced people (for example, by the HCR).

The United Nations Charter stipulates that each primary organ of the UN can establish various specialized agencies to fulfil its duties.

Membership

With the addition of Montenegro on 28 June 2006, there are currently 192 United Nations member states, including all fully recognized independent states apart from Vatican City (the Holy See, which holds sovereignty over the state of Vatican City, is a permanent observer).

The United Nations Charter outlines the rules for membership:

1. Membership in the United Nations is open to all other peace-loving states which accept the obligations contained in the present Charter and, in the judgment of the Organization, are able and willing to carry out these obligations.
2. The admission of any such state to membership in the United Nations will be effected by a decision of the General Assembly upon the recommendation of the Security Council.

Group of 77

The Group of 77 at the UN is a loose coalition of developing nations, designed to promote its members' collective economic interests and create an enhanced joint negotiating capacity in the United Nations. There were 77 founding members of the organization, but the organization has since expanded to 130 member countries. The group was founded on 15 June 1964 by the "Joint Declaration of the Seventy-Seven Countries" issued at the United Nations Conference on Trade and Development (UNCTAD). The first major meeting was in Algiers in 1967, where the *Charter of Algiers* was adopted and the basis for permanent institutional structures was begun.

Functions

Peacekeeping and Security

The UN, after approval by the Security Council, sends peacekeepers to regions where armed conflict has recently ceased or paused to enforce the terms of peace agreements and to discourage combatants from resuming hostilities. Since the UN does not maintain its own military, peacekeeping forces are voluntarily provided by member states of the UN. The forces, also called the "Blue Helmets", who enforce UN accords are awarded United Nations Medals, which are considered international decorations instead of military decorations. The peacekeeping force as a whole received the Nobel Peace Prize in 1988. The founders of the UN had envisaged that the organization would act to prevent conflicts between nations and make future wars impossible, however the outbreak of the Cold War made peacekeeping agreements extremely difficult because of the division of the world into hostile camps. Following the end of the Cold War, there were renewed calls for the UN to become the agency for achieving world peace, as there are several dozen ongoing conflicts that continue to rage around the globe.

A 2005 RAND Corp study found the UN to be successful in two out of three peacekeeping efforts. It compared UN nation-building efforts to those of the United States, and found that seven out of eight UN cases are at peace, as compared with four out of eight US cases at peace. Also in 2005, the Human Security Report documented a decline in the number of wars, genocides and human rights abuses since the end of the Cold War, and presented evidence, albeit circumstantial, that international activism—mostly spearheaded by the UN—has been the main cause of the decline in armed conflict since the end of the Cold War. Situations where the UN has not only acted to keep the peace but also occasionally intervened include the Korean War (1950–1953), and the authorization of intervention in Iraq after the Persian Gulf War in 1990.

The UN has also drawn criticism for perceived failures. In many cases, member states have shown reluctance to achieve or enforce Security Council resolutions, an issue that stems from the UN's intergovernmental nature—seen by some as simply an association of 192 member states who must reach consensus, not an independent organization. Disagreements in the Security Council about military action and intervention are seen as having failed to prevent the 1994 Rwandan Genocide, failed to provide humanitarian aid and intervene in the Second Congo War, failed to intervene in the 1995 Srebrenica massacre and protect a refugee haven by the authorizing the peacekeepers to use force, failure to deliver food to starving people in Somalia, failure to implement provisions of Security Council resolutions related to the Israeli-Palestinian conflict, and continuing failure to prevent genocide or provide assistance in Darfur. UN peacekeepers have also been accused of child rape, sexual abuse or soliciting prostitutes during various peacekeeping missions, starting in 2003, in the Congo, Haiti, Liberia, Sudan, Burundi and Côte d'Ivoire. In 2004, former Israeli ambassador to the UN Dore Gold criticized what it called the organization's moral relativism in the face of (and occasional support of) genocide and terrorism that occurred between the moral clarity of its founding period and the present day. Gold specifically mentions Yasser Arafat's 1988 invitation to address the General Assembly as a low point in the UN's history.

In addition to peacekeeping, the UN is also active in encouraging disarmament. Regulation of armaments was included in the writing of the UN Charter in 1945 and was envisioned as a way of limiting the use of human and economic resources for the creation of them. However, the advent of nuclear weapons came only weeks after the signing of the charter and immediately halted concepts of arms limitation and disarmament, resulting in the first resolution of the first ever General Assembly meeting calling for specific proposals for "the elimination from national armaments of atomic weapons and of all other major weapons adaptable to mass destruction". The principal forums for disarmament issues are the General Assembly First Committee, the UN Disarmament Commission, and the Conference on Disarmament, and considerations have been made of the merits of a ban on testing nuclear weapons, outer space arms control, the banning of chemical weapons and land mines, nuclear and conventional disarmament, nuclear-weapon-free zones, the reduction of military budgets, and measures to strengthen international security.

The UN is one of the official supporters of the World Security Forum, a major international conference on the effects of global catastrophes and disasters, taking place in the United Arab Emirates, in October 2008.

Role of the United Nations

As the most representative inter-governmental organization of the world today, the United Nations' role in world affairs is irreplaceable by any other international or regional organizations. The United Nations has made enormous positive contributions in maintaining international peace and security, promoting cooperation among states and international development. Today, people of the world still face the two major issues of peace and development. Only by international cooperation can mankind meet the challenges of the global and regional issues. The United Nations can play a pivotal and positive role in this regard. Strengthening the role of the United Nations in the new century and promoting the establishment of a just and reasonable international political and economic order goes along with the trend of history and is in the interest of all nations.

In order to strengthen the role of the United Nations, efforts should be made to uphold the purposes and principles of the Charter of the United Nations. The authority of the Security Council in maintaining international peace and security must be preserved and role of the United Nations in development area should be strengthened. To strengthen the role of the United Nations, it is essential to ensure to all Member States of the United Nations the right to equal participation in international affairs and the rights and interests of the developing countries should be safeguarded.

Objectives and Strategy-United Nations

Declaration of the Rights of Mentally Retarded Persons, 20 December 1971

The General Assembly,

Proclaims this Declaration on the Rights of Mentally Retarded Persons and calls for national and international action to ensure that it will be used as a common basis and frame of reference for the protection of these rights:

1. The mentally retarded person has, to the maximum degree of feasibility, the same rights as other human beings.
2. The mentally retarded person has a right to proper medical care and physical therapy and to such education, training, rehabilitation and guidance as will enable him to develop his ability and maximum potential.
3. The mentally retarded person has a right to economic security and to a decent standard of living. He has a right to perform productive work or to engage in any other meaningful occupation to the fullest possible extent of his capabilities.

Declaration on the Rights of Disabled Persons, 9 December 1975

The General Assembly,

Proclaims this Declaration on the Rights of Disabled Persons and calls for national and international action to ensure that it will be used as a common basis and frame of reference for the protection of these rights:

1. The term "disabled person" means any person unable to ensure by himself or herself, wholly or partly, the necessities of a normal individual and/or social life, as a result of deficiency, either congenital or not, in his or her physical or mental capabilities.
2. Disabled persons shall enjoy all the rights set forth in this Declaration. These rights shall be granted to all disabled persons without any exception whatsoever and without distinction or discrimination on the basis of race, colour, sex, language, religion, political or other opinions, national or social origin, state of wealth, birth or any other situation applying either to the disabled person himself or herself or to his or her family.
3. Disabled persons have the inherent right to respect for their human dignity. Disabled persons, whatever the origin, nature and seriousness of their handicaps and disabilities, have the same fundamental rights as their fellow-citizens of the same age, which implies first and foremost the right to enjoy a decent life, as normal and full as possible.
4. Disabled persons have the same civil and political rights as other human beings; paragraph 7 of the Declaration on the Rights of Mentally Retarded Persons applies to any possible limitation or suppression of those rights for mentally disabled persons.
5. Disabled persons are entitled to the measures designed to enable them to become as self-reliant as possible.
6. Disabled persons have the right to medical, psychological and functional treatment, including prosthetic and orthetic appliances, to medical and social rehabilitation, education, vocational training and rehabilitation, aid, counselling,

placement services and other services which will enable them to develop their capabilities and skills to the maximum and will hasten the processes of their social integration or reintegration.

7. Disabled persons have the right to economic and social security and to a decent level of living. They have the right, according to their capabilities, to secure and retain employment or to engage in a useful, productive and remunerative occupation and to join trade unions.
8. Disabled persons are entitled to have their special needs taken into consideration at all stages of economic and social planning.
9. Disabled persons have the right to live with their families or with foster parents and to participate in all social, creative or recreational activities. No disabled person shall be subjected, as far as his or her residence is concerned, to differential treatment other than that required by his or her condition or by the improvement which he or she may derive therefrom. If the stay of a disabled person in a specialized establishment is indispensable, the environment and living conditions therein shall be as close as possible to those of the normal life of a person of his or her age.
10. Disabled persons shall be protected against all exploitation, all regulations and all treatment of a discriminatory, abusive or degrading nature.
11. Disabled persons shall be able to avail themselves of qualified legal aid when such aid proves indispensable for the protection of their persons and property. If judicial proceedings are instituted against them, the legal procedure applied shall take their physical and mental condition fully into account.
12. Organizations of disabled persons may be usefully consulted in all matters regarding the rights of disabled persons.
13. Disabled persons, their families and communities shall be fully informed, by all appropriate means, of the rights contained in this Declaration.

Resolution on the International Year for Disabled Persons, 16 December 1976

The General Assembly,

1. Proclaims the year 1981 International Year for Disabled Persons, with the theme "full participation";
2. Decides to devote that year to the realization of a set of objectives, including:
   a. Helping disabled persons in their physical and psychological adjustment to society;
   b. Promoting all national and international efforts to provide disabled persons with proper assistance, training, care and guidance, to make available to the opportunities for suitable work and to ensure their full integration in society;
   c. Encouraging study and research projects designed to facilitate the practical participation of disabled persons in daily life, for example by improving their access to public buildings and transportation systems;
   d. Educating and informing the public of the rights of disabled persons to participate in and contribute to various aspects of economic, social and political life;
   e. Promoting effective measures for the prevention of disability and for the rehabilitation of disabled persons;
3. Invites all Member States and the organizations concerned to give their attention to the establishment of measures and programmes to implement the objectives of the International Year for Disabled Persons;

World Programme of Action Concerning Disabled Persons, 3 December 1982

Objectives, Background and Concepts

Objectives: The purpose of the World Programme of Action concerning Disabled Persons is to promote effective measures for prevention of disability, rehabilitation and the realization of the goals of 'full participation' of disabled persons in social life and development, and of 'equality'. This means opportunities equal to those of the whole population and an equal share in the improvement in living conditions resulting from social and economic development. These concepts should apply with the same scope and with the same urgency to all countries, regardless of their level of development.

Rehabilitation: Rehabilitation usually includes the following types of services:

- Early detection, diagnosis and intervention;
- Medical care and treatment;
- Social, psychological and other types of counselling and assistance;
- Training in self-care activities, including mobility, communication and daily living skills, with special provisions as needed, e g., for the hearing impaired, the visually impaired and the mentally retarded;
- Provision of technical and mobility aids and other devices;
- Specialized education services;
- Vocational rehabilitation services (including vocational guidance), vocational training, placement in open or sheltered employment;
- Follow-up.

In all rehabilitation efforts, emphasis should be placed on the abilities of the individual, whose integrity and dignity must be respected. The normal development and maturation process of disabled children should be given the maximum attention. The capacities of disabled adults to perform work and other activities should be utilized.

Important resources for rehabilitation exist in the families of disabled persons and in their communities. In helping disabled persons, every effort should be made to keep their families together, to enable them to live in their own communities and to support family and community groups who are working with this objective. In planning rehabilitation and supportive programmes, it is essential to take into account the customs and structures of the family and community and to promote their abilities to respond to the needs of the disabled individual.

Services for disabled persons should be provided, whenever possible, within the existing social, health, education and labour structures of society. These include all levels of health care; primary, secondary and higher-education, general programmes of vocational training and placement in employment; and measures of social security and social services. Rehabilitation services are aimed at facilitating the participation of disabled persons in regular community services and activities. Rehabilitation should take place in the natural environment, supported by community-based services and specialized institutions. Large institutions should be avoided. Specialized institutions, where they are necessary, should be organized so as to ensure an early and lasting integration of disabled persons into society.

Rehabilitation programmes should make it possible for disabled persons to take part in designing and organizing the services that they and their families consider necessary. Procedures for the participation of disabled persons in the decision-making relating to their rehabilitation should be provided for within the system. When people such as the severely mentally disabled may not be able to represent themselves adequately in decisions affecting their lives, family members or legally designated agents should take part in planning and decision-making.

Efforts should be increased to develop rehabilitation services integrated in other services and make them more readily available. These should not rely on imported costly equipment, raw material and technology. The transfer of technology among nations should be enhanced and should concentrate on methods that are functional and relate to prevailing conditions.

Equalization of Opportunities

To achieve the goals of "full participation and equality", rehabilitation measures aimed at the disabled individual are not sufficient. Experience shows that it is largely the environment which determines the effect of an impairment or a disability on a person`s daily life. A person is handicapped when he or she is denied the opportunities generally available in the community that are necessary for the fundamental elements of living, including family life, education, employment, housing, financial and personal security, participation in social and political groups, religious activity, intimate and sexual relationships, access to public facilities, freedom of movement and the general style of daily living.

Societies sometimes cater only to people who are in full possession of all their physical and mental faculties. They have to recognize the fact that, despite preventive efforts, there will always be a number of people with impairments and disabilities, and that societies have to identify and remove obstacles to their full participation. Thus, whenever pedagogically possible, education should take place in the ordinary school system, work be provided through open employment and housing be made available as to the population in general. It is the duty of every Government to ensure that the benefits of development programmes also reach disabled citizens. Measures to this effect should be incorporated into the general planning process and the administrative structure of every society. Extra services which disabled persons might need should, as far as possible, be part of the general services of a country.

The above does not apply merely to Governments. Anyone in charge of any kind of enterprise should make it accessible to people with disabilities. This applies to public agencies at various levels, to non-governmental organizations, to firms and to private individuals. It also applies to the international level. People with permanent disabilities who are in need of community support services, aids and equipment to enable them to live as normally as possible both at home and in the community should have access to such services. Those who live with such disabled persons and help them in their daily activities should themselves receive support to enable them to have adequate rest and relaxation and an opportunity to take care of their own needs

The principle of equal rights for the disabled and non-disabled implies that the needs of each and every individual are of equal importance, that these needs must be made the basis for the planning of societies, and that all resources must be employed in such a way as to ensure, for every individual, equal opportunity for participation. Disability policies should ensure the access of the disabled to all community services. As disabled persons have equal rights, they also have equal obligations. It Is their duty to take part in the building of society. Societies must raise the level of expectation as far as disabled persons are concerned, and in so doing mobilize their full resources for social change. This means, among other things, that young disabled persons should be provided with career and vocational opportunities-not early retirement pensions or public assistance.

Persons with disabilities should be expected to fulfil their role in society and meet their obligations as adults. The image of disabled persons depends on social attitudes based on different factors that may be the greatest barrier to participation and equality. We see the disability, shown by the white caner crutches, hearing aids and wheelchairs, but not the person. What is required is to focus on the ability, not on the disability of disabled persons. All over the world, disabled persons have started to unite in organizations as advocates for their own rights to influence decision-makers in Governments and all sectors of society. The role of these organizations includes providing a voice of their own, identifying needs, expressing views on priorities, evaluating services and advocating change and public awareness. As a vehicle of self-development, these organizations provide the opportunity to develop skills in the negotiation process, organizational abilities, mutual support, information-sharing and often vocational skills and opportunities. In view of their vital importance in the process of participation, it is imperative that their development be encouraged.

Mentally handicapped people are now beginning to demand a voice of their own and insisting on their right to take part in decision-making and discussion. Even those with limited communication skills have shown themselves able to express their point of view. In this respect, they have much to learn from the self-advocacy movement of persons with other disabilities. This development should be encouraged.

Information should be prepared and disseminated to improve the situation of disabled persons. The cooperation of all public media should be sought to bring about presentations that will promote an understanding of the rights of disabled persons aimed at the public and the persons with disabilities themselves, and that will avoid reinforcing traditional stereotypes and prejudices.

10

Regional Organizations

Introduction

Regional Organisations (ROs) are in a sense, international organizations (IOs), as they incorporate international membership and encompass geopolitical entities that operationally transcend a single nation state. However, their membership is characterized by boundaries and demarcations characteristic to a defined and unique geography, such as continents, or geopolitics, such as economic blocks. They have been established to foster cooperation and political and economic integration or dialogue amongst states or entities within a restrictive geographical or geopolitical boundary. They both reflect common patters of development and history that have been fostered since the end of World War II as well as the fragmentation inherent in globalization. Most ROs tend to work alongside well-established multilateral organizations such as the United Nations. While in many instances a regional organizations are simply referred as international organizations, in many other it makes sense to use the ROs term to stress the more limited scope of a particular membership.

Examples of ROs include the African Union (AU), European Union (EU), the Organization of American States (OAS), the Arab League, and Association of Southeast Asian Nations (ASEAN), South Asian Association for Regional Cooperation (SAARC).

Arab League

The Arab League, officially called the League of Arab States, is a regional organization of Arab states in Southwest Asia, and North and Northeast Africa. It was formed in Cairo on March 22,

1945 with six members: Egypt, Iraq, Transjordan (renamed Jordan after 1946), Lebanon, Saudi Arabia, and Syria. Yemen joined as a member on May 5, 1945. The Arab League currently has 22 members and four observers. The main goal of the league is to "draw closer the relations between member States and co-ordinate collaboration between them, to safeguard their independence and sovereignty, and to consider in a general way the affairs and interests of the Arab countries."

Through institutions such as the Arab League Educational, Cultural and Scientific Organization (ALESCO) and the Economic and Social Council of the Arab League's Council of Arab Economic Unity (CAEU), the Arab League facilitates political, economic, cultural, scientific and social programs designed to promote the interests of the Arab world. It has served as a forum for the member states to coordinate their policy positions, to deliberate on matters of common concern, to settle some Arab disputes, and to limit conflicts such as the 1958 Lebanon crisis. The League has served as a platform for the drafting and conclusion of many landmark documents promoting economic integration. One example is the *Joint Arab Economic Action Charter* which sets out the principles for economic activities in the region.

Each member state has one vote in the *League Council,* while decisions are binding only for those states that have voted for them. The aims of the league in 1945 were to strengthen and coordinate the political, cultural, economic, and social programs of its members, and to mediate disputes among them or between them and third parties. Furthermore, the signing of an agreement on *Joint Defence and Economic Cooperation* on April 13, 1950 committed the signatories to coordination of military defence measures. The Arab league has played an important role in shaping school curricula, advancing the role of women in the Arab societies, promoting child welfare, encouraging youth and sports programs, preserving Arab cultural heritage, and fostering cultural exchanges between the member states. Literacy campaigns have been launched, intellectual works reproduced, and modern technical terminology is translated for the use within member states. The league encourages measures against crime and drug abuse, and deals with labor issues—particularly among the emigrant Arab workforce.

Arab League and its Members

The Arab League was founded in Cairo in 1945 by Egypt, Iraq, Lebanon, Saudi Arabia, Syria, Transjordan (Jordan from 1946), and Yemen. There was a continual increase in membership during the second half of the 20th century, with additional 15 Arab states and 4 observers being admitted.

Egypt's membership was suspended in 1979 after it signed the Egyptian–Israeli Peace Treaty, and the League's headquarters were moved from Cairo to Tunis. In 1987, Arab countries restored diplomatic relations with Egypt and the country was readmitted to the league in 1989 while the league's headquarters moved back to Cairo. In September 2006, Venezuela was accepted as an observer, and India in 2007.

Israel is not a member despite 20% of its population being of Arab origin, nearly half the Jewish population being descended from Jews from Arab countries, and Arabic being an official language. Neither is Chad a member, although Arabic is in both official and vernacular use there.

Four countries are observer states — a status that entitles them to express their opinion and give advice but denies them voting rights.

The current members and *observers* of the Arab League are listed below along with their admission dates.

Geography

The area of members of the Arab League covers around 14 million km^2 and straddles two continents: Western Asia as well as Northern and Northeastern Africa. The area consists of large arid deserts, namely the Sahara. Nevertheless, it also contains several very fertile lands, such as the Nile Valley, the High Atlas Mountains, and the Fertile Crescent which stretches from Iraq over Syria and Lebanon to Palestine. The area comprises also deep forests in southern Arabia and southern Sudan as well as the major parts of the world's longest river—the Nile.

The area has witnessed the rise and fall of many ancient civilizations: Ancient Egypt, Rome, Ancient Israel, Assyria, Babylon, Phoenicia, Carthage, Kush, and Nabateans.

Governance

The Charter of the Arab League endorsed the principle of an Arab homeland while respecting the sovereignty of the individual member states. The internal regulations of the Council of the League and the committees were agreed in October 1951. Those of the Secretariat-General were agreed in May 1953.

Since then, governance of the Arab League has been based on the duality of supernational institutions and the sovereignty of the member states. Preservation of individual statehood derived its strengths from the natural preference of ruling elites to maintain their power and independence in decision making. Moreover, the fear of the richer that the poorer may share their wealth in the name of Arab nationalism, the feuds among Arab rulers, and the influence of external powers that might oppose Arab unity can be seen as obstacles towards a deeper integration of the league.

Economy

The Arab League is rich in resources, with enormous oil and natural gas resources; it also has great fertile lands in South of the Sudan, usually referred to as the food basket of the Arab World. The region's instability has not affected its tourism industry, that is considered the fastest growing industry in the region, with Egypt, UAE, Algeria, Tunisia, and Jordan leading the way. Another industry that is growing steadily in the Arab League is telecommunications. Within less than a decade, local companies such as Orascom and Etisalat have managed to compete internationally.

Economic achievements initiated by the League amongst member states have been less impressive than those achieved by other smaller Arab organizations such as the Gulf Cooperation Council (GCC). However, several promising major economic projects are set to be completed soon. Among them is the Arab Gas Pipeline, scheduled to be accomplished in 2010. It will transport Egyptian and Iraqi gas to Jordan, Syria, Lebanon, and Turkey. The Greater Arab Free Trade Area (GAFTA), planned to come into effect on January 1, 2008, will render 95% of all Arab products free of customs.

Economic development in the Arab League is very disparate. Significant difference in wealth and economic conditions exist between the rich oil states of UAE, Qatar, Kuwait, and Algeria on the one hand, and poor countries like the Comoros, Mauritania, and Djibouti on the other hand. Arab economic funding is under development. As an example, the Arab League agreed to support the Sudanese region of Darfur with 500 million dollars, and Egyptian and Libyan companies are planning to build several wells in this dry area.

List of member states by GDP (PPP)

This following table lists the gross domestic product (GDP) of the Arab League and its member states based on purchasing power parity (PPP) and measured in US dollar. If not indicated otherwise, the figures are based on the 2008 data published by the International Monetary Fund, World Economic Outlook Database, in April 2008.

Education

In collecting literacy data, many countries estimate the number of literate people based on self-reported data. Some use educational attainment data as a proxy, but measures of school attendance or grade completion may differ. Because definitions and data collection methods vary across countries, literacy estimates should be used with caution. | United Nations Development Programme Report 2009.

Status of Palestine

Mindful of their previous announcements in support of the Arabs of Palestine the framers of the Pact were determined to include them within the league from its inauguration. This was done by means of an annex that declared:

> "Even though Palestine was not able to control her own destiny, it was on the basis of the recognition of her independence that the Covenant of the League of Nations determined a system of government for her. Her existence and her independence among the nations can, therefore, no more be questioned *de jure* than the independence of any of the other Arab States. [...] Therefore, the States signatory to the Pact of the Arab League consider that in view of Palestine's special circumstances, the Council of

the League should designate an Arab delegate from Palestine to participate in its work until this country enjoys actual independence"

At the Cairo Summit of 1964, the Arab League initiated the creation of an organization representing the Palestinian people. The first Palestinian National Council convened in East Jerusalem on May 29, 1964. The Palestinian Liberation Organization was founded during this meeting on June 2, 1964.

At the Beirut Summit on March 28, 2002 the league adopted the Arab Peace Initiative, a Saudi-inspired peace plan for the Arab–Israeli conflict. The initiative offered full normalization of the relations with Israel. In exchange, Israel was demanded to withdraw from all occupied territories, including the Golan Heights, to recognize an independent Palestinian state in the West Bank and the Gaza Strip with East Jerusalem as its capital, as well as a "just solution" for the Palestinian refugees.

The Peace Initiative was again endorsed at 2007 in the Riyadh Summit. In July 2007, the Arab League sent a mission, consisting of the Jordanian and Egyptian foreign ministers, to Israel to promote the initiative. The mission was welcomed with reservations by Israel.

Following Venezuela's move to expel the resident Israeli diplomats amid the 2008–2009 Israel–Gaza conflict, Kuwaiti member of parliament Waleed al-Tabtabai made a public plea to move the Arab League headquarters from Cairo to Caracas, Venezuela.

Demographics

The Arab League is a culturally and ethnically diverse association of 22 member states, although a vast majority of the league consist of Arab people. As of January 1, 2007, about 314,000,000 people live in the states of the Arab League. Its population grows faster than in most other global regions. This threatens to diminish the slow economic expansion expected in the league's developing countries.

The most populous member state is Egypt, with a population of about 80 million. The least populated is Djibouti, with about 500,000 inhabitants. Most of the Persian Gulf Arab states have large populations of foreign labourers. The UAE's Arab population counts for less than 20% of its total population, while 50% originate from South-and Southeast Asia, although they are not citizens. Some Persian Gulf Arab states also import cheap Arab labor, mainly from Egypt, Yemen, and Somalia.

Since large parts of the Arab League are deserts, the population is concentrated in and around cities where most the trade and industry are located. The largest Arab cities are Cairo, followed by Baghdad, Khartoum, Giza, Damascus, Riyadh, and Casablanca.

Comparisons with other organizations

The Arab League resembles the Organization of American States, Celtic League, the Council of Europe, and the African Union, in that it has primarily political aims. However, membership in the league is based on culture rather than geographical location. In this respect, the Arab League resembles organizations such as the Latin Union or the Caribbean Community.

The Arab League differs notably from the European Union, in that it has not achieved a significant degree of regional integration and the organization itself has no direct relations with the citizens of its member states. However, the Arab League is based on principles that support and promote a unified Arab nationalism and a common position among Arabic states on various issues.

All Arab League members are also members of the Organisation of the Islamic Conference. In turn, the memberships of the smaller GCC and Arab Maghreb Union organizations are subsets of that of the league.

Secretary Generals

Abdul Rahman Azzam	1945 to 1952
Abdul Khalek Hassouna	1952 to 1972
Mahmoud Riad	1972 to 1979
Chedli Klibi	1979 to 1990
Assad al-Assad	1990 to 1991
Ahmad Esmat Abd al Meguid	1991 to 2001
Amr Moussa	2001 to date

Organization of American States (OAS)

The Organization of American States (OAS, or, as it is known in the three other official languages, OEA) is an international organization, headquartered in Washington, D.C., United States. Its members are the thirty-five independent states of the Americas with two countries suspended. Honduras recently withdrew from the organization; Cuba was suspended until recently.

History

The notion of closer hemispheric union in the Americas was first put forward by Simón Bolívar who, at the 1826 Congress of Panama, proposed creating a league of American republics, with a common military, a mutual defence pact, and a supranational parliamentary assembly. This meeting was attended by representatives of Gran Colombia (comprising the modern-day nations of Colombia, Ecuador, Panama, and Venezuela), Peru, the United Provinces of Central America, and Mexico, but the grandly titled "Treaty of Union, League, and Perpetual Confederation" was ultimately only ratified by Gran Colombia. Bolívar's dream soon floundered with civil war in Gran Colombia, the disintegration of Central America, and the emergence of national rather than continental outlooks in the newly independent American republics. Bolívar's dream of American unity was meant to unify Latin American nations against imperial domination by external power.

The pursuit of regional solidarity and cooperation again came to the forefront in 1889–90, at the First International Conference of American States. Gathered together in Washington, D.C., 18 nations resolved to found the International Union of American Republics, served by a permanent secretariat called the Commercial Bureau of the American Republics (renamed the "International Commercial Bureau" at the Second International Conference in 1901–02). These two bodies, in existence as of 14 April 1890, represent the point of inception to which today's OAS and its General Secretariat trace their origins.

At the Fourth International Conference of American States (Buenos Aires, 1910), the name of the organization was changed to the "Union of American Republics" and the Bureau became the "Pan American Union".

The experience of World War II convinced hemispheric governments that unilateral action could not ensure the territorial integrity of the American nations in the event of extra-continental aggression. To meet the challenges of global conflict in the postwar world and to contain conflicts within the hemisphere, they adopted a system of collective security, the Inter-American Treaty of Reciprocal Assistance (Rio Treaty) signed in 1947 in Rio de Janeiro.

The Ninth International Conference of American States was held in Bogotá between March and May 1948 and led by United States Secretary of State George Marshall, a meeting which led to a pledge by members to fight communism in America. This was the event that saw the birth of the OAS as it stands today, with the signature by 21 American countries of the Charter of the Organization of American States on 30 April 1948 (in effect since December 1951). The meeting also adopted the American Declaration of the Rights and Duties of Man, the world's first general human rights instrument.

The transition from the Pan American Union to OAS was smooth. The Director General of the former, Alberto Lleras Camargo, became the Organization's first Secretary General. The current Secretary General is former Chilean foreign minister José Miguel Insulza.

Significant milestones in the history of the OAS since the signing of the Charter have included the following:

- 1959: Inter-American Commission on Human Rights created.
- 1961: Charter of Punta del Este signed, launching the Alliance for Progress.
- 1962: OAS suspends Cuba
- 1969: American Convention on Human Rights signed (in force since 1978).
- 1970: OAS General Assembly established as the Organization's supreme decision-making body.
- 1979: Inter-American Court of Human Rights created.
- 1991: Adoption of Resolution 1080, which requires the Secretary General to convene the Permanent Council within ten days of a coup d'état in any member country.

- 1994: First Summit of the Americas (Miami), which resolved to establish a Free Trade Area of the Americas by 2005.
- 2001: Inter-American Democratic Charter adopted.
- 2009: OAS revokes 1962 suspension of Cuba
- 2009: OAS suspends Honduras due to the coup which ousted president Manuel Zelaya.

Goals and Purpose

In the words of Article 1 of the Charter, the goal of the member nations in creating the OAS was "to achieve an order of peace and justice, to promote their solidarity, to strengthen their collaboration, and to defend their sovereignty, their territorial integrity, and their independence." Article 2 then defines eight essential purposes:

- To strengthen the peace and security of the continent.
- To promote and consolidate representative democracy, with due respect for the principle of nonintervention.
- To prevent possible causes of difficulties and to ensure the pacific settlement of disputes that may arise among the member states.
- To provide for common action on the part of those states in the event of aggression.
- To seek the solution of political, judicial, and economic problems that may arise among them
- To promote, by cooperative action, their economic, social, and cultural development.
- To eradicate extreme poverty, which constitutes an obstacle to the full democratic development of the peoples of the hemisphere.
- To achieve an effective limitation of conventional weapons that will make it possible to devote the largest amount of resources to the economic and social development of the member states.

Over the course of the 1990s, with the end of the Cold War, the return to democracy in Latin America, and the thrust toward globalization, the OAS made major efforts to reinvent itself to fit the new context. Its stated priorities now include the following:

- Strengthening democracy: Between 1962 and 2002, the

Organization sent multinational observation missions to oversee free and fair elections in the member states on more than 100 occasions. The OAS also works to strengthen national and local government and electoral agencies, to promote democratic practices and values, and to help countries detect and defuse official corruption.

- Working for peace: Special OAS missions have supported peace processes in Nicaragua, Suriname, Haiti, and Guatemala. The Organization has played a leading part in the removal of landmines deployed in the Americas and it has led negotiations to resolve the continent's remaining border disputes (Guatemala/Belize; Peru/Ecuador). Work is also underway on the construction of a common inter-American counter-terrorism front.
- Defending human rights: The agencies of the inter-American human rights system provide a venue for the denunciation and resolution of human rights violations in individual cases. They also monitor and report on the general human rights situation in the member states.
- Fostering free trade: The OAS is one of the three agencies currently engaged in drafting a treaty that will establish a hemispheric free trade area from Alaska to Tierra del Fuego.
- Fighting the drugs trade: The Inter-American Drug Abuse Control Commission was established in 1986 to coordinate efforts and crossborder cooperation in this area.
- Promoting sustainable development: The goal of the OAS's Inter-American Council for Integral Development is to promote economic development and combating poverty. OAS technical cooperation programs address such areas as river basin management, the conservation of biodiversity, preservation of cultural diversity, planning for global climate change, sustainable tourism, and natural disaster mitigation.

Article 19 of the OAS Charter prohibits any State from interfering with the internal or external affairs of a member state. Article 21 prohibits any State from the military occupation—even temporarily—of a Member State's territory. The Charter subscribes to international law but goes further, saying that Charter rights depend not on power but follow from the existence of the state. The United States is signatory to the OAS Charter, meaning that the U.S. (like other Members) is legally bound by Article 19, 21, and other Charter provisions.

Organizational Structure

The OAS is composed of a Permanent Council, and a number of committees, including: General Secretariat; Secretariat on Juridical and Political Affairs; Executive Secretariat for Integral Development; Secretariat on Administrative and Budgetary Affairs; Secretariat on Hemispheric Security; Secretariat on Inter-American Summits Management; as well as Civil Society Participation in OAS Activities.

General Assembly

- Thirty-ninth regular session: San Pedro Sula, Honduras, June 2009.
- Thirty-eight regular session: Medellín, Colombia, June 2008.
- Thirty-seventh regular session: Panama City, Republic of Panama, June 2007.
- Thirty-sixth regular session: Santo Domingo, Dominican Republic, June 2006.
- Thirty-fifth regular session: Fort Lauderdale, United States, June 2005.
- Thirty-fourth regular session: Quito, Ecuador, June 2004.
- Thirty-third regular session: Santiago, Chile, June 2003.
- Thirty-second regular session: Bridgetown, Barbados, June 2002.
- Thirty-first regular session: San José, Costa Rica, June 2001.
- Thirtieth regular session: Windsor, Canada, June 2000.
- Twenty-ninth regular session: Guatemala City, Guatemala, June 1999.
- Twenty-eight regular session: Caracas, Venezuela, June 1998.
- Twenty-seventh regular session: Lima, Peru, June 1997.
- Twenty-sixth regular session: Panama City, Republic of Panama, June 1996.

- Twenty-fifth regular session: Montrouis, Haiti, June 1995.
- Twenty-fourth regular session: Belém do Pará, Brazil, June 1994.
- Twenty-third regular session: Managua, Nicaragua, June 1993.
- Twenty-second regular session: Nassau, The Bahamas, May 1992.
- Twenty-first regular session: Santiago, Chile, June 1991.
- Twentieth regular session: Asunción, Paraguay, June 1990.
- Nineteenth regular session: Washington, D.C., United States, November 1989.
- Eighteenth regular session: San Salvador, El Salvador, November 1988.
- Seventeenth regular session: Washington, D.C., United States, November 1987.
- Sixteenth regular session: Guatemala City, Guatemala, November 1986.
- Fifteenth regular session: Cartagena de Indias, Colombia, December 1985.
- Fourteenth regular session: Brasília, Brazil, November 1984.
- Thirteenth regular session: Washington, D.C., United States, November 1983.
- Twelfth regular session: Washington, D.C., United States, November 1982.
- Eleventh regular session: Castries, Saint Lucia, December 1981.
- Tenth regular session: Washington, D.C., United States, November 1980.
- Ninth regular session: La Paz, Bolivia, October 1979.
- Eighth regular session: Washington, D.C., United States, June/July 1978.
- Seventh regular session: St. George's, Grenada, June 1977.
- Sixth regular session: Santiago, Chile, June 1976.
- Fifth regular session: Washington, D.C., United States, May 1975.
- Fourth regular session: Atlanta, United States, April/May 1974.

- Third regular session: Washington, D.C., United States, April 1973.
- Second regular session: Washington, D.C., United States, April 1972.
- First regular session: San José, Costa Rica, April 1971.

Membership and Adhesions

All 35 independent nations of the Americas are members of the OAS. Upon foundation on 5 May 1948 there were 21 members:

- Argentina
- Bolivia
- Brazil
- Chile
- Colombia
- Costa Rica
- Cuba
- Dominican Republic
- Ecuador
- El Salvador
- Guatemala
- Haiti
- Honduras
- Mexico
- Nicaragua
- Panama
- Paraguay
- Peru
- United States
- Uruguay
- Venezuela.

The later expansion of the OAS included the newly independent nations of the Caribbean (most of whom gained independence only after World War II) and Canada. Members with later admission dates (sorted chronologically):

- Barbados (member since 1967)

- Trinidad and Tobago (1967)
- Jamaica (1969)
- Grenada (1975)
- Suriname (1977)
- Dominica (1979)
- Saint Lucia (1979)
- Antigua and Barbuda (1981)
- Saint Vincent and the Grenadines (1981)
- Bahamas (1982)
- Saint Kitts and Nevis (1984)
- Canada (1990)
- Belize (1991)
- Guyana (1991).

ASEAN

The Association of Southeast Asian Nations, commonly abbreviated ASEAN, is a geopolitical and economic organisation of 10 countries located in Southeast Asia, which was formed on 8 August 1967 by Indonesia, Malaysia, the Philippines, Singapore and Thailand. Since then, membership has expanded to include Brunei, Burma (Myanmar), Cambodia, Laos, and Vietnam. Its aims include the acceleration of economic growth, social progress, cultural development among its members, the protection of the peace and stability of the region, and to provide opportunities for member countries to discuss differences peacefully.

In 2005, the bloc spanned over an area of 4.46 million km^2 with a combined GDP (Nominal/PPP) of about USD$896.5 billion/ $2,728 billion growing at an average rate of around 5.6% per annum. In 2008, its combined GDP had grown to more than USD $1.5 trillion with a population of approximately 580 million people (8.7% of the world population)

History

ASEAN was preceded by an organisation called the Association of Southeast Asia, commonly called ASA, an alliance consisting of the Philippines, Malaysia and Thailand that was formed in 1961. The bloc itself, however, was established on 8

August 1967, when foreign ministers of five countries– Indonesia, Malaysia, the Philippines, Singapore, and Thailand– met at the Thai Department of Foreign Affairs building in Bangkok and signed the ASEAN Declaration, more commonly known as the Bangkok Declaration. The five foreign ministers– Adam Malik of Indonesia, Narciso Ramos of the Philippines, Abdul Razak of Malaysia, S. Rajaratnam of Singapore, and Thanat Khoman of Thailand– are considered as the organisation's Founding Fathers.

The motivations for the birth of ASEAN were so that its members' governing elite could concentrate on nation building), the common fear of communism, reduced faith in or mistrust of external powers in the 1960s, as well as a desire for economic development; not to mention Indonesia's ambition to become a regional hegemon through regional cooperation and the hope on the part of Malaysia and Singapore to constrain Indonesia and bring it into a more cooperative framework.

In 1976, the Melanesian state of Papua New Guinea was accorded observer status. Throughout the 1970s, the organisation embarked on a program of economic cooperation, following the Bali Summit of 1976. This floundered in the mid-1980s and was only revived around 1991 due to a Thai proposal for a regional free trade area. The bloc then grew when Brunei Darussalam became the sixth member after it joined on 8 January 1984, barely a week after the country became independent on 1 January.

On 28 July 1995, Vietnam became the seventh member. Laos and Burma (Myanmar) joined two years later in 23 July 1997. Cambodia was to have joined together with Laos and Myanmar, but was deferred due to the country's internal political struggle. The country later joined on 30 April 1999, following the stabilisation of its government.

During the 1990s, the bloc experienced an increase in both membership as well as in the drive for further integration. In 1990, Malaysia proposed the creation of an East Asia Economic Caucus composing the then-members of ASEAN as well as the People's Republic of China, Japan, and South Korea, with the intention of counterbalancing the growing influence of the United States in the Asia-Pacific Economic Cooperation (APEC) as well as in the Asian region as a whole. This proposal, however, failed since it faced heavy opposition from Japan and the United States. Despite this failure, member states continued to work for further integration. In 1992, the Common Effective Preferential Tariff (CEPT) scheme was signed as a schedule for phasing tariffs and as a goal to increase the *region's competitive advantage as a production base geared for the world market*. This law would act as the framework for the ASEAN Free Trade Area. After the East Asian Financial Crisis of 1997, a revival of the Malaysian proposal was established in Chiang Mai, known as the Chiang Mai Initiative, which calls for better integration between the economies of ASEAN as well as the ASEAN Plus Three countries (China, Japan, and South Korea).

Aside from improving each member state's economies, the bloc also focused on peace and stability in the region. On 15 December 1995, the Southeast Asian Nuclear-Weapon-Free Zone Treaty was signed with the intention of turning Southeast Asia into a Nuclear-Weapon-Free Zone. The treaty took effect on 28 March 1997 after all but one of the member states have ratified it. It became fully effective on 21 June 2001, after the Philippines ratified it, effectively banning all nuclear weapons in the region.

At the turn of the 21st century, issues shifted to involve a more environmental perspective. The organisation started to discuss environmental agreements. These included the signing of the ASEAN Agreement on Transboundary Haze Pollution in 2002 as an attempt to control haze pollution in Southeast Asia. Unfortunately, this was unsuccessful due to the outbreaks of the 2005 Malaysian haze and the 2006 Southeast Asian haze. Other environmental treaties introduced by the organisation include the Cebu Declaration on East Asian Energy Security, the ASEAN-Wildlife Enforcement Network in 2005, and the Asia-Pacific Partnership on Clean Development and Climate, both of which are responses to the potential effects of climate change. Climate change is of current interest.

Through the Bali Concord II in 2003, ASEAN has subscribed to the notion of democratic peace, which means all member countries believe democratic processes will promote regional peace and stability. Also, the non-democratic members all agreed that it was something all member states should aspire to.

The leaders of each country, particularly Mahathir Mohamad of Malaysia, also felt the need to further integrate the region.

Beginning in 1997, the bloc began creating organisations within its framework with the intention of achieving this goal. ASEAN Plus Three was the first of these and was created to improve existing ties with the People's Republic of China, Japan, and South Korea.

This was followed by the even larger East Asia Summit, which included these countries as well as India, Australia, and New Zealand. This new grouping acted as a prerequisite for the planned East Asia Community, which was supposedly patterned after the now-defunct European Community. The ASEAN Eminent Persons Group was created to study the possible successes and failures of this policy as well as the possibility of drafting an ASEAN Charter.

In 2006, ASEAN was given observer status at the United Nations General Assembly. As a response, the organisation awarded the status of "dialogue partner" to the United Nations. Furthermore, on 23 July that year, José Ramos-Horta, then Prime Minister of East Timor, signed a formal request for membership and expected the accession process to last at least five years before the then-observer state became a full member.

In 2007, ASEAN celebrated its 40th anniversary since its inception, and 30 years of diplomatic relations with the United States. On 26 August 2007, ASEAN stated that it aims to complete all its free trade agreements with China, Japan, South Korea, India, Australia and New Zealand by 2013, in line with the establishment of the ASEAN Economic Community by 2015. In November 2007 the ASEAN members signed the ASEAN Charter, a constitution governing relations among the ASEAN members and establishing ASEAN itself as an international legal entity. During the same year, the Cebu Declaration on East Asian Energy Security in Cebu on 15 January 2007, by ASEAN and the other members of the EAS (Australia, People's Republic of China, India, Japan, New Zealand, South Korea), which promotes energy security by finding energy alternatives to conventional fuels.

On February 27, 2009 a Free Trade Agreement with the ASEAN regional block of 10 countries and New Zealand and its close partner Australia was signed, it is estimated that this FTA would boost aggregate GDP across the 12 countries by more than US. billion over the period 2000-2020.

The ASEAN Way

In the 1960s, the push for decolonisation promoted the sovereignty of Indonesia and Malaysia among others. Since nation building is often messy and vulnerable to foreign intervention, the governing elite wanted to be free to implement independent policies with the knowledge that neighbours would refrain from interfering in their domestic affairs. Territorially small members such as Singapore and Brunei were consciously fearful of force and coercive measures from much bigger neighbours like Indonesia and Malaysia. "Through political dialogue and confidence building, no tension has escalated into armed confrontation among ASEAN member countries since its establishment more than three decades ago".

The ASEAN way can be traced back to the signing of the Treaty of Amity and Cooperation in South East Asian. "Fundamental principles adopted from this included: mutual respect for the independence, sovereignty, equality, territorial integrity, and national identity of all nations;

- the right of every State to lead its national existence free from external interference, subversion or coercion;
- non-interference in the internal affairs of one another;
- settlement of differences or disputes by peaceful manner;
- renunciation of the threat or use of force; and
- effective cooperation among themselves".

On the surface, the process of consultations and consensus is supposed to be a democratic approach to decision making, but the ASEAN process has been managed through close interpersonal contacts among the top leaders only, who often share a reluctance to institutionalise and legalise cooperation which can undermine their regime's control over the conduct of regional cooperation. Thus, the organisation is chaired by the secretariat.

All of these features, namely non-interference, informality, minimal institutionalisation, consultation and consensus, non-use of force and non-confrontation have constituted what is called the ASEAN Way.

Since the late 1990s, many scholars have argued that the principle of non-interference has blunted ASEAN efforts in handling the problem of Myanmar, human rights abuses and haze pollution in the region. Meanwhile, with the consensus-based approach, every member in fact has a veto and decisions are usually reduced to the lowest common denominator. There has been a widespread belief that ASEAN members should have a less rigid view on these two cardinal principles when they wish to be seen as a cohesive and relevant community.

Policies

Apart from consultations and consensus, ASEAN's agenda-setting and decision-making processes can be usefully understood in terms of the so-called Track I and Track II. Track I refers to the practice of diplomacy among government channels. The participants stand as representatives of their respective states and reflect the official positions of their governments during negotiations and discussions. All official decisions are made in Track I. Therefore, "Track I refers to intergovernmental processes". Track II differs slightly from Track I, involving civil society groups and other individuals with various links who work alongside governments. This track enables governments to discuss controversial issues and test new ideas without making official statements or binding commitments, and, if necessary, backtrack on positions.

Although Track II dialogues are sometimes cited as examples of the involvement of civil society in regional decision-making process by governments and other second track actors, NGOs have rarely got access to this track, meanwhile participants from the academic community are a dozen think-tanks. However, these think-tanks are, in most cases, very much linked to their respective governments, and dependent on government funding for their academic and policy-relevant activities, and many working in Track II have previous bureaucratic experience. Their recommendations, especially in economic integration, are often closer to ASEAN's decisions than the rest of civil society's positions.

The track that acts as a forum for civil society in Southeast Asia is called Track III. Track III participants are generally civil society groups who represent a particular idea or brand. Track III networks claim to represent communities and people who are largely marginalised from political power centres and unable to achieve positive change without outside assistance. This track tries to influence government policies indirectly by lobbying, generating pressure through the media. Third-track actors also organise and/or attend meetings as well as conferences to get access to Track I officials.

While Track II meetings and interactions with Track I actors have increased and intensified, rarely has the rest of civil society had the opportunity to interface with Track II. Those with Track I have been even rarer.

Looking at the three tracks, it is clear that until now, ASEAN has been run by government officials who, as far as ASEAN matters are concerned, are accountable only to their governments and not the people. In a lecture on the occasion of ASEAN's 38th anniversary, the incumbent Indonesian President Dr. Susilo Bambang Yudhoyono admitted:

"All the decisions about treaties and free trade areas, about declarations and plans of action, are made by Heads of Government, ministers and senior officials. And the fact that among the masses, there is little knowledge, let alone appreciation, of the large initiatives that ASEAN is taking on their behalf."

Meetings

ASEAN Summit

The organisation holds meetings, known as the ASEAN Summit, where heads of government of each member meet to discuss and resolve regional issues, as well as to conduct other meetings with other countries outside of the bloc with the intention of promoting external relations.

The ASEAN Leaders' Formal Summit was first held in Bali, Indonesia in 1976. Its third meeting was held in Manila in 1987 and during this meeting, it was decided that the leaders would meet every five years. Consequently, the fourth meeting was held in Singapore in 1992 where the leaders again agreed to meet more frequently, deciding to hold the summit every three years. In 2001, it was decided to meet annually to address urgent issues affecting the region. Member nations were assigned to be the summit host in alphabetical order except in the case of Myanmar which dropped its 2006 hosting rights in 2004 due to pressure from the United States and the European Union. By December 2008, the ASEAN Charter came into force and with it, the ASEAN Summit will be held twice in a year. The formal summit meets for three days. The usual itinerary is as follows:

- Leaders of member states would hold an internal organisation meeting.
- Leaders of member states would hold a conference together with foreign ministers of the ASEAN Regional Forum.
- A meeting, known as ASEAN Plus Three, is set for leaders of three Dialogue Partners (People's Republic of China, Japan, South Korea)
- A separate meeting, known as ASEAN-CER, is set for another set of leaders of two Dialogue Partners (Australia, New Zealand).

ASEAN Formal Summits

	Date	Country	Host
1st	23–24 February, 1976	Indonesia	Bali
2nd	4–5 August, 1977	Malaysia	Kuala Lumpur
3rd	14–15 December, 1987	Philippines	Manila
4th	27 29 January, 1992	Singapore	Singapore
5th	14 15 December, 1995	Thailand	Bangkok
6th	15 16 December, 1998	Vietnam	Hanoi
7th	5 6 November, 2001	Brunei	Bandar Seri Begawan
8th	4 5 November, 2002	Cambodia	Phnom Penh
9th	7 8 October, 2003	Indonesia	Bali
10th	29 30 November, 2004	Laos	Vientiane
11th	12 14 December, 2005	Malaysia	Kuala Lumpur
12th	11 14 January, 2007	Philippines	Cebu
13th	18 22 November, 2007	Singapore	Singapore
14th[3]	27 February-1 March, 2009		
	10-11 April 2009	Thailand Pattaya	Cha Am, Hua Hin
15th	23 October 2009	Thailand	Cha Am, Hua Hin
16th	2010	Vietnam	Hanoi

[1] Postponed from 10 14 December, 2006 due to Typhoon Seniang.

[2] hosted the summit because Myanmar backed out due to enormous pressure from US and EU

[3] This summit consisted of two parts.

The first part was moved from 12 17 December, 2008 due to the 2008 Thai political crisis. The second part was aborted on April 11 due to protesters entering the summit venue.

During the fifth Summit in Bangkok, the leaders decided to meet "informally" between each formal summit:

ASEAN Informal Summits

	Date	Country	Host
1st	30 November 1996	Indonesia	Jakarta
2nd	14 16 December, 1997	Malaysia	Kuala Lumpur
3rd	27 28 November, 1999	Philippines	Manila
4th	22 25 November, 2000	Singapore	Singapore

Cultural activities

The organisation hosts cultural activities in an attempt to further integrate the region. These include sports and educational activities as well as writing awards. Examples of these include the ASEAN University Network, the ASEAN Centre for Biodiversity, the ASEAN Outstanding Scientist and Technologist Award, and the Singapore-sponsored ASEAN Scholarship.

Heritage Parks

ASEAN Heritage Parks is a list of nature parks launched 1984 and relaunched in 2004. It aims to protect the region's natural treasures. There are now 35 such protected areas, including the Tubbataha Reef Marine Park and the Kinabalu National Park.

Scholarship

The ASEAN Scholarship is a scholarship program offered by Singapore to the 9 other member states for secondary school, junior college, and university education. It covers accommodation, food, medical benefits & accident insurance, school fees, and examination fees.

South Asian Association for Regional Cooperation (SAARC)

The South Asian Association for Regional Cooperation (SAARC) is an economic and political organization of eight countries in Southern Asia. In terms of population, its sphere of influence is the largest of any regional organization: almost 1.5 billion people, the combined population of its member states. It was established on December 8, 1985 by Bangladesh, Bhutan, Maldives, Nepal, Pakistan, India and Sri Lanka. In April 2007, at the Association's 14th summit, Afghanistan became its eighth member.

History

In the late 1970s, Bangladeshi President Ziaur Rahman proposed the creation of a trade bloc consisting of South Asian countries. The idea of regional cooperation in South Asia was again mooted in May 1980. The foreign secretaries of the seven countries met for the first time in Colombo in April 1981. The Committee of the Whole, which met in Colombo in August 1981, identified five broad areas for regional cooperation. New areas of cooperation were added in the following years.

The objectives of the Association as defined in the Charter are:

- to promote the welfare of the people of South Asia and to improve their quality of life;
- to accelerate economic growth, social progress and cultural development in the region and to provide all individuals the opportunity to live in dignity and to realize their full potential;
- to promote and strengthen collective self-reliance among the countries of South Asia;
- to contribute to mutual trust, understanding and appreciation of one another's problems;
- to promote active collaboration and mutual assistance in the economic, social, cultural, technical and scientific fields;
- to strengthen cooperation with other developing countries;
- to strengthen cooperation among themselves in international forums on matters of common interest; and
- to cooperate with international and regional organisations with similar aims and purposes.

The Declaration on South Asian Regional Cooperation was adopted by the Foreign Ministers in 1983 in New Delhi. During the meeting, the Ministers also launched the Integrated Programme of Action (IPA) in nine agreed areas, namely, Agriculture; Rural Development; Telecommunications; Meteorology; Health and Population Activities; Transport; Postal Services; Science and Technology; and Sports, Arts and Culture. The South Asian Association for Regional Cooperation (SAARC) was established when its Charter was formally adopted on 8 December 1985 by the Heads of State or Government of Bangladesh, Bhutan, India, Maldives, Nepal, Pakistan and Sri Lanka.

Afghanistan was added to the regional grouping at the behest of India on 13 November 2005, and became a member on 3 April 2007. With the addition of Afghanistan, the total number of member states were raised to eight (8). In April 2006, the United States of America and South Korea made formal requests to be granted observer status. The European Union has also indicated interest in being given observer status, and made a formal request for the same to the SAARC Council of Ministers meeting in July 2006. On 2 August 2006 the foreign ministers of the SAARC countries agreed in principle to grant observer status to the US, South Korea and the European Union. On 4 March 2007, Iran requested observer status. Followed shortly by the entrance of Mauritius.

Secretariat

The SAARC Secretariat was established in Kathmandu on 16 January 1987 and was inaugurated by Late King Birendra Bir Bikram Shah of Nepal.

It is headed by a Secretary General appointed by the Council of Ministers from Member Countries in alphabetical order for a three-year term. He is assisted by the Professional and the General Services Staff, and also an appropriate number of functional units called Divisions assigned to Directors on deputation from Member States. The Secretariat coordinates and monitors implementation of activities, prepares for and services meetings, and serves as a channel of communication between the Association and its Member States as well as other regional organizations.

The Memorandum of Understanding on the establishment of the Secretariat which was signed by Foreign Ministers of member countries on 17 November 1986 at Bangalore, India contains various clauses concerning the role, structure and administration of the SAARC Secretariat as well as the powers of the Secretary-General.

In several recent meetings the heads of state or government of member states of SAARC have taken some important decisions and bold initiatives to strengthen the organisation and to widen and deepen regional cooperation.

The SAARC Secretariat and Member States observe 8 December as the SAARC Charter Day1..

Criticism

Not enough is being done to for rapid economic integration of the region. Apart from the fact that the recently approved south asian university and the creation of new rail lines linking the region, people to people contacts and connectivity of region needs to be strengthened.

Political issues

SAARC has intentionally laid more stress on "core issues" mentioned above rather than more decisive political issues like the Kashmir dispute and the Sri Lankan civil war. However, political dialogue is often conducted on the margins of SAARC meetings. SAARC has also refrained itself from interfering in the internal matters of its member states. During the 12th and 13th SAARC summits, extreme emphasis was laid upon greater cooperation between the SAARC members to fight terrorism.

Free trade agreement

Over the years, the SAARC members have expressed their unwillingness on signing a free trade agreement. Though India has several trade pacts with Maldives, Nepal, Bhutan and Sri Lanka, similar trade agreements with Pakistan and Bangladesh have been stalled due to political and economic concerns on both sides. India has been constructing a barrier across its borders with Bangladesh and Pakistan. In 1993, SAARC countries signed an agreement to gradually lower tariffs within the region, in Dhaka. Eleven years later, at the 12th SAARC Summit at Islamabad, SAARC countries devised the South Asia Free Trade Agreement which created a framework for the establishment of a free trade area covering 1.4 billion people. This agreement went into force on January 1, 2006. Under this agreement, SAARC members will bring their duties down to 20 per cent by 2007.

Dhaka 2005 Summit

The summit accorded observer status to People's Republic of China, Japan, South Korea and United States of America. The nations also agreed to organize development funds under a single financial institution with a permanent secretariat, that would cover all SAARC programs and also ranging from social, to infrastructure, to economic ones.

Asia-Pacific Economic Cooperation

Asia-Pacific Economic Cooperation (APEC) is a forum for 21 Pacific Rim countries (styled 'member economies') to cooperate on regional trade and investment liberalisation and facilitation. APEC's objective is to enhance economic growth and prosperity in the region and to strengthen the Asia-Pacific community. Members account for approximately 40% of the world's population, approximately 54% of world GDP and about 44% of world trade. An annual APEC Economic Leaders' Meeting, attended by the heads of government of all APEC members (with the exception of Chinese Taipei which is represented by a ministerial-level official). The location of the meeting rotates annually among the member economies, and a famous tradition involves the attending Leaders dressing in a national costume of the host member.

History

In January 1989, Australian Prime Minister Bob Hawke called for more effective economic cooperation across the Pacific Rim region. This led to the first meeting of APEC in the Australian capital Canberra in November, chaired by Australian Foreign Affairs Minister Gareth Evans. Attended by political ministers from twelve countries, the meeting concluded with commitments for future annual meetings in Singapore and South Korea. The initial proposal was opposed by countries of the Association of Southeast Asian Nations (ASEAN) which instead proposed the East Asia Economic Caucus which would exclude non-Asian countries such as the United States, Canada, Australia and New Zealand. The plan was opposed and strongly criticised by Japan and the United States.

The first APEC Economic Leaders' Meeting occurred in 1993 when US president Bill Clinton, after discussions with Australian prime minister Paul Keating, invited the heads of government from member economies to a summit on Blake Island. He believed it would help bring the stalled Uruguay Round of trade talks on track.

At the meeting, some leaders called for continued reduction of barriers to trade and investment, envisioning a community in the Asia-Pacific region that might promote prosperity through cooperation. The APEC Secretariat, based in Singapore, was established to coordinate the activities of the organisation.

During the meeting in 1994 in Bogor, Indonesia, APEC Leaders adopted the Bogor Goals that aim for free and open trade and investment in the Asia-Pacific by 2010 for industrialised economies and by 2020 for developing economies. In 1995, APEC established a business advisory body named the APEC Business Advisory Council (ABAC), composed of three business executives from each member economy.

Member economies

APEC currently has 21 members, including most countries with a coastline on the Pacific Ocean. By convention, APEC uses the term *member economy* to refer to one of its members.

India has requested membership in APEC, and received initial support from the United States, Japan and Australia. Officials have decided not to allow India to join for various reasons. However, the decision was made not to admit more members until 2010.

Moreover, India does not border the Pacific which all members do. The Philippines trade negotiator was quoted as saying that there is concern that "Once the Indians come in, the (Asian) weighting would become heavier in this part of the world."

In addition to India, Mongolia, Pakistan, Laos, Bangladesh, Colombia, and Ecuador, are among a dozen countries seeking membership in APEC by 2008. Colombia applied for APEC's membership as early as in 1995, but its bid was halted as the organization stopped accepting new members from 1993 to 1996, and the moratorium was further prolonged to 2007 due to the 1997 Asian Financial Crisis. Colombia and Ecuador hope to become members in 2010. Guam has also been actively seeking a separate membership, citing the example of Hong Kong, but the request is opposed by the United States, which currently represents Guam. APEC is one of the few international level organizations that Taiwan is allowed to join, albeit under the name Chinese Taipei.

Member economy	Date of accession
Australia	1989
Brunei	1989
Canada	1989
Indonesia	1989
Japan	1989
Republic of Korea	1989
Malaysia	1989
New Zealand	1989
Philippines	1989
Singapore	1989
Thailand	1989
United States	1989
Chinese Taipei	1991
Hong Kong, China	1991
People's Republic of China	1991
Mexico	1993
Papua New Guinea	1993
Chile	1994
Peru	1998
Russia	1998
Vietnam	1998

APEC Business Advisory Council

The APEC Business Advisory Council (ABAC) was created by the APEC Economic Leaders in November 1995 with the aim of providing advice to the APEC Economic Leaders on ways to achieve the Bogor Goals and other specific business sector priorities, and to provide the business perspective on specific areas of cooperation. Each economy nominates up to three members from the private sector to ABAC. These business leaders represent a wide range of industry sectors. ABAC provides an annual report to APEC Economic Leaders containing recommendations to improve the business and investment environment in the Asia-Pacific region, and outlining business views about priority regional issues. ABAC is also the only non-governmental organisation that is on the official agenda of the APEC Economic Leader's Meeting.

Annual APEC Economic Leaders' Meetings

Since its formation in 1989, APEC has held annual meetings with representatives from all member economies. The first four annual meetings were attended by ministerial-level officials. Beginning in 1993, the annual meetings are named APEC Economic Leaders' Meetings and are attended by the heads of government from all member economies except Taiwan, which is represented by a ministerial-level official. The annual Leaders' Meetings are not called summits. The location of the meeting is rotated annually among the members. As a tradition, the leaders attending the meeting participate in a photo op in which they dress in a costume that reflects the culture of the host member.

11

New International Economic Order (NIEO)

Economic and Social Development-New International Economic Order

In September 1973, in Algiers, the Arab petroleum-exporting countries discussed the possible uses of oil as a political weapon. When a new Arab-Israeli conflict broke out on 6 October, the Arab countries reduced the flow of oil to Europe and Japan and suspended exports to the US, the Netherlands, and Portugal. The embargo against the US was lifted in March 1974, that against the Netherlands in July 1974, and that against Portugal after a new regime instituted a policy leading to independence for African territories under Portuguese administration in 1974 and 1975. However, the measures taken by the petroleum-exporting countries marked a turning point for the world economy. Members of the Organization of Petroleum-Exporting Countries (OPEC) undertook a long-term study of the collective fixing of oil prices and increased them periodically thereafter.

On 31 January 1974, President Boumedienne of Algeria requested a special session of the General Assembly to consider the question of all raw materials and relations between developed industrial and developing states. Within two weeks, 70 nations endorsed his proposal.

Sixth Special Session of the General Assembly. The special session, held in April–May 1974, adopted a declaration and program of action on the establishment of a new international economic order. The declaration and program of action called for a fundamental change in the international economic order, in the absence of which the gap between developing and developed countries would only continue to widen. Such a change would require the industrial countries to make adjustments in their policies and economies for the benefit of the poorer countries, which in turn were determined to control their own resources. The program of action called for efforts to link the prices of exports of developing countries to the prices of their imports from developed countries. It suggested the formation of producers' associations, orderly commodity trading, increased export income for producing developing countries, and improvement in their terms of trade. It also looked to the evolution of an equitable relationship between the prices of raw materials, primary commodities, and semi-manufactured goods exported by developing countries and the raw materials, primary commodities, food, manufactured and semimanufactured goods, and capital equipment imported by them. In the declaration, UN member states proclaimed their determination to work urgently for "the establishment of a new international economic order based on equity, sovereign equality, interdependence, common interest, and cooperation among all states, irrespective of their economic and social systems, which shall correct inequalities and redress existing injustices, make it possible to eliminate the widening gap between the developed and the developing countries and ensure steadily accelerating economic and social development in peace and justice for present and future generations."

Though the program and declaration were adopted without a vote and enthusiastically supported by almost all developing and socialist countries, most Western European and other industrialized states with market economies entered reservations, often very far-reaching. They warned against constraints to the flow of trade that might result from the establishment of producers' associations and argued that nationalization should be carried out in accordance with the existing rules of international law.

Charter of Economic Rights and Duties of States. At its regular session in 1974, the General Assembly adopted a charter of Economic Rights and Duties of States. The charter affirmed that every state has the right to exercise freely full permanent sovereignty over its wealth and natural resources, to regulate foreign investment within its national jurisdiction, and to nationalize, expropriate, or transfer the ownership of foreign property. The charter provided that appropriate compensation should be paid in cases of nationalization and that any controversies should be settled under the domestic laws of the nationalizing states unless all states concerned agree to other peaceful means. It also set forth the right of states to associate in organizations of primary producers in order to develop their national economies.

Seventh Special Session of the General Assembly. The General Assembly held a seventh special session devoted to development and international cooperation in September 1975. The polemical atmosphere in which the program and declaration on the new international economic order and the charter on the economic rights and duties of states had been adopted was replaced by a pragmatic approach. Negotiations were carried on chiefly in private meetings between "contact groups" representing the developing countries and the Western European and other states with market economies. Since the market economy states were the buyers of approximately three-quarters of the exports of the developing countries, agreement between the two groups was essential to significant progress. At the close of the session, Secretary-General Kurt Waldheim declared that it had been "about *change* rather than the smoother management of the status quo."

The results of the special session were embodied in a resolution that proposed a large number of initiatives and was unanimously adopted by the General Assembly. It reaffirmed the target, originally defined in the strategy for the second Development Decade, of 1% of the GNP of developed countries to be devoted to official assistance to the developing countries, and it called for the accumulation of buffer stocks of commodities in order to offset market fluctuations, combat inflationary tendencies, and ensure grain and food security. In 1979, the General Assembly called for the launching, at the third special session on development in 1980, of a round of global and sustained negotiations on international economic cooperation for development. The negotiations, however, failed to achieve the hoped-for progress at the special session held in September 1980, but at the regular session that year, an international development strategy for the third UN Development Decade was adopted.

Economic aspects of the New International Order

1. The prerequisites of a more rapid, further economic advance of the developing countries are their continued

industrialization and their increase in the volume of non-traditional exports of manufactured goods. The aim would be to overcome the economic disadvantages resulting low differentiation, i.e. specialization in the production of agriculture and raw materials. Furthermore, a rise in export earnings is essential to enable developing countries to cover the heavy service payments due on their external debt.

2. The process of industrialization of developing countries requires adequate industrial strategies of the advanced countries, e.g. reduction of labour-intensive industries and protectionist policies by advanced countries.
3. The developing countries aided by the developed countries should aim at improvements in their agricultural sector and the stabilization of primary product markets.
4. Developed and less developed countries should strive for an internationally managed economic solution embracing the main factors determining the pattern of domestic and international productive investment.
5. The importance was stressed for the developing countries to aim at greater economic independence by financing a larger percentage of investment out of increased domestic savings. The ability to do so will be closely correlated with their export potential and size of per capita income.
6. To consolidate the existing external debt of developing countries into a more appropriate maturity structure.
7. To match more appropriately than has been the case in the recent past the financial needs of the less developed countries (e.g. for short-term balance-of-payments finance, trade finance, project finance, infrastructure and social investment, etc.) and the particular type of financial provision (short and medium-term bank credit, IMF lending, long-term development agency finance, etc.).

Global aspects of the New International Economic Order

1. The concept of the New International Economic Order must be seen as part of a global pattern of cultural development.
2. Therefore, a holistic or systemic approach is indicated as the only legitimate approach.

3. A scientific approach should include: a. reliance on fact-finding; b. inductive reference; c. cross-cultural comparison.
4. The principles as expressed in the resolution of the United Nations concerning the establishment of a New International Economic Order should not only be discussed in an abstract and formal manner. Those principles should be transformed into rules of international law. Special emphasis should be given to the recognition of the fundamental social rights-as part of the system of human rights-, not only on a national level, but as guiding rule of the transnational responsibility of states.
5. Any global approach has to include not only the aspect of fact-finding (descriptive level), but above all the aspect of ethics (normative level).
6. Therefore, the system of international economic relations is not exclusively related to "pure" (immanent) economic concepts, but it is linked, in its very essence, with ethical principles of mutual responsibility on a transnational level.
7. It will be necessary, therefore, that commonly accepted principles of "social" policy, already accepted on the level of national governments, will be implemented as rules of the economic and diplomatic relations between sovereign states. The global interdependence will make it necessary to give up the traditional *do ut des* principle as guiding rule of foreign policy; it should be replaced by the multi-dimensional concept of solidarity.
8. A prerequisite for the establishment of a New International Economic Order lies in tolerance and in a spiritual predisposition to open oneself to a dialogue with the members of the human community, as the present day mankind has to live with antinomies and with the fact of complex and not entirely soluble conflicts, without prejudice to constant search for peace and global development.
9. A dramatic change of attitudes and mind-especially in the developed and former colonialist countries-is required to the effect of a shifting the emphasis from having to being, and from consumption to quality of life.

The general consensus reached at this meeting of experts was that this conference should be the first step to influence-by scientific means-the international public opinion (especially in the developed countries) in regard to a new and multi-dimensional concept of development which will include not only the economic progress, but all forms of cultural self-realization of nations. The participants have expressed the hope that this might lead to overcoming the evil consequences of colonialism and to establish international relations based on the principles of equality and solidarity. The International Progress Organization was asked to continue its strife for this new system of international cooperation.

Toward a New International Economic Order

The financial crisis which started in east Asia in mid-1997 has continued to spread throughout 1998. Russia has undergone a financial collapse. Brazil has been hit by the financial wobbles, and has had to raise interest rates to a level which will ensure a 1999 recession there and in the rest of Latin America. The same also holds for South Africa, which is Africa's largest economy.

At the beginning of this year east Asia's woes were viewed by many as having little consequence for the U.S. economy. Indeed, Chairman Greenspan even mused that it might be "salutary" in that it would slightly restrain economic activity, thereby avoiding the need for the Federal Reserve to raise interest rates. This Panglossian view has now dissipated, and with recent moves by the Fed to cut the federal funds rate by three quarters of a percent has come official recognition that the troubles sparked by east Asia's financial collapse pose a real danger to U.S. economic well-being.

The crisis and its subsequent spread have raised two distinct sets of issues. One set of issues has concerned how to react immediately to the crisis and prevent it from deepening. Here, the focus has been on the appropriateness of the IMF's policy recommendations for east Asia and the need for global reflation. The IMF initially recommended a dose of fiscal and monetary austerity in the afflicted economies (Thailand, South Korea, and Indonesia), while the Federal Reserve viewed the crisis as exclusively regional in impact. The IMF's policies threatened to worsen east Asia's deflation, and it has now been grudgingly compelled to allow east Asian governments to run deficits, and interest rates have also been lowered somewhat. Meanwhile, the Fed has grudgingly come to recognize the U.S. economy's own exposure to east Asia's misfortune, and it has cut interest rates. However, there is a real danger of Federal Reserve policy being a matter of "too little, too late." In particular, the Fed continues to claim that rates cut have been needed to calm financial markets which indicates it may not yet have recognized the scale of weakening global demand. A second set of issues concerns the structure of the international economic order. Here, the question is to what extent are fundamental flaws in the structure responsible for the crisis, and to what extent are they responsible for the trend slow down in economic development and worsening of global income distribution.

This second set of issues is at the heart of the debate over the international financial architecture, and its resolution will critically determine the path of future prosperity. Though IMF policy in east Asia and Federal Reserve interest rate policy have both shifted in a more expansionary direction, this advance risks being short lived unless accompanied by recognition of the fundamentally flawed character of the existing global economic order. This is because the thinking that gave rise to the IMF's initial mistaken diagnosis of and prescription for east Asia's collapse is the same thinking that has guided the construction of the existing order.

Absent a rejection of this thinking, the world economy will remain brutally exposed to unstable deflationary forces, while policy makers will ineluctably be drawn back toward policies of contraction. Indeed, this is already evident in Brazil, where IMF sponsored high interest rates and fiscal austerity may manage to save the Brazilian currency, but only at the cost of deep recession. Moreover, this in turn threatens to pull down the Argentine economy. The lesson is clear: applied to enough countries, IMF contractionary policies will trigger a global recession.

The differences in thinking regarding the validity of the existing global economic order are reflected in disagreements over the interpretation of the current crisis. On one hand, there is the IMF-Treasury view which interprets it as a narrow crisis of international financial markets: hence, Treasury Secretary Rubin's call to "modernize the architecture of the international financial markets." On the other hand there is a view that reads the situation as a full-fledged crisis of globalization that has revealed deep flaws in the design of the existing global economic order. The narrow financial markets crisis view is promoted by supporters of the "Washington Consensus" which has dominated economic policy making for the last twenty years. It maintains that global economic growth is best furthered by more open trade, export-led growth, greater deregulation, and more liberalized financial markets. It is epitomized by the IMF, which has sought to characterize the crisis as resulting from inadequate financial transparency, and in the aftermath of the crisis the IMF has actually called for greater liberalization of international financial capital flows. All that is required is a minor tune-up of the international financial system, combined with some learning from experience. Thus, "sequencing of reforms" has become a hot new issue, the argument being that countries like South Korea engaged in wrong sequencing whereby they mistakenly liberalized short term capital flows before long term flows. Learning means that policy makers will not make this mistake next time, but meanwhile the underlying recommendations of the Washington consensus remain correct.

The Treasury view is a blood cousin of that of the IMF. Both the Treasury and the IMF were slow to recognize that east Asia's troubles were triggered by a bank run that had foreign investors rushing to repatriate funds. They therefore both initially supported mistaken policies of economic austerity predicated upon high interest rates, government spending cuts and higher taxes. Since then, both have reversed these policy prescriptions to a significant degree. However, they continue to see the long run solution in terms of limited financial market reforms. Thus, Secretary Rubin's claim that "(T)hese reform programs have at their core strengthening financial systems, improving transparency and supervision, eliminating the inter-relationships between banks, the government, and commercial entities, opening capital markets, and appropriate monetary and fiscal policies." A view that straddles the debate is that of Jeffrey Sachs. Sachs was one of the early architects of Washington consensus "shock" therapy in eastern Europe, the premise of which was that the old command style economies had to be opened to the bracing wind of the market by rapid privatization and deregulation. However, he has broken with the Washington Consensus over east Asia's crisis, and was one of the first to point out that austerity was the wrong response to a bank run.

A key difference between the IMF-Treasury view and Sachs concerns the relationship between stabilization and growth. All are for growth. However, the IMF-Treasury view maintains that stabilization must come first, and only then will growth be possible; hence, the inclination to high interest rates and fiscal austerity to placate financial markets. Sachs implicitly argues that stabilization is not possible without growth. Policy makers must therefore focus on jump starting the world economy through a variety of initiatives from coordinated interest rate cuts to debt relief and development assistance.

This growth versus stabilization difference is important, but in all other regards Sachs shares the Washington consensus. In particular, he is committed to "fast track" style free trade which fosters an international race to the bottom. International wage competition and shifting of jobs in response to cross-country differences in work place and environmental standards are legitimate dimensions of free trade. At the macroeconomic level, export-led growth which has countries relying on foreign demand to ensure full employment, is also legitimate. Moreover, this is so even if exports are achieved through reliance on depreciated currencies.

Whereas proponents of the Washington consensus think that the existing model of globalization merely needs a tune-up, there is a "Washington alternative" which thinks the model fundamentally unsound. The issue is not one of recalibrating the model, but rather one of designing a new model that is stable, equitable, and pro-growth. For the last fifteen years, the Washington consensus approach has dominated, yet global economic growth has been slower and inequality has risen. In industrialized countries, wages have stagnated, workers are working longer hours, and there has been an increase in job insecurity. Rather than being an isolated event, east Asia's financial crisis represents one more in a succession of crises. As World Bank chief economist Joseph Stiglitz puts it, the world economy has been having "a boom in busts."

At the most abstract level, the Washington alternative challenges the notion that markets and the process of globalization are natural phenomena that are to be fatalistically accepted. Thus, John Sweeney, President of the AFL-CIO, has said "The global economy is not a natural outgrowth of the workings of an invisible hand. It is an act of man, not of god." All markets and all economies operate on rules, and this applies as much to the markets that have been fashioned by the Washington consensus as it did to markets fashioned under the New Deal. The problem is that the new global economy has been made to benefit some at the expense of others. Thus, President Sweeney notes that it has been "created by government muscle, welded behind closed doors, largely on behalf of the most powerful corporate and financial interests."

The Washington alternative also seeks to modernize the financial architecture, and it also sees the restoration of expansionary demand conditions as critical to restoring stability and growth. In this, it shares elements with both the Treasury-IMF and the Sachs views. However, that said, it maintains that these measures are nothing near enough. Instead, they are but part of a more fundamental reconfiguration of the international economic order. The conversation cannot be narrowly restricted to discussion of financial markets. Trade, finance, economic growth, and income distribution are all intimately connected, and this means much more must be on the table.

Though notionally agreeing on the need for a new financial architecture, discussion of specifics quickly reveals fundamental differences. The Washington consensus seeks more capital liberalization, more financial transparency and disclosure, and more IMF market surveillance: the claim is that more daylight and more market openness will ensure that market discipline produces efficiency and stability. The Washington alternative says that more financial transparency and disclosure are indeed needed, but there is also a need to reduce speculation and get investors to invest with an eye to the long term and with proper regard to risk. Measures such as Tobin taxes (which tax buying and selling in currency markets) that reduce currency speculation, and Chilean style speed bumps that oblige investors to commit for a minimum time period, are also needed. To the Washington consensus these are interventions that distort the market's natural rythms: to the Washington alternative these are rules that harness the strengths of markets for the benefits of all.

There is also notional agreement on the need to strengthen demand conditions to foster growth, but again there is fundamental disagreement on the specifics. Thus, whereas the Washington consensus sees export-led growth as a solution to each country's demand problem, the Washington alternative sees it as a source of deflation. Export-led growth must be replaced with domestic demand-led growth. One country's exports are another country's imports which means that all can not rely on export-led growth. Attempts to do so result in a beggar-thy-neighbour world that risks plunging the global economy into a deflationary spiral. The way out is domestic demand-led growth. This is a strategy that lifts all boats since demand growth in one country pulls in exports from others, so that all grow together.

Achieving domestic demand-led growth in turn requires strengthening domestic demand, and this brings to the fore even deeper divisions between the Washington consensus and the Washington alternative. Growing domestic demand calls for rising wages to support domestic consumption, and achieving this will require restoring the balance of power between capital and labor. Core labor standards that give workers rights of free association allowing them to form unions and bargain collectively are essential. Rather than being a market distortion, independent trade unions are the private sector solution to the imbalance of power created by capital's new found ability to roam the globe in search of the cheapest most exploitable workers.

The intelligence and humanity that mark Treasury Secretary Rubin have placed him on record as supporting such core labor standards and human rights for ethical reasons, but the problem is that this issue remains peripheral in the Treasury's economic construction of the current crisis. The reality is that it is central: escaping the trap of export-led growth and making globalization work for all can only happen if the playing field between workers and capital is levelled.

Moreover, there is another reason why human rights, labor rights, and strong independent trade unions are vital. The IMF has emphasized the problem of political corruption and economic cronyism which has given rise to misallocation of borrowed resources. It has proposed solving this problem through increased market discipline imposed by increased financial transparency and increased financial liberalization. The argument is that market competition will compete cronyism away. This belief is mistaken. The reality is that these behaviors are politically sponsored, and changing them requires political reform. This in turn requires putting in place countervailing forces that can block such behaviour. Human and labor rights that give workers the right of free association and confer the ability to organize independent trade unions, are the foundation of such reforms. Strong well-functioning democracy is needed to prevent economic cronyism, and unions are an essential ingredient for such an outcome.

Debt relief for developing countries is another measure that can help shift the world economy toward a path of domestic demand-led growth. Debt service burdens now hinder much of the developing world from following an equitable pro-growth agenda. They also force the third world to focus on export-led growth, which has contributed to deteriorating terms of trade, as well as causing job loss in developed countries.

What is true for workers also holds for governments. Just as footloose capital is able to threaten workers, so too it can threaten governments. As a result of their increased mobility, corporations are increasingly able to win tax exemptions by threatening to move jobs overseas. This has contributed to shifting the tax burden on to working households. The same process threatens to undermine environmental and work place safety standards. Thus, with business perceiving these measures as a cost, the threat of relocation will be used to get such standards repealed. This is the hallmark of race to the bottom that has been unleashed by globalization Washington consensus style.

The Washington alternative seeks to remake the globalization process in a way that addresses these problems. Opponents call it interventionist and protectionist. The reality is that it embraces open markets when the rules have been designed such that there is a level playing field between workers and capital, and when business cannot engage in competition that puts work place and environmental standards in play.

East Asia's crisis has provided an opportunity to break with the Washington consensus and replace it with the Washington alternative. This alternative can shift the global economy away from its current path of deflation and rising inequality, back on to an earlier path of equitable growth with full employment. It is time to say goodbye Washington, hello Washington alternative.

Bibliography

Ahmad, Imtiaz: *State and Foreign Policy: India's Role in South Asia*, New Delhi, Vikas, 1993.

Appleby, Paul H.: *Policy and Administration*, Birmingham, AL: University of Alabama Press, 1949.

Baran, Paul A.: *The Political Economy of Growth*, New York, Modern Reader Paperbacks, 1975.

Barill, C.: *Social and Political Ideas of B.R. Ambedkar*, Jaipur, Aalekh Publishers, 1977.

Borcherding, K., : *Contemporary Issues in Decision Making*, Amsterdam, North-Holland, 1990.

Brown, Judith M.: *Modern India: The Origins of an Asian Democracy*, New Delhi, Oxford University Press, 1985.

Carl J. Friedrich: *Constitutional Government and Democracy in International Relations*, Boston, Ginn, 1950.

Carroll, John M., and Herring, George C.: *Modern American Diplomacy*, Wilmington, Del., 1996.

Chomsky, Noam: *World Orders Old and New*. New York, 1994.

Dikshit, D.P.: *Political History of the Chalukyas of Badami*, New Delhi, Abhinav, 1980.

Eldridge, P.J.: *The Politics of Foreign Aid in India*, New York, Schocken, 1970.

English, Barbara: *The War for a Persian Lady*, Boston, Houghton Mifflin, 1971.

Gardner, Lloyd C.: *Spheres of Influence: The Great Powers Partition Europe, from Munich to Yalta*. Chicago, 1993.

Gorbachev, Mikhail: *Perestroika: New Thinking for Our Country and the World*. New York, 1987.

Gul, F. and Pesendorfer, W.: *The Foundations of Positive and Normative Economics*, New York, Oxford University Press 2008.

Hamilton, J.R.: *Alexander the Great*, Oxford, Clarendon Press, 1965.

Hunter, Allen: *Rethinking the Cold War*. Philadelphia, 1998.

Jack Peltason: *Federal Courts in the Political Process,* New York, Random House, 1955.

Jenkins, Rob: *Democratic Politics and Economic Reform in India,* New York, Cambridge University Press, 1999.

Jones, W.H.: *The Government and Politics of India,* London, Hutchinson, 1971.

Leslie, J.: *Toward Empowerment: Women and Politics in India,* Colorado, Westview Press, 1992.

Loomes, G.: *Current Issues in Microeconomics,* New York: St. Martin's Press, 1989.

Mary, W.: *Asian Power and Politics: the Cultural Dimensions of Authority,* Cambridge, Belknap Press, 1985.

Nelson, Judy A.: *Feminism, Objectivity and Economics,* London and New York, Routledge, 1996.

Pye, Lucian W. and Mary W.: *Asian Power and Politics: the Cultural Dimensions of Authority,* Cambridge, Mass, Belknap Press, 1985.

Rappaport, A.: *Creating Shareholder Value, The New Standard for Business Performance,* New York, Free Press, 1986.

Robert D. Schulzinger: *Henry Kissinger: Doctor of Diplomacy,* New York: Columbia University Press, 1989.

Robert, W.: *Public Bureaucracy and the Incentive Problem,* Washington, D.C., World Bank, 1994.

Schmidhauser, R.: *Supreme Court: Its Politics, Personalities and Procedures,* New York, Holt, 1960.

Schumpeter, J. A., *The Theory of Economic Development,* Harvard University Press,Cambridge, Massachusetts, 1934.

Sullivan, Ezra N.: *Bureaucrats and Policy Making,* New York, Holmes & Meier, 1984.

Victor G. : *Law as a Political Instrument,* New York, Random House, 1955.

Warwick, D. P.: *A Theory of Public Bureaucracy,* Cambridge, MA: Harvard University Press, 1975.

Weber, M.: *The Theory of Social and Economic Organizations,* New York, Oxford University Press, 1947.

Index

O

P

R

□□□